D1711983

P8-cTF-637

The Comic Matrix of
Shakespeare's Tragedies

The Comic Matrix of Shakespeare's Tragedies

Romeo and Juliet, Hamlet, Othello, and King Lear

Susan Snyder

Princeton University Press
Princeton, New Jersey

Copyright © 1979 by Princeton University Press
Published by Princeton University Press, Princeton, New Jersey.
In the United Kingdom: Princeton University Press, Guildford, Surrey.

All Rights Reserved. Library of Congress Cataloging in Publication Data
will be found on the last printed page of this book.

This book has been composed in VIP Bembo.
Clothbound editions of Princeton University Press books
are printed on acid-free paper, and binding materials are
chosen for strength and durability.

Printed in the United States of America by Princeton
University Press, Princeton, New Jersey.

To my Swarthmore students,
who have inspired, collaborated,
and criticized in Shakespeare classes and
seminars for more than a decade:
this is their book.

Contents

Acknowledgments	ix
Introduction	3
1. A World Elsewhere	15
2. Beyond Comedy: *Romeo and Juliet* and *Othello*	56
3. The Tragedy of Multiplicity: *Hamlet*	91
4. Between the Divine and the Absurd: *King Lear*	137
Index	181

Acknowledgments

Work on this study has been facilitated by a senior fellowship from the Folger Shakespeare Library and a summer stipend from the National Endowment for the Humanities, as well as by the generous leave policy of Swarthmore College. My sincere thanks to all three institutions. Special appreciation is due to the Folger, where the incomparable resources include a most supportive community of scholars. In particular, Jeanne Addison Roberts and Gail Kern Paster read all or part of this book at some stage of its evolution. I am grateful to them for their counsel and encouragement and also to Samuel Hynes, who interrupted his own sabbatical work to scrutinize the first three chapters and offer a wealth of detailed comment and valuable suggestion.

Parts of Chapter 2 have been published earlier in somewhat different form. I wish to thank the editors of *Essays in Criticism* and *Renaissance Drama* for permission to use this material.

My thinking about tragedy and comedy owes a great deal to the work of Northrop Frye, Susanne K. Langer, and Maynard Mack. They are cited occasionally in the pages that follow, but this seems the proper place to acknowledge in a more comprehensive way the shaping force of their ideas on mine. Another kind of stimulus, no less important, is recorded in the dedication.

The Comic Matrix of

Shakespeare's Tragedies

Introduction

"*Shakespears* genius lay for Comedy and Humour. In Tragedy he appears quite out of his Element." Not an unexpected judgment from Thomas Rymer,[1] whose view of tragedy was "short" in more senses than he knew—too narrowly focused on conventional consistency and poetic justice to take in the complex vision of an *Othello* or a *Julius Caesar*. It is a surprise, though, to find the more humane and unblinkered Johnson agreeing with Rymer. In an age accustomed to seeing Shakespeare's highest art in the great tragedies, we can make little of Johnson's conclusion that they show the dramatist working in an uncongenial mode to produce labored scenes in which "there is always something wanting."[2] But we may depart from Johnson to admire Shakespeare's splendid achievements in the development of tragedy and still gain a valuable perspective on these achievements from that initial notion that comedy came more naturally to him than tragedy.

Certainly mastery of comedy came earlier. By the generally accepted dating, Shakespeare in the first decade of his career as a playwright wrote eight comedies but attempted tragedy, as distinct from history with tragic elements, only twice.[3] Although *Love's Labour's Lost* was written at most only a year after *Titus Andronicus*, the fourth comedy presents none of the problems in

---

[1] *A Short View of Tragedy*, in *The Critical Works of Thomas Rymer*, ed. Curt A. Zimansky (New Haven, 1956), p. 169.

[2] *Johnson on Shakespeare*, ed. Arthur Sherbo, *The Works of Samuel Johnson*, Yale ed., VII (New Haven and London, 1968), 69.

[3] The Riverside edition lists for comedy before 1599 *The Comedy of Errors* (1592-94), *The Taming of the Shrew* (1593-94), *Two Gentlemen of Verona* (1594), *Love's Labour's Lost* (1594-95), *A Midsummer Night's Dream* (1595-96), *The Merchant of Venice* (1596-97), *The Merry Wives of Windsor* (1597), and *Much Ado About Nothing* (1598-99); for tragedy *Titus Andronicus* (1593-94), and *Romeo and Juliet* (1595-96). On the dating of *Merry Wives* see H. J. Oliver's introduction to the New Arden edition (London, 1971), pp. xliv-lviii.

4   INTRODUCTION

moral and dramatic direction, in control of tone and adjustment of language to action, that are so evident in the first tragedy. Rhetoric and situation could not be more perfectly fused in *Love's Labour's Lost*, and Shakespeare is already at ease within the comic formulas to the point of playing sophisticated tricks with them.[4] The narrative poems from these same years can also be seen as exercises in comedy and tragedy—for although *Venus and Adonis* ends in Adonis's death, it is hard to quarrel with F. T. Prince's conclusion that the poem treats sexual desire "in the spirit of romantic comedy," as *Lucrece* treats it tragically. Again, Shakespeare's hand is much surer in the comic mode. Indeed, Prince specifically cites Johnson on Shakespeare's natural bent for comedy when he compares the deft success of *Venus and Adonis* with the elaborate failure of *Lucrece*.[5] A year or two later, *Romeo and Juliet* strikes out in a new tragic direction, with considerable effect. Still, the bare bones of construction show through at times as they never do in the contemporary, and structurally more complex, *Midsummer Night's Dream*. Shakespeare waited four years before writing his next tragedy, and by the time the great tragic phase was well under way he had behind him no fewer than ten successful comedies.

Shakespeare, then, had thoroughly explored and mastered the comic mode while he was still finding his way in tragedy. Add to that the taste for mixing comic with serious that was part of his theatrical heritage, and it seems probable that he would use the dramatic convention in which he was most at home, the world of romantic comedy, as a point of reference and departure in developing tragic forms. It is this hypothesis that underlies my studies of four tragedies, from the early experiment *Romeo and Juliet* through *Hamlet* and *Othello* to *King Lear*.

In these plays, I believe, traditional comic structures and assumptions operate in several ways to shape tragedy. (Here and throughout, I use the word *comic* to mean "pertaining to comedy," not—or not necessarily—"funny.") I have in mind relationships more organic than that implied in the notion, much attacked of late but apparently indestructible, of "comic relief."

[4] See below, pp. 20-21.
[5] *The Poems*, New Arden ed. (London, 1960), pp. xxxiv-xxxv.

INTRODUCTION

Addressing only humorous interludes in serious action and justifying them as a kind of loosening of the screws that allows the audience time to breathe and readjust mentally, the concept of comic relief takes in too few possibilities of comedy in tragedy and explains even these few too mechanically. A simple formula of tension alternating with relaxation can tell us very little about the gravediggers' scene in *Hamlet* or the trial of Goneril and Regan in *Lear*, and nothing at all about the extended comic movement toward marriage as social regeneration that molds the first half of *Romeo and Juliet*. Better, as A. P. Rossiter has suggested, to think of "relief" as in sculpture: "low-relief or high-relief, whereby the figures are 'brought out' by being laid against a something, or an absence of something, so that the two effects interact, to produce a unified but complex reaction of the mind."[6] Romantic comedy offers both "something," in its multiple possibilities held in harmonious balance, and also "an absence of something," in its anarchic dislocations of order and identity. In either aspect, positive or negative, comedy can become the ground from which, or against which, tragedy develops. By evoking the world where lovers always win, death always loses, and nothing is irrevocable, a dramatist can set up false expectations of a comic resolution so as to reinforce by sharp contrast the movement into tragic inevitability. Comic characters can define the tragic situation by their very unawareness and irrelevance. The formulas of comedy and their underlying assumptions can serve as the foundations of tragic dilemma: deeper probing reveals that accepted comic goods like multiple awareness and self-completion through mating have their paradoxical shadow-sides. Finally, comedy can become part of the tragedy itself, providing in its long-range, leveling, anti-individual perspective the most radical challenge to heroic distinction.

From *Romeo* to *Lear* one can see Shakespeare moving through these possibilities in the order I have just set out: that is, comedy and tragedy functioning first as polar opposites, later as two sides of the same coin, and finally as two elements in a single compound. There is, however, no straightforward sequence.

---

[6] *Angel with Horns and Other Shakespeare Lectures* (London, 1961), p. 281.

6   INTRODUCTION

Lear as well as *Romeo* encourages anticipations of a happy outcome only to thwart them, and it is *Hamlet* rather than the later
Othello that looks forward most clearly to the jar of heroic
against absurd in *Lear*. Nor do I envision Shakespeare system-
atically following some program of deliberate exploitation of the
comic for tragic purposes. The materials from which he was
working when he composed these plays could certainly have re-
called his own comedies in their different ways. *Romeo* and
Othello derive from *novelle* of courtship and sexual intrigue;
Hamlet from the tale of a wise fool, a clever avenger who rights
his wrongs by feigning and manipulation; and *Lear* from a
tragicomedy of evil purposes thwarted and suffering redeemed
in final happiness. How consciously did Shakespeare follow up
these suggestions? As with most questions of authorial intention, we know too little about the circumstances of the creative
process to give a satisfactory answer. If we could, it would not
be the same in each case. In *Hamlet* the comic roots of Polonius
and Osric are unmistakable; Hamlet's own affinities with the
eiron figures of comedy are less obvious—and therefore, let it be
admitted, proportionately more likely to be my invention rather
than Shakespeare's. It is not possible, and I do not think it is
necessary, to draw a firm line between comedy as Shakespeare's
starting point in creation and comedy as my vantage point in interpretation. Ultimately all questions of Shakespeare's artistic
purpose lead us back to the results, the plays themselves, and the
justification of my approach must be what it can offer to illuminate *Romeo*, *Hamlet*, *Othello*, and *Lear*.

  That illumination of the chosen plays is my object in this
study, rather than an exhaustive canvass of comic devices in
Shakespearean tragedy. No analysis of a complex work of art
can approach completeness, of course. Any mode of entry en-
tails its own emphases and omissions. Still, I have tried to see
these plays as dramatic wholes, and not as quarries for examples
in the service of a thesis or a set of categories. Surveying every
incidence of the comic in every tragedy, it seemed to me, would
increase the ever-present risk of critical distortion and would
necessitate going over quite a lot of ground already well trodden
by others. My approach offered less prospect of fresh discovery
in a play like *Antony and Cleopatra*, where the comic elements

INTRODUCTION   7

have attracted considerable comment in recent studies.[7] Rather
than include *Antony* for the sake of completeness and rehearse
and modify others' positions accordingly, I chose instead to con-
centrate on a few plays in which the approach through comedy
did lead me in new critical directions.

Comedy is a broad term which has gathered various implications in its long journey down to us from the Greeks. While it is
possible to extract a common denominator for Aristophanes and
Dante, Molière and the Marx Brothers, one has to stand at a
considerable distance to do it, and the result will be fairly
abstract. In seeking what a working dramatist like Shakespeare
might *use* as point of departure or system of reference in a
tragedy, we need to get at something more immediate and concrete, a set of signs whose meaning was familiar to a particular
audience at a particular time. My first chapter therefore takes as
its focus the popular comedies that survive from the years
(1588-95) just before Shakespeare wrote *Romeo and Juliet*—years
which saw a distinctive genre of romantic comedy taking hold
on the public stage.[8] I occasionally will cite comedies written
after 1595 as well, for although Jonson and Chapman were then
popularizing satiric comedy, Shakespeare and others carried on
the romantic tradition without altering it essentially.[9] The comic
conventions that Shakespeare invokes in *Hamlet*, *Othello*, and
King Lear are those established in the theater of the late 1580s and
early 1590s. I have had to examine these comedies of the formative years in a fairly detailed way in order to identify the compo-
nents of the comic "world" and the assumptions that connect
one component with another in a coherent sense of life. Although what emerges from this examination often may bear on
comedy in general, it is meant primarily as the ground of the fol-

[7] See, for example, Janet Adelman, *The Common Liar: An Essay on "Antony
and Cleopatra"* (New Haven and London, 1973), pp. 50-52 and chap. 1 passim;
J. L. Simmons, *Shakespeare's Pagan World: The Roman Tragedies* (Charlottesville,
Va., 1973), pp. 149-163; Philip J. Traci, *The Love Play of Antony and Cleopatra: A
Critical Study of Shakespeare's Play* (The Hague and Paris, 1970), chap. 3.

[8] Madeleine Doran notes a heightened sense of genre differentiation in the
drama of the later Elizabethans and discusses the role of Roman models for comedy and tragedy in this development. *Endeavors of Art: A Study of Form in
Elizabethan Drama* (Madison, Wis., 1954), pp. 137, 105, and 116-185 passim.

[9] On romantic and satiric comedy, see below, chap. 1, n. 41.

8INTRODUCTION

lowing chapters, in Rossiter's sculpture-sense: the foundation from which or against which the gestures of tragedy stand out in higher relief.

In a study based on genre distinctions, generalizations about comedy call for some complementary exposition of tragedy. I must stress, though, that in this study the two genres are seen in different ways: the comic as a common raw material, and the tragic as a series of individually shaped expressions. Comedy may suggest the same device in two plays—both Mercutio and Polonius as comic characters project alternatives to the tragic dynamic and ironically become relevant to that dynamic only by dying—but the recurrence only points up how different are the internal laws by which *Romeo* and *Hamlet* develop. Extracting and synthesizing the features common to contemporary trage-dies, as I have done for the comedies, would be beside the point, which is not to pour all four plays into a single mold called "tragedy" but to explore each one's distinctive qualities. It seems appropriate, therefore, to sketch in generally the assump-tions about tragedy that inform my discussions of the individual plays, with the understanding that the discussions in their turn will refine and qualify these broad statements.

Tragedy is usually characterized in terms of emotional effect. One is tempted to blame this unusual state of affairs on historical accident: Aristotle in the *Poetics* felt obliged to defend tragedy against Plato's charge (*Republic* 10) that it stirred up potentially destructive passions, and the solution he found—the catharsis of pity and fear—by the very difficulties it presented to interpreters loomed larger than it should have on the critical horizons of later generations. But Plato would not have singled out the tragic poets for condemnation if he had not perceived in their work a special emotive power. And the continuing argument about what to make of *eleos* and *phobos*, or what to offer in their place, suggests that the emotions are indeed involved in some special way in tragedy. What holds most constant in all the defining and redefining from Aristotle to modern critics is the notion of *oppo-site* emotions, positive and negative, coexisting in tension. The impulse to retreat is poised against the impulse to advance (I. A. Richards), or awe at necessity against admiration for the hero's *grandeur d'âme* (D. D. Raphael), or "a fearful sense of rightness

INTRODUCTION   9

(the hero must fall)" against "a pitying sense of wrongness (it is too bad that he falls)" (Northrop Frye).[10]

What these strong paradoxical feelings are ultimately responding to is the universal fact of mortality. The highest human potential cannot be infinite; the greatest human achievement must be cut short by death. We know this. Our vulnerable bodies remind us of it, as do logic and experience. But we cannot really take it in. Who can imagine himself not being? (Who, that is, born into a Western culture that assumes each human life is unique?) Thus we sense death as natural and unnatural all at once, something both inherent in us and imposed on us from without. Our myth of how death came into the world bodies forth this tension. Recognition of death's rightness and resistance to its wrongness clash in the very manner of the Fall. Inevitability is clear in the pattern of prohibition, disobedience, and punishment: "Of the tree of the knowledge of good and evil you shall not eat, for in the day that you eat of it you shall die. . . . She took of its fruit and ate; and she also gave some to her husband, and he ate. . . . You are dust, and to dust you shall return."[11] God's sentence, by linking man's fate to his beginnings, dust to dust, strengthens our sense of rightness. It must be so. Yet within this clear causal pattern responsibility is curiously displaced. The story is arranged so that Adam, guilty as he doubtless is, can nevertheless plead in extenuation "the woman whom thou gavest to be with me," and Eve in her turn can offer the excuse "the serpent beguiled me." The serpent who began it all is not asked for an explanation of his motives, and he gives none. The effect is that the "just" death verdict is also felt as arbitrary, not so much proceeding from man's own imperfection as imposed on his naturally immortal state by a mysteriously malevolent outside force.[12]

[10] Richards, *Principles of Literary Criticism* (London, 1925), pp. 245-248; Raphael, *The Paradox of Tragedy* (London, 1960), chap. 1; Frye, *Anatomy of Criticism* (Princeton, 1957), p. 214. Terms like *balance*, *equilibrium*, and *paradox* recur frequently in discussions of tragedy.

[11] Gen. 2:17, 3:6, 19 (Revised Standard Version).

[12] Cf. Northrop Frye, *Fools of Time: Studies in Shakespearean Tragedy* (Toronto, 1967), p. 3: "The mood of tragedy preserves our ambiguous and paradoxical feeling about death; it is inevitable and always happens, and yet, when it does happen, it carries with it some sense of the unnatural and premature." In

10   INTRODUCTION

This is not to say that tragedies are "about" death or that all tragic heroes must die—though Shakespeare's all do, and he like his contemporaries associated the terms *tragic* and *tragedy* with death.[13] It is what death makes concrete and absolute that matters: the failure of power, the end of hope. Physical death as a plot event is less essential than the cadential movement. Aristotle was not consistent in his preference for the tragic plot that begins in happiness and ends in misery,[14] but the downward movement is all-important in Roman and medieval traditions of tragedy. Yet even tragedies that end with the hero and others dead need not address death explicitly. Hamlet contemplates it at some length, Lear does not; but *Lear* is not therefore less tragic than *Hamlet*. Rather, tragic conventions of action and character relate to our ambivalent attitude to death in the way of Susanne Langer's "significant form," which articulates symbolically patterns of human feeling.[15]

Aristotle's conclusions on the most effective incidents for a tragic plot (*Poetics* 9) make sense from this point of view. They should grow logically one from the other (death is inevitable, the natural outcome of human imperfection), yet they should surprise us (death is unnatural, imposed from outside). The kind of *peripeteia* he admired, an action designed toward one end which brings forth a completely opposite result, reflects the ironic causal relation of life to death. We shall die *because* we live: the process of life itself brings the end of life. When the very greatness of an Oedipus or an Othello contains the seeds of his destruction, this paradox finds full expression. It is there as well in tragic ironies of a smaller scale: the action of destroying what one most wished to save, the words that prove true in senses

---

Anatomy of Criticism Frye discusses Adam as the archetypal tragic hero who forfeits a godlike destiny "in a way which suggests moral responsibility to some and a conspiracy of fate to others" (p. 212). He is thinking more of *Paradise Lost* than of Genesis, however, and more of freedom exchanged for constraint and law than of death *per se*.

[13] J. V. Cunningham, "*Tragedy* in Shakespeare," *ELH*, 17 (1950), 36-46; cf. Theodore Spencer, *Death and Elizabethan Tragedy* (Cambridge, Mass., 1936), pp. 232-233, and also below, pp. 19-20.

[14] His approval in *Poetics* 13 is qualified in 14 when he praises plays like *Iphigenia in Tauris* in which last-minute recognition forestalls disaster.

[15] *Feeling and Form: A Theory of Art* (New York, 1953), chap. 3.

INTRODUCTION   11

quite opposite to the speaker's intention.[16] So, too, there is a
logic underneath the apparently arbitrary dicta on tragedy that
were passed on to generations of Renaissance students in their
Terence texts under the name of "Donatus."[17] Tragedy begins
in tranquillity but ends in sorrow or death. Tragic events must
be fearsome and tragic characters of great estate, because only
the extraordinary can express for the individual his unique self,
his never-to-be-repeated life. Tragedies are appropriately based
on history rather than on fiction, because the truth they express
has the fated quality of what has already happened and cannot be
changed or evaded. Even the debatable proposition that tragedy
teaches us to reject life rather than embrace it affirms in its way
the primary tragic impulse to come to terms with the emotions
of death.

   Broadly speaking, tragedy expresses the two sides of the
paradoxical attitude I have been exploring—recognition of
necessity and resistance to the cutting off of human possibility—through plot and character, respectively. The arc of tragic
action incorporates death's inevitability, against which develops
that special dimension of the protagonist that we call heroic. Ultimately this division is too strict, failing as it does to take account of heroism expressed *through* tragic action. The hero may
propel events toward disaster by persisting in his ways, and yet
realize his potential more fully in the process than if he had
played safe. Blake's Proverb of Hell applies: "If the fool would
persist in his folly he would become wise." Nevertheless,
Shakespeare's tragic plots do tend to back the hero into a corner,

   [16] Rossiter observes that " 'tragic irony' is really verbal *peripeteia.*" *Angel with
Horns*, p. 267n.
   [17] "De fabula hoc est de comoedia," attributed to Aelius Donatus but probably the work of Evanthius (fourth century): "Inter tragoediam autem et com-
oediam cum multa tum inprimis hoc distat, quod in comoedia mediocres for-
tunae hominum, parvi impetus periculorum laetique sunt exitus actionum, at in
tragoedia omnia contra, ingentes personae, magni timores, exitus funesti haben-
tur; et illic prima turbulenta tranquilla ultima, in tragoedia contrario ordine res
aguntur; tum quod in tragoedia fugienda vita, in comoedia capessenda ex-
primitur; postremo quod omnis comoedia de fictis est argumentis, tragoedia
saepe de historica fide petitur." *Comicorum graecorum fragmenta*, ed. G. Kaibel
(Berlin, 1899), I, i, 66, cited from Doran, *Endeavors*, p. 415, n.18. I have regularized *u* and *v*.

spiritually and sometimes physically as well. They often mark the limits of the hero's power by moving him out of his realm of natural competence into a situation demanding another, perhaps diametrically opposed, kind of competence. Othello and Coriolanus must leave the straightforward hostilities of war for the concealed rivalries of peace; Brutus and Hamlet, the amplitude of uncommitted speculation for a world of action that asks decisive deeds. More voluntarily, Macbeth goes from an honorable subordination to an absolute power he cannot wield righteously, and Lear in the other direction, from supreme authority to dependence. In the sequence that usually follows, one event grows out of the other by the logic of the situation and of the hero's nature, until he and those around him are destroyed. Here, however, even so general a formulation must be qualified by the distinctive directions of some tragedies, especially those that have a pronounced element of comedy. The initial comic movement of *Romeo and Juliet* and the characters in the second half of the play who are left over from that movement make evident that play's untypical scheme, which is to impose tragic inevitability from outside, without reference to the nature of the protagonists. And *Lear* creates a special kind of inevitability, one of absurdity rather than of logic, by revealing underneath an apparently redemptive comic pattern of action a patternless universe. In *Hamlet*, the narrowing of options is itself a term in Hamlet's tragic dilemma: it is what he must do to accomplish his revenge, and what he cannot do without denying part of his own consciousness. Even so, these plays participate in the basic tragic rhythm of act and consequence (Romeo's slaying of Tybalt, Lear's transfer of power to his children, Hamlet's withholding the sword from Claudius only to kill Polonius instead—all are fateful); and these tragic heroes share with others the refusal to compromise that separates their kind from the survivors of this world.

This integrity is the hallmark of the heroic. The hero comes up against the hard walls of limitation and necessary failure, uncushioned by civilized forms and comfortable beliefs, unaccommodated but also unaccommodating. To locate in the hero the center of tragedy's protest against the snuffing out of human greatness is not to insist that he struggle actively against his fate.

INTRODUCTION   13

He may do so, but heroism emerges in endurance as well as in
defiance. Like Macduff confronting his suffering, the tragic hero
may dispute it like a man but he must certainly feel it like a man.
When the refusal to accommodate does not come through in
defiance, it finds more indirect expression in the hero's energy of
spirit to react, his ability in pain and despair to realize more and
more of himself. Maynard Mack has observed in Shakespeare's
mature tragedies a rhythm of self-definition, by which the hero
under stress passes into his own antithesis, and then into a re-
covery that is a synthesis as well. We see him in this final phase
"exhibiting one or more aspects of his original, or—since these
may not coincide—his better self."[18] The heroic self is in a process of expansion, even of creation. Tragic conventions underline
the hero's uniqueness and irreplaceability in various ways, jux-
taposing his single self with pairs and groups—Job's counsellors,
the Roman mob, Rosencrantz and Guildenstern—and of course
elevating him through language. The speech used by and about
the tragic hero invokes absolutes and superlatives; reaches out to
the exalted, the fearsome, the exotic; and sweeps the whole universe into its frame of reference. It is this language that con-
vinces us emotionally of his importance.

The hero's suffering and defeat are articulated as nobly as his
power, or more so. Langer saw self-realization and failure as sequential, the tragic error marking the end of the protagonist's
development.[19] But her formula ignores the equilibrium tragedy
sets up between internal and external action: one broadens out
while the other narrows down. The arch-tragedy of Genesis
shows this equilibrium in the paradoxical results of the Fall.
After eating of the tree of knowledge, Adam and Eve realize
their own nakedness; they feel the need for the protection of
clothing and try to hide from God among the trees. Recognition
and reaction suggest anxiety, a sense of their own frailty before
God's power. Yet according to that same God, man's attainment
to the knowledge of good and evil has made him "like one of

---

[18] "The Jacobean Shakespeare," in *Jacobean Theatre*, ed. J. Russell Brown and
Bernard Harris, Stratford-upon-Avon Studies, 1 (London, 1960), p. 37; Mack
discusses the antithesis phase on pp. 33-36.

[19] *Feeling and Form*, p. 358.

14   INTRODUCTION

us"—not farther from godhead but closer to it. Immortality is within his reach.[20] Tragic action exposes the nakedness of the hero (sometimes literally, as with Adam and Lear) but also fulfills more of his godlike potential. It grants him a kind of divinity with one hand even while striking him down with the other. It is just because we can relate the ineluctable events so closely to self-expansion, can see them as the same action, that the defeats of tragedy do not leave us feeling passive and depressed. When he banished tragedy from his republic, Plato felt in it only the grief without the balancing, energizing pride.

Tragedy is too many-sided and problematic a topic to cope with in a volume, let alone a few pages. But these suggestions, though incomplete and oversimplified, are perhaps sufficient to start this study on its way in a rhythm of alternation. From tragedy in general, we move to comedy generalized from actual Elizabethan practice, and then back to tragedies, plural, in all their own particularity.

[20] "Then the Lord God said, 'Behold, the man has become like one of us, knowing good and evil; and now, lest he put forth his hand and take also of the tree of life, and eat, and live forever'—therefore the Lord God sent him forth from the garden of Eden, to till the ground from which he was taken. He drove out the man; and at the east of the garden of Eden he placed the cherubim, and a flaming sword which turned every way, to guard the way to the tree of life." Gen. 3:22-24.

[1]

A World Elsewhere

When Coriolanus's Roman career has reached a dead end in rejection and banishment, he shouts back defiantly at the mob that there are alternatives to Rome: "Despising / For you the city, thus I turn my back; / There is a world elsewhere" (III.iii.135-137).[1] It is not true. Rome is the only world for Coriolanus, and his tragedy is that he can live neither with it nor without it. But the alternative worlds that are not available to Shakespeare's tragic heroes are eminently available to their creator. The comic conventions, in particular, offer a world apart from tragedy, which may be called forth to sharpen or deepen tragic thrust in several ways.

A developed literary convention can be valuable to any writer, whether he proposes to work inside it or against it. It allows him to call up a whole world-view with a few signs, to provide tellingly but economically a rich context for his words. Take, for example, the first line of Donne's "The Indifferent":

> I can love both faire and browne.[2]

With the first-person pronoun and its verb, "I . . . love," Donne appeals to his contemporary readers' familiarity with the dominant convention of subjective love poetry, Petrarch's lifelong adoration of the unique and unattainable Laura, and all the accompanying features of stance and style that had held sway for so long in the European love lyric. Having invited the reader to supply this tradition, Donne then stands it on its head. He loves *both fair and brown*, though tradition dictates that he love only the

---

[1] Shakespeare references throughout are to *The Complete Works*, ed. Peter Alexander (London and Glasgow, 1951).

[2] Donne is quoted from *The Elegies and The Songs and Sonnets*, ed. Helen Gardner (Oxford, 1965). In old-spelling citations throughout I have silently expanded abbreviations and regularized *i/j* and *u/v*.

16   A WORLD ELSEWHERE

fair, and only one fair at that. With a minimum of effort, the
poet has begun the comic counterpoint of the poem—between
libertine self-indulgence and the devout fidelity of the Petrarchan lover—and established the poetic voice as individual and
iconoclastic.

Another kind of effect occurs when Donne looks at the Petrarchan convention not just to mock and discard it but to probe
below its surface silliness. In "Loves Deitie" he attacks that silliness with impatient common sense, deploring the elevation of
Love into divinity and especially the tyranny of the love-god in
his demand "That I should love, who loves not mee." But beneath the conventions so easily dismissed—blind Cupid and adoration eternally unrewarded—is a fact of human nature: love is
not controlled by common sense, and we do find it hard to stop
loving even when our love is not returned. Thus the restive
speaker, who threatened to "ungod this child againe," turns on
himself in the last stanza with charges of rebellion and atheism,
and reaffirms the values of love and fidelity almost in spite of
himself. Donne has flouted tradition only to discover, apparently afresh, its underlying truth. Shakespeare does the same
thing in Sonnet 130, "My mistress' eyes are nothing like the
sun." Here too the rejections of Petrarchan metaphor finally
serve to underline his loving enslavement: "And yet, by heaven,
I think my love as rare / As any she belied with false compare."

Accepting the general premise that literary convention can
operate to shape and enrich a work that is moving in a direction
opposite to that convention, we must still, before looking at
Shakespeare's use of comedy in his tragedies, ask two questions.
First, to what extent had popular comedy developed, by the
time Shakespeare was trying his hand at tragedy, a convention
or set of conventions that the knowledgeable audience could
recognize from generic clues? Second, if there were such conventions, what sort of world did they evoke for the audience?
Why these recurrent character types, this kind of plot, this use of
language, and not others? How do the conventions of plot,
character, and language connect with one another, and what
sense of life informs them? The second question has more
ramifications, and the latter part of this chapter is addressed to it.

A WORLD ELSEWHERE 17

But first we must find out if the comedies that survive from the years before Shakespeare wrote the first tragedy I shall be considering, *Romeo and Juliet*, have enough in common to justify speaking of Elizabethan comic conventions at all.

The Elizabethan theater inherited a welter of dramatic forms, from jigs and maskings to interlude-debates, morality plays, and scriptural cycles. The sense of genre evolved slowly, and contemporary designations of plays do not tell a clear story of that evolution. A study of title pages and running titles of plays printed between 1560 and 1599[3] shows that the terms *comedy* and *tragedy* came into frequent use only in the 1570s, before which the commonest designation for a play was *interlude*. But throughout these four decades many plays that we would call comedies—*Friar Bacon and Friar Bungay*, *The Taming of a Shrew*, *Mother Bombie*, and others—are called *histories*, or are given no label at all. Conversely, the term *comedy* was applied to morality plays as well as to such romantic pieces as *Fair Em* and *Mucedorus*. As a group, the plays labeled comedies have not much in common except a happy ending, and even this is conspicuously lacking in the first version of Nathaniel Woodes' *The Conflict of Conscience* (printed in 1581), an "excellent new Commedie" that ends with the protagonist's suicide and eternal damnation.[4] On the same title page the *Conflict* is redefined as a "lamentable Hystorie." Such wavering between categories is typical of the whole period. Designations like "comedy or interlude," "pitiful comedy," and even "tragical comedy" are not unusual. It is fair to say that only translations are labeled with any consistent sense of genre.

Nevertheless, the drama surviving from the late 1580s and early 1590s does show a coalescing of elements from theatrical, festival, and literary tradition into a recognizable genre, romantic comedy. An *idea* of comedy was current, if not a carefully applied nomenclature. Shakespeare himself had a great deal to do with both the development of the idea and its dominance.

---

[3] W. W. Greg, *A Bibliography of the English Printed Drama to the Restoration*, vol. I (London, 1939).

[4] Title page, first issue; in a second issue the same year cancel sheets changed the ending from suicide to repentance and a holy death.

18   A WORLD ELSEWHERE

But along with his early comedies—*The Comedy of Errors*, *The Two Gentlemen of Verona*, *The Taming of the Shrew*, *Love's Labour's Lost*, and *A Midsummer Night's Dream*—other plays of the popular theater must be considered: *The Two Angry Women of Abington*, *Friar Bacon and Friar Bungay*, *John a Kent and John a Cumber*, *The Taming of a Shrew*, *Fair Em*, *Mucedorus*, *The Pinner of Wakefield*, *James the Fourth*, *The Old Wives' Tale*, *Orlando Furioso*, *John of Bordeaux*, *A Knack to Know a Knave*, *A Knack to Know an Honest Man*. These, at least, are the popular comedies and tragicomedies that have come down to us from the years 1588-95, according to the dating of the Harbage-Schoenbaum *Annals*.[5] I have not included in this list Lyly's and other plays performed privately or at court, although they share many preoccupations and formulas with the popular comedies. The question here is what audiences in the public theaters were familiar with, what they expected when they went to see a comedy.

My discussion of comic conventions of this period is limited in two ways. First, my conclusions will be based on the eighteen plays I have listed above, with some reference to Shakespeare's later comedies in the same vein. I shall at times use the general terms *comedy* and *comic* to avoid cumbersome designations of romantic-comedy-in-the-late-1580s-and-1590s, but this is simply a convenience. I do not mean to offer a comprehensive theory of comedy, or even of English Renaissance comedy. Some of the generalizations that emerge seem to me to apply to comedies of all sorts and of all times, but others clearly do not fit comedies of a satiric bent like Jonson's.[6] Second, in attempting to isolate and interpret conventions I have naturally had to seek out the common denominators of these plays rather than their distinctive individual qualities. Some readers may feel that I neglect Shakespeare's verse and the other excellences that set his

[5] Alfred Harbage, *Annals of English Drama, 975-1700*, rev. S. Schoenbaum (London, 1964; supplements 1966, 1970). Besides plays designated there as comedy, romantic comedy, and romance, I have included two plays labeled in the *Annals* as history (*James the Fourth*) and pseudohistory (*John a Kent and John a Cumber*) which have strong affinities with the others in structure and mode. Dates in parentheses for non-Shakespearean plays are from Harbage-Schoenbaum unless otherwise noted.

[6] See n. 41, below, on differences between Jonson's mode and the romantic-comic.

A WORLD ELSEWHERE   19

comedies so far above most of the others discussed. To this I
plead guilty in advance. My purpose is not to show the superiority of *A Midsummer Night's Dream*, or for that matter of *The Old
Wives' Tale*, to such awkward efforts as *Orlando Furioso*. It is to
discover what audiences of the time were used to in comedies,
good and bad.

One thing they must have expected, for they always got it,
was a love story. Courtship is usually the mainspring of the action, even in an otherwise quite unromantic play like *Two Angry
Women*. In the rare cases where the main action turns on some
other motive, the obligatory courtship becomes a subplot, as in
Comedy of Errors and *Knack to Know a Knave*. Contemporary
comment confirms this identification of comedy with love. Lyly
in the prologue to *Midas* takes it for granted. So, in a less agree-
able spirit, does Stephen Gosson, grumbling to those who defend plays as delightful teachers of morality that in fact comedies
teach nothing but love and wooing. Love, concurs Bacon, is
"ever matter of comedies." It identifies the genre, as death identifies tragedy. Facing death, Pamela in Sidney's *Arcadia* calls her
plight a tragedy; but when Anaxius offers to make love to her,
she says, "Thou plaiest worse thy Comedy, then thy Tragedy."[7]

The author of *Soliman and Perseda* (1602) singles out another,
related element in the comic formula when he has Death reserve
tragedy for himself and order not only Love but Fortune off to
play in comedies.[8] Fortune—the fortuitous, the chance, the
unexpected—is a strong force in most of these romantic comedies, working through chance and coincidence to ward off disaster and bring the favored courtships to happy conclusions.
Death is evoked, for the most part, only to be evaded or out-
witted.

A villain like Sacrepant in *Orlando Furioso*, or minor characters

[7] Lyly, prologue to *Midas* (1589): "At our exercises, Souldiers call for
Tragedies, their object is bloud: Courtiers for Commedies, their subject is love"
(1592 ed.), A2r; Gosson, *Playes Confuted in Five Actions* (London, 1582), C6r; Ba-
con, "Of Love" (first printed in 1612 ed. of *Essays*); Sidney, *The Countesse of
Pembrokes Arcadia*, ed. Albert Feuillerat (Cambridge, 1922), pp. 503, 507. In *Not
Wisely But Too Well* (San Marino, Calif., 1957), Franklin Dickey cites Sidney's
Defense of Poesie, Puttenham, Heywood, and Burton as well as Bacon to support
the conventional association of love with comedy (pp. 3-6).

[8] 1599 ed., I2v.

20   A WORLD ELSEWHERE

like the suitors and scholars in *Friar Bacon*, may die; but more
typical is Sempronio in *Knack to Know an Honest Man*. Apparently killed early in the play (indeed, his murder sets off all
following events), he turns up whole and well later on, having
been rescued and cured by a convenient hermit. Another who
bleeds but is not killed is Dorothea in *James the Fourth*. Her reappearance after being reported dead seems, of course, like a
miraculous resurrection to her repentant husband. The device
anticipates a long line of near deaths and faked deaths in later
Shakespearean comedy. Peele's *Old Wives' Tale* shows how
thoroughgoing this generic refusal of mortality can be: the town
drunk is well and truly dead before the play begins, but that does
not prevent him from taking a lively part in the action.[9]

It is with these conventional expectations—that death would
be kept at a distance and that the affairs of heroes and heroines
would conclude in joyous union—that audiences must have
reacted to Berowne's complaint in the last scene of *Love's
Labour's Lost*:

> Our wooing doth not end like an old play:
> Jack hath not Jill. These ladies' courtesy
> Might well have made our sport a comedy.
>   (v.ii.862-864)

Shakespeare has his reasons for violating the convention in
Love's Labour's Lost. He puts off the traditional marriages for a
year (too long, as Berowne says, for a play), as he untradi-

---

[9] *The Dead Man's Fortune* (1590), which survives only in a playhouse "plot,"
has a stage direction for the final scene that might serve as an emblem for the
comic way with death: "Enter kinge Egereon, Allgeryus, Tesephon, with
lordes, the executioner with his sworde and blocke and offycers with holberds.
To them Carynus and Prelior. Then after that the musicke plaies and ther enters
3 antique faires [fairies] dancynge on after a nother. The firste takes the sworde
from the executioner and sendes him a waye. The other caryes a waie the blocke
and the third sends a waie the offycers and unbindes Allgeryus and Tesiphon and
as they entred,so they depart." Transcription by W. W. Greg, ed., *Dramatic Documents from the Elizabethan Playhouses*, vol. II (Oxford, 1931); I have supplied
some capitalization and punctuation for clarity. Cf. the prologue to *Mucedorus*,
which pits a personified Comedy against Envy: while Envy plots to turn happy
auguries into sorrow and disaster, Comedy prepares to defend her actors from
death.

A WORLD ELSEWHERE   21

tionally introduces the blunt realities of birth and death, in order
to carry on the process by which the young men are freed from
artifice and affectation. And he deliberately reminds his audience
of the comic norm in order to make his point more emphatically.

Berowne's speech points to another common feature of these
comedies. The events of *Love's Labour's Lost* are set in motion
by Fortune, who presumably directed the arrival of the Princess
and her ladies just when the men had renounced love for study;
but most of the ensuing action is controlled by "these ladies,"
and it is also they who decide to delay the happy ending. The
ladies have many counterparts in contemporary comedies, not
necessarily female, manipulators of persons and events who as-
sist Fortune or even take over her function entirely—as in the
case of the Petruchio figures in the two *Shrew* plays. From one
point of view, to be sure, the stratagems of Petruchio or the dis-
guisings of the wooers in *Fair Em* are quite different from the
operations of Fortune, since they imply that, far from being
pawns of chance, the characters have the power to contrive their
own happiness. But ultimately the two kinds of action express
the same thing, a kind of natural law of comedy whereby consequences are not irrevocable, second chances are given, death is
not final, and barriers between true lovers are no more permanent than the mobile Wall of Peter Quince's "Pyramus and
Thisbe" play. Jack shall have Jill, nought shall go ill.

One sort of manipulator, the magician, was enjoying a vogue
in the period we are considering. Friar Bacon, something of a
mischief-maker in *Friar Bacon and Friar Bungay*, reforms suffi-
ciently in *John of Bordeaux* to help the worthy hero and heroine
with his supernatural powers and to foil by stronger spells the
efforts of his rival Vandermast on behalf of illicit love. John a
Kent gives similar service to two young couples in *John a Kent
and John a Cumber*. Oberon in *Midsummer Night's Dream* exerts
his magical powers to smooth the course of true love not only
for Helena but for himself.

In the absence of such powers, purely human characters with
an impulse to manipulate events typically resort to disguise.
Mucedorus, for example, wishes before consenting to an arranged marriage to test love actively. This desire to act as person

22 A WORLD ELSEWHERE

rather than prince leads to his first disguise as a shepherd, and
when the ensuing complications threaten romance and life itself,
he gains the necessary freedom of action by switching from
shepherd to hermit. Other temporary hermits are John a Kent
and the Pinner of Wakefield, who uses his disguise to foil rebellion while his boy Wily dresses as a "sempster's maid" to further
the Pinner's romantic designs. In *Love's Labour's Lost* the ladies'
control of events is expressed in part by their superior disguises:
they easily see through the false Muscovites, but the men are totally fooled by the exchanging of masks. Each man shows the
untested, superficial nature of his attraction by ardently wooing
the mask instead of the girl.

Of course, even in these comedies magic and disguise are not
always in the service of order and true love. Sorcerers are active
in bad causes as well as good ones—for example, John a
Cumber, Vandermast in *Friar Bacon*, Sacrapant in *Old Wives'
Tale*. The magic flower in Puck's hands brings confusion and
pain to the lovers of *Midsummer Night's Dream* before Oberon directs its proper use. Disguise, too, may aggravate the problem
rather than solve it. In *Two Gentlemen of Verona*, Julia's assumed
identity as page to the faithless Proteus does nothing to restore
his love to her (this comes about by other means) but, rather,
intensifies her suffering. Comic playwrights clearly found sorcery and disguising useful in their plots to generate complications as well as solutions. John a Kent brings out the dual
potential of his powers when, early in the play, he plans com-
prehensively to "help, hinder, give, take back, turne, over-
turne, / deceive, bestowe, breed pleasure, discontent. / yet
comickly conclude."[10] He will, in short, play both Puck and
Oberon.

Two points should be noticed here. It seems clear that romantic comedy has some basic affinity with magic and disguise, two
ways of transforming the "real," that goes deeper than their
convenience as agents of benevolent fortune. Indeed, they may
be inserted for their own sake, as part of the atmosphere; this
seems to be the case in *James the Fourth*, where Oberon's magic

[10] Anthony Munday, *John a Kent and John a Cumber*, ed. M. St. C. Byrne,
Malone Society Reprints (Oxford, 1923), ll. 134-136.

A WORLD ELSEWHERE   23

powers and Ateukin's charms do not affect the plot at all. Beyond that, there are disturbing possibilities in a transforming power that *may* serve good ends but need not. Controlled by comedy's overarching natural law, the power will "comickly conclude," but nothing in its nature makes it do so. This is one of several areas where the comic muse skates on thin ice, areas that will especially invite further exploration when the shaping mode is tragic instead of comic.

It may be objected that, since disguise and magic do not appear exclusively in comedy, they should not be specially linked with the comic convention. But in the case of magic the only real exception in the period under discussion is *Doctor Faustus*, and magic in this case is less a means of shaping the action than the particular expression first of Faustus's temptation and then of his degradation. Magic in operation produces the comic transformations of the middle of the play; in the tragic beginning and end it is an idea rather than an agent, an appropriately tragic idea in that it embodies both human aspiration and human limitation.[11]

Disguise is also rare in Elizabethan tragedy until about 1600. In the formative period I am considering, it was associated with romantic comedy. After the turn of the century, disguise is frequent enough in tragedies of intrigue and revenge to blur the generic distinction, although Chapman in 1602 could still joke about a "change of a hat or a cloak" as the comic playwright's cliché.[12] Chapman, in fact, used disguise in such tragedies as *Bussy D'Ambois* as well as in his comedies. Shakespeare, on the other hand, kept up the older distinction very consistently.

---

[11] After the turn of the century, portrayal of supernatural arts in drama would be complicated in various ways by scepticism about their efficacy, by an increased appetite for the sensational and the macabre onstage, and by some attention to the tragic possibilities of witchcraft and sorcery as manifestations of evil. But for the time being the sorcerer's powers were assured, and his natural home was romantic comedy. His arts and their source posed no moral issue, except in *Friar Bacon*—and even here Bacon's repentance near the play's end comes as a surprise, an unexpected intrusion of morality. Through most of the action his conjurings have been presented to call forth not moral reaction but pure enjoyment.

[12] *May Day* II.i.480-481, in *The Plays and Poems of George Chapman*, ed. T. M. Parrott, vol. II (London, 1914).

24   A WORLD ELSEWHERE

Characters assume other identities in almost all of his comedies, in almost none of his tragedies. *Hamlet*, where the hero takes on / is taken over by the role of madman, and *King Lear*, where Kent and Edgar are Caius and Poor Tom for most of the action, are the exceptions;[13] and I shall argue in the chapters on *Hamlet* and *Lear* that Shakespeare meant this device to remind us of comedy and to call its assumptions into play for his own special purposes.

Most characters in comedy are not manipulators and do little to control events. Their role is to respond to events, welcoming the good fortune and meeting adverse turns either by some evasive action or by adapting to them. Thus such characters as the King of Scots in *James the Fourth* and Fortunio in *Honest Man*, having pursued evil ends throughout their actions, adapt to exposure with sudden but sincere repentance. Another sort of comic accommodation reaches an extreme in *Fair Em*: both Em and Duke William in their respective plots abandon unpromising love affairs to fall in love, as the situation requires, with more possible mates. This is perhaps the purest instance of the adaptability we also witness in Prince Edward of *Friar Bacon* and Proteus in *Two Gentlemen*, both shamed into giving up their unsuitable loves for suitable ones. For those whose loves are suitable

---

[13] In *Titus Andronicus*, the disguises of Tamora and her sons as Revenge, Rape, and Murder do not fool Titus and are not really alternative identities. Titus himself points out the close connection between Tamora, Chiron, and Demetrius and their allegorical labels (v.ii.98-109). It is not clear in *Coriolanus* whether Marcius's "disguise" when entering Antium is intentional, as in Plutarch, or simply the result of his destitute state, as Dover Wilson suggests in his note to IV.iv in the New Cambridge edition (1960). In any case, the main point about his role as poor nobody is that he cannot sustain it; patrician arrogance breaks through almost immediately when he is among the servants, and he can hardly wait to reveal his name and history to Aufidius. Other tragedies show identities concealed by deception (Iago) or threatened with disintegration (Othello, Antony) but not identities taken on as alternatives to the original selves.

Of the comedies only *Errors* has no disguising. Even there, Syracusan Antipholus has another identity thrust upon him by his resemblance to his brother. Bottom's "translation" in *Dream* is also involuntary, and Margaret in *Much Ado* does not mean to put on Hero's identity with her clothes, but in both cases the effect is a temporarily changed identity with important consequences for the plot.

A WORLD ELSEWHERE

but are blocked by circumstances or human malevolence, the proper response is different. They must not adapt but find some circumventing stratagem, or at the very least stay stubbornly faithful. It is presumably by this rule that Vallingford finally wins Fair Em. He starts out in the courtship stakes on a par with Mountney and well behind Em's initial favorite Manvile, but he perseveres in love, and ingenuity, after Manvile is faithless and Mountney gives up.

The favored characters of comedy, true of heart or sharp of wit (occasionally they are both), must often endure a confusion verging on chaos before receiving their rewards. Again we have some extreme cases: Delya (*Old Wives' Tale*) forgets who she is, and Orlando (*Orlando Furioso*) runs mad. But chaos threatens in other plays as well. Kate in the *Shrew* plays must learn to call the sun the moon; *Two Angry Women* is a free-for-all of compounded mistaken identities; and the high point of confusion in *Comedy of Errors* is marked not only by unsettled identities but by imprisonment in the dark and fears of demonic possession. Here is another patch of thin ice in the conventional world of romantic comedy—the potential terror of a completely fluid reality where no loyalty or identity is secure. Many will recall the moment in Peter Brook's production of *Midsummer Night's Dream* when Hermia awoke to find herself inexplicably deserted by Lysander in the dark forest. As coils of wire swirled about and entangled her, the audience could feel the sudden panic of one whose sureties had vanished while she slept.

Still, audience involvement with Ephesian Antipholus's frustration or Hermia's fear is momentary, a parenthetic *frisson*. We know that for all the apparent chaos of the situation the appropriate sorting-out devices are at hand—a long-lost twin and a benevolent Fairy King. This is the natural law that comedy never violates. Laws in the more usual sense—the social rules imposed by custom or authority—come off badly in romantic comedy. They are restraints which the characters have to evade, stretch, or break in order to get what they want. But here we should perhaps add the qualification "Shakespearean" to "romantic comedy," for this motif of the law to be got round or overturned is a notable feature of his early comedies and may be

26   A WORLD ELSEWHERE

his own contribution to the convention of the early 1590s.[14] At
the end of *Two Gentlemen*, one would expect Valentine's
banishment to be revoked when the Duke cools off; it is surprising that he extends the pardon to Valentine's criminal companions. It is more surprising when the dukes of Ephesus (in
Comedy of Errors) and Athens (in *Midsummer Night's Dream*),
who invoke harsh, unbreakable laws for alien merchants and
disobedient daughters, find in the face of family reunions and
happily paired lovers that the legal obstacles can after all be
brushed aside quite easily.

> It shall not need; thy father hath his life.
>
> > > > > > > > > > (*Err*. v.i.389)
>
> Egeus, I will overbear your will.
>
> > > > > > > > > (*Dream* iv.i.176)

In both these cases the law is wrong for the particular situation,
although possibly appropriate or necessary for general circumstances. Even self-imposed law can be wrong for those who impose it if it is alien to their nature or time of life. The young
scholars of *Love's Labour's Lost* must lose their oaths to find
themselves. Law is usually felt as extrinsic, imposed from without indiscriminately on a whole group, and therefore alterable in
individual circumstances. The device is not exclusively Shakespeare's, of course. Most of the complications in *Honest Man* derive from two laws, that against murder, which is applied to
Lelio even though he has been wronged by his victim Sempronio, and that forbidding assistance to a murderer. In the latter
case, the actions of Lelio's father-in-law and others who flout the
law to help him are clearly approved. As for the law against
murder, abrogation here might have posed some difficulties;
these are avoided when Sempronio turns out to be alive after all.

Established social hierarchies fare as badly as laws. Servants
vie with masters in wit and initiative, as do women with men;
and, as in *Love's Labour's Lost*, the supposed inferiors often come
out on top. Costard and even Holofernes and Armado display in
the end more sense of reality and human obligation than
Navarre and his young nobles, who are also led by the nose al-

---

[14] Frye, *Anatomy of Criticism*, p. 166.

A WORLD ELSEWHERE   27

most from the start by the visiting ladies. Female supremacy in
consciousness and power is not so clearly established in these
comedies as in some of Shakespeare's later ones: the powerful
characters in *Taming of the Shrew* and *Midsummer Night's Dream*
are male, while the Abbess in *Comedy of Errors* and Julia and
Silvia in *Two Gentlemen* only begin to adumbrate Portia and
Rosalind. Nevertheless, one can see the beginning of a comic
tradition of the aware, aggressive woman which is not confined
to Shakespeare. In *Fair Em*, the heroine resourcefully feigns
blindness and deafness to discourage her unwanted suitors,
while another woman character, Mariana, initiates the bride-
substitution that resolves the subplot. Dorothea in *James the
Fourth* develops from helpless victim at a low point in midplay to
disguiser and engineer of the final reconciliation, taking over the
position of dramatic power first held by her royal husband.
Others show their strength and independence in wit-battles
rather than by stratagems. Mall in *Two Angry Women* tests her
lover's powers of repartee before accepting his suit, as her
brother had warned him she would:

> Sirra sheel bowe the mettall of your wits,
> And if they cracke she will not hold ye currant,
> Nay she will way your wit as men way angels,
> And if it lacke a graine, she will not change with ye.[15]

This preeminence of women doubtless harks back to the festival
roots of comedy, those rites of spring in which women played a
prominent part. May queens were more common in English vil-
lage festivals than May kings.[16] And courtship, the standard
situation of romantic comedy, was one of the few situations in
which women could, in literary tradition and sometimes in fact,
exercise power over men. What is most important to note here is
that this elevation of women and servants over their betters, like

---

[15] Henry Porter, *The Two Angry Women of Abington*, ed. W. W. Greg, Malone
Society Reprints (Oxford, 1912), ll. 1471-1474.

[16] E. K. Chambers, *The Medieval Stage* (Oxford, 1903), I, 144. C. L. Barber in
Shakespeare's Festive Comedy (Princeton, 1959), pp. 20-21, cites in connection
with the May game a couplet from the medieval English lyric "Lenten is come
with love to toune": "Wormés woweth under cloude, / Wymmen waxeth
wounder proud."

28 A WORLD ELSEWHERE

comedy's cavalier treatment of the law, was quite at odds with the prevailing social values.

Time in these comedies is as flexible and accommodating as law. Events may spread out over years or rush breakneck through a single city day or woodland night, but deadlines are always met. The Antipholus brothers find each other and their father before sundown ends his term of grace; Orlando arrives at Angelica's trial by combat in time to be her champion; Lord Lacy of *Friar Bacon* returns to Fressingfield just before the nunnery doors close on his love Margaret—another comic lawbreaker who then cheerfully forswears her "vow which may not be revok'd."[17] "Too late" is not in the comic vocabulary. There is always time to keep the appointment, to undo the mistake, or even to neglect the action altogether for a display of wit or clowning. In tragedy, our sense that time is limited and precious grows with our perception of an inevitable outcome, time cut off. In comedy, short-term urgencies are played against a dominant expansiveness as we move toward a conclusion of "all the time in the world."

In some comedies the elasticity of time affects temporal logic as well. Barriers between different time periods tend to break down. Ignorance or carelessness may account for Greene's setting of *James the Fourth* in 1520, seven years after the historical James IV was killed at Flodden. But the whole play is characterized by blurred time distinctions, from the induction onward. Here Bohan sends his sons Slipper and Nano off to make their fortunes; yet the main action, in which they try to do so, is presented by Bohan to Oberon as his memory of the past, long before the time of the induction. Later it is not a memory but a creation of Bohan's imagination. Slipper wanders at will between the temporally separate frame scenes and the play proper; and Oberon, who is watching Bohan's presentation of these past—or fictional—events, at one point steps into the main plot to save Slipper from hanging. There is a similar crossover from frame to play and from one time to another in *Old Wives' Tale*. The story happened "once upon a time," but when Madge starts

[17] Robert Greene, *Friar Bacon and Friar Bungay*, ed. Daniel Seltzer, Regents Renaissance Drama Series (Lincoln, Nebr., 1963), xiv.78.

A WORLD ELSEWHERE   29

to tell it, two of its characters come on stage and take over the presentation.

Frame actions and multiple plots are themselves important features of the comic convention. *Mucedorus* and the two *Shrew* plays have inductions, as do *James the Fourth* and *Old Wives' Tale*. In fact, out of the eighteen plays I have been considering, only five lack some defined additional action, frame play, or subplot. Three of these five—*Two Angry Women*, *John a Kent*, and *Two Gentlemen of Verona*—have well-developed servant scenes that without being separate plots give a similar effect of multiplicity. So does the madness interlude in *Orlando Furioso*: Orlando's deranged dealings with the fiddler and the clowns are somewhat separate from the main plot of love and war, and suggest a kind of mad parody on that plot. Even *Honest Man*, more a tragicomedy than a romantic comedy, has its rustic and servant characters in counterpoint to the lofty ideals and motives of the main action.

Here again we need to ask if the taste for additional actions was in fact a special feature of comedy or simply a general function of the Elizabethan passion for variety. After all, tragedies such as *Gorboduc*, *Locrine*, and *The Spanish Tragedy* have inductions too. But these, whether they body forth allegorically the forces at work in the play or represent antecedent events, are fully focused on the tragic action to come.[18] Comedy developed other kinds of induction, notably the frame play. The frame typically presents a contrast to the main action, not a commentary on it. There are connections, but they are indirect. In both *Shrew* plays, for example, the transformation of Christopher Sly from tinker to lord sets the scene for Kate's transformation in the play proper; yet the immediate effect is of two quite separate worlds—tavern doings in England as opposed to courtship amidst merchant affluence in Italy. (The second world itself soon subdivides, conventional romance surrounding the Bianca action while Petruchio and Kate live in an earthier environment of

---

[18] Thus the dumb show, with its interpretive emblems, was felt to be appropriate to tragedy but never became part of the comic convention. Dieter Mehl notes that the rare dumb shows in English comedy function mainly to parody the grand manner of tragedy. *The Elizabethan Dumb Show* (London, 1965), p. xii.

30 A WORLD ELSEWHERE

blows, beef and mustard, and horses that slip in the mud.) The *Shrew* plays suggest that the comic induction differs from the tragic in presenting an alternative to the main play world rather than an adjunct to it. The other comedies in our group bear out this distinction fairly well: *James the Fourth* frames its intrigues with music and magic; *Old Wives' Tale* offers homely Madge and Clunch to set off the romantic, improbable tale. Only the *Mucedorus* induction, a struggle between Comedy and Envy that comments on the events of the play to follow, is an exception.

If presenting disparate worlds was a comic desideratum, it is not surprising that several of the earlier comedies I am examining go beyond the relatively simple dualities of plot/subplot or induction/play to multiply actions further. In Shakespeare's work, *Midsummer Night's Dream* comes immediately to mind, but we should also note that *Shrew* has three plots (although the Sly one is left unresolved), and that *Love's Labour's Lost* combines with the main courtship action the low-life version played by Costard, Armado, and Jacquenetta; the Nine Worthies pageant; and a kind of overplot concerning the Princess as emissary of her royal father and ending with his death. Even *Comedy of Errors* manages to cram into fewer than 1,800 lines a complicated double twin plot, an overarching romance plot of family separation and reunion, and the two less developed actions of Syracusan Antipholus's wooing of Luciana and Syracusan Dromio's entanglement with the kitchen-wench. *James the Fourth*, *Knack to Know a Knave*, and *Pinner of Wakefield* are similarly generous with plots; and *Old Wives' Tale* is positively prodigal.

In itself, plot proliferation does not guarantee variety of tone. The kinds of plots developed in these comedies, however, indicate that such variety was desired. The commonest device, so common as to constitute a cliché of the convention, was to ground different plots in different social realms. Country bumpkins are set against princes and princesses, yeoman wooings against affairs of state, rude mechanicals against courtly lovers and creatures of the fairy world.

The low-life characters typically manage to stand apart from the main action, even when they are not actively pursuing plots of their own. Whether or not they, like the clowns Hamlet de-

A WORLD ELSEWHERE   31

plored, spoke more than was set down for them, the written
script shows them full of their own concerns, which seldom
coincide for long with those of their social betters. Mouse in
Mucedorus is a willing enough servant, but he has never heard of
the king, and his real obsession is not romance and revenge but
cakes and ale. Slipper in *James the Fourth*, Pierce in *John of Bordeaux*, Miles in *Friar Bacon*, Sly in the *Shrew* plays, Speed in *Two
Gentlemen*, the whole corps of servants in *Two Angry Women*, all
are similarly preoccupied. Gnatto of *Honest Man* voices the simple creed of all comic servants and rustics: "Tis better to be
dronken and drousie, / Than hunger starved and lousie."[19] Like
Bottom, they can easily forgo romance for a peck of provender.
Sex comes up frequently, to be sure, in their own lives or as matter for comment in the lives of others, but always as a placket-
and-codpiece affair. It is accepted, like hunger, as a physical
need. "Such is the simplicity of man," says Costard, "to hearken
after the flesh" (*LLL* I.i.212-213). Happiness for comedy clowns
is the gratification of animal appetites. Fittingly enough, clowns
tend to hobnob with animals. One thinks at once of Launce and
his dog Crab, who in *Two Gentlemen* carry on a relationship almost as complicated as the affairs of the gentlemen themselves.
The shepherd in *Honest Man* is not given a name, but his dog is
individualized as Slip—not to be confused with Craft, who is
Goodman Corydon's dog. Jenkin in *Pinner of Wakefield* holds
converse with horses, and one of the poor men in *Knave* is of like
mind: "Wel neighbor, we wil have the horse examined before an
officer, and my boy Jack shall write what the horse speaks."[20]
Talking animals are not unknown in romance, of course, but the
point here is not magic but simple affinity. The ass's head fixed
on Bottom expresses part of the nature of his world.

With clown scenes usually interspersed throughout the doings
of lovers, rulers, and magicians, no value or perspective is allowed to hold sway for very long. Exchanges like the following,
from *Old Wives' Tale*, remind us that a single view of life cannot
tell all:

[19] *A Knack to Know an Honest Man*, ed. H. DeVocht, Malone Society Reprints
(Oxford, 1910), ll. 658-659.
[20] *A Knack to Know a Knave*, ed. G. R. Proudfoot, Malone Society Reprints
(Oxford, 1964), ll. 1016-1017.

32   A WORLD ELSEWHERE

> *Old Woman*: Once upon a time there was a King or a
> Lord, or a Duke that had a faire daughter, the fairest
> that ever was; as white as snowe, and as redd as bloud:
> and once uppon a time his daughter was stollen away,
> and hee sent all his men to seeke out his daughter, and
> hee sent so long, that he sent all his men out of his
> Land.
> *Frolicke*: Who drest his dinner then?[21]

Hearkening after the flesh is not merely a matter of food and
sex, and its uses to comment on romantic motives are various.
Ideal heroism in the *Pinner of Wakefield* is balanced against Jenkin's comic cowardice. Romantic courtship is set off by the
earthier modes of Launce in *Two Gentlemen*, Costard in *Love's
Labour's Lost*, and Trotter in *Fair Em*, who manifests his lovesickness with a head-kerchief and a urinal. The problems of
clowns tend to be concrete. While highborn folk in *Old Wives'
Tale* worry about spells and prophecies, the friends of Jack, the
deceased town drunk, are stuck with a body to bury and no
money to pay the sexton. This obsession with the concrete is
often the basis for the comic counterpoint between clowns and
great ones. We would doubtless never have been told that Craft
is Goodman Corydon's dog (who Goodman Corydon is, we
never do find out), except that this news is all the bewildered
shepherd can come up with when First Senator philosophizes in
abstractions: "Craft often lurketh in a shepheards coate" (*Honest
Man*, ll. 193-196). We see the same literalism in Trotter's ker-
chief and urinal, and in Costard's discovery that *remuneration*
means three farthings while *guerdon* is eleven-pence farthing better.

Costard's role in the word games of *Love's Labour's Lost* is
to deflate linguistic pretensions all about him with perfect good
will and almost perfect ignorance. Many of his fellows in other
comedies seem to have a special option on verbal fun. Any one
of them is likely to bring the action to a temporary halt while he
bandies insults, strings along comic catalogues, chops logic, and
generally indulges himself without much thought for his task of

---

[21] *The Old Wives' Tale*, ll. 110-116, in *The Life and Works of George Peele*, ed.
C. T. Prouty et al., vol. III (New Haven and London, 1970).

A WORLD ELSEWHERE   33

the moment. That expandable time of comedy, which insures
last-minute rescues and reunions, also allows such digressions in
the middle of the most urgent events. Sometimes a digression is
involuntary, as the clown fails to see the point through a haze of
malapropisms and mistakings, but the effect on the audience is
deflective in any case. In *Two Angry Women*, not all the plans for
future marriage and troubles with current ones can divert
Nicholas from his happy flow of proverbs. Even murder, it
seems, is not too pressing a mission to interrupt with verbal
humor: Jaques in *James the Fourth*, hired to kill the virtuous
queen Dorothea, chatters through the attempt in Franglais.

It is not only clowns who make a pastime of words, of course.
They are centers of linguistic foolery, but frequently they draw
their masters into the game, and sometimes the masters—and
mistresses—play on their own. Courtship, the staple of comic
plots, can be a battle of wits, as in *Two Angry Women*, *Taming of
the Shrew*, and especially *Love's Labour's Lost*, where the wordplay reaches epidemic dimensions and involves all levels of society.

Again a question arises about generic distinction. Does the
wordplay of comic speech differ from verbal wit in tragic
speech? It is not unusual in Shakespearean tragedy to find punning at moments of high seriousness, as in Antony's words over
the bleeding body of Caesar:

> O world, thou wast the forest to this hart;
> And this indeed, O world, the heart of thee!
> <div align="right">(<i>JC</i> iii.i.208-209)</div>

Generalizations must be tentative here, but I think one can draw
a broad distinction between tragic wordplay, where the crucial
element is the *word*, and comic wordplay, where it is the *play*.
That is, in tragic speech (as opposed to comic speech in a
tragedy, like Mercutio's Queen Mab speech in *Romeo and Juliet*),
the primary function of the pun is to illuminate by its conjunction of meanings some aspect of the tragic action. The heart/hart
pun contains in little a central paradox of *Julius Caesar*, that
Caesar is spiritually as vital to Rome as the heart is to the body
but is physically a vulnerable animal. While some kinds of wit
can be used effectively in either comedy or tragedy, it is still pos-

34   A WORLD ELSEWHERE

sible to see, opposed to the tragic pun, a distinctively comic use
of wordplay. It may make indirect comment on the action,
much as the *Shrew* induction glances obliquely at the play
proper, but essentially it is self-contained. Characters and audience alike enjoy multiple meanings and mind-expanding juxtapositions within their own system of reference rather than as
focusers of larger significance. Extended wit-passages are typical
of comedy but not of tragedy, where their self-propulsion, their
virtuoso quality, would deflect emotional concentration from
the tragic situation. In any kind of play, to be sure, the virtuoso
instinct might get out of hand and threaten dramatic integrity;
the point is that it was the Kempes who had license to extem-
porize, not the Burbages and Alleyns.

It follows that comic wit-passages often strike us as in a way
detachable from their immediate context. They may well have
their place in the play's imaginative world, especially as parody
or clarifying alternative vision, but their true relation to the
thrust of plot is like the relation of play to ongoing life in
Huizinga's formulation. Play is self-contained, nonutilitarian,
not imposed by necessity; "it stands outside the immediate satisfaction of wants, indeed it interrupts the appetitive process. It
interpolates itself as a temporary activity satisfying in itself and
ending there."[22] This is a good description of what is happening
when Slipper in *James the Fourth* interrupts his announced haste
to bandy logic with Sir Bartram, or when in *Two Gentlemen*
Launce rollicks through some eighty-five lines of punning and
comic inventory before telling Speed, "Thy master stays for
thee at the Northgate" (III.i.362). Even when passages of wit advance the comic action, as they sometimes do in courtship
scenes, the manner is still more important than the matter.

Verbal wit involves a certain kind of awareness, a consciousness of disparate meanings and disparate ways of seeing. It is
particularly at home in comedies, which characteristically not
only reward those characters who are most fully aware but en-
courage multiple awareness in the audience. Much of the spectators' pleasure derives from their knowledge of what characters

---

[22] Johan Huizinga, *Homo Ludens: A Study of the Play Element in Culture*, introd.
G. Steiner (New York and Evanston, 1970), p. 27.

A WORLD ELSEWHERE 35

onstage don't know—that Ephesian Antipholus is berating the wrong Dromio, that murder victim Sempronio is not really dead (*Honest Man*), that the youth whom Lady Anderson finds so attractive is really Dorothea in disguise (*James the Fourth*). Allusions to the business of playmaking and play production can give the audience an extra awareness, of itself as a group of real persons watching a piece of make-believe. Both *Shrew* inductions, for example, remind the spectators that what they are seeing is highly artificial: boys dressed as women, players who might as well perform other parts as these. The audience can see in Sly both its representative (especially in *A Shrew*, where he welcomes the prospect of a play) and its inferior. His comments are at best simpleminded, allowing the spectators to feel their own sophistication by contrast. They are the real gentry, so to speak, while they know that Sly is only a make-believe lord. One among them who is truly sophisticated may sense beyond this a kind of ironic identification with Sly, for the playmaker-deceivers are to assume a temporary power over him as the lord and his servants do with Sly, drawing him into their world to make of him what they will. The *James the Fourth* induction is less complex in effect, but in presenting the main action as a demonstration and sometimes as Bohan's fiction it also calls attention to the artifice of the play and the contrasting reality of the spectators. Oberon, the stage audience, is a kind of intermediary. He has a world of his own that is different from both the play world and the audience world.

The popular device of the play within the play can make the audience similarly self-conscious. This is the effect of the Nine Worthies pageant in *Love's Labour's Lost* and the "Pyramus and Thisbe" play in *Midsummer Night's Dream*—but not, I think, of "Soliman and Perseda" in *The Spanish Tragedy* or "The Murder of Gonzago" in *Hamlet*. In these tragedies we are concentrating on the *content* of the inserted plays: the stabbings that fulfill Hieronymo's long-sought revenge and the reenactment of Claudius's crime. In the comedies it is the *process* of playacting that compels our attention, partly because it is so badly done. The actors are miscast; they mistake or forget their lines; they cannot submerge their own identities, or their everyday relationships with the nobles looking on, enough to sustain any

36   A WORLD ELSEWHERE

dramatic illusion. Nor do the nobles themselves cooperate by
suspending disbelief. On the contrary, they keep refusing to accept the convention by which a clown can be a conquering general or a man can be a wall.[23] They have little to say about what
is being presented, but a great deal about how it is being presented. On the other hand, in the Mousetrap scene of *Hamlet*,
the prince, who earlier talked much of acting styles and techniques, directs our attention while the play is actually going on
not to process but to content. "That's wormwood. . . . If she
should break it now! . . . You shall see anon how the murderer
gets the love of Gonzago's wife" (III.ii.176, 219, 258-259). In
The Spanish Tragedy the principals in the main action are the actors in the "play"; the passions they voice and their deaths at the
end are real. The two tragedies offer plays of their own genre
closely fused with their own actions and competently acted. The
two comedies offer a heroic pageant and a tragedy, comically at
odds with their own actions and acted so as to remind the audience constantly that it is watching a play. The generic distinction
is like that I drew earlier between *word*play (emphasis on content) in tragedy and word*play* (emphasis on process) in comedy.
Certainly the play within the play can function in other ways
which have nothing to do with generic differences. But when its
handling invites audience self-awareness, it has a special affinity
for the comic.

To sum up: the knowledgeable theatergoer of the early 1590s,
when he went to see a comedy, anticipated a love story with a
happy ending, in which the obstacles to the marriage of true
minds were removed by providential chance and human ingenuity. He would expect disguise, magic, and all manner of
quick changes of appearance and heart. When disaster threatened
the principals, he could feel secure under any momentary agitation, trusting the playwright to reverse the course of events and
even, if necessary, to resurrect the dead. He would be used to
seeing the playwright overturn his everyday verities—the demands of retributive justice, the inexorable progress of time, the
authority of parents over children, the superiority of men over
women, the law of averages, even the basic processes of cause

[23] Anne Righter, *Shakespeare and the Idea of the Play* (London, 1962), pp. 109-
111.

A WORLD ELSEWHERE

and effect—seeing this not with discomfort but with delight. He would look forward to diversity of action and character, and though he might enjoy scenes of romantic wooing and high policy, he would be pleased by sudden switches to servants in the pantry or rustics in the field. Like Gossip Tattle in Jonson's *Staple of News*, he would fain see the Fool. He might indeed not agree with that lady that the fool or clown "is the finest man i' the company . . . and has all the wit,"[24] but he would expect him to have a good deal of it. Our theatergoer would enjoy puns, malapropisms, and insult contests for their own sake, not worrying overmuch about the plot, which obligingly slowed down to make room for them. He could take pleasure both in lofty idealism and in the earthy practicality that recognizes no ideal higher than the belly, in *James the Fourth* rejoice both at Dorothea's highminded fidelity and Slipper's different philosophy: "I cannot abide a full cup unkissed, a fat capon uncarved, a full purse unpicked."[25]

For the literate among the audience, these expectations would be reinforced at several points by acquaintance with Roman comedy and with prose romance, especially the translations and imitations of Greek and Spanish romances. Playwrights drew directly on the romances—Gosson in the 1580s cites *Amadís de Gaul*, Heliodorus's *Aethiopian History*, and the Arthurian tales as major sources for the drama[26]—but apart from such direct borrowing the widespread popularity of prose romance helped solidify the stage conventions of comedy by parallel emphases. The world of Heliodorus's Theagenes and Chariclea, of Sidney's Pyrocles and Musidorus, of Amadís and Palmerin and their progeny, is much like the milieu we have been examining in romantic comedy.[27] Here too actions are propelled by love and end in lovers' unions. Fortune provides both near-catastrophes and providential escapes in a world full of strange chances yet

[24] *The Staple of News*, first intermean, ll. 23-24, in *Ben Jonson*, ed. C. H. Herford, P. Simpson, and E. Simpson, vol. VI (Oxford, 1938).

[25] Robert Greene, *The Scottish History of James the Fourth*, ed. Norman Sanders (London, 1970), I.ii.21-23.

[26] *Playes Confuted*, D5v.

[27] Moses Hadas attributes the emphasis in Greek prose romance on love, intrigue, and recognition to the influence of New Comedy. *Three Greek Romances* (Indianapolis, 1964), p. vii.

38   A WORLD ELSEWHERE

ultimately benevolent to faithful lovers. Children are regularly
exposed in the wilderness yet always survive. Rapes are attempted yet never accomplished. Shipwrecks are not fatal, and
pirates never kill anyone important. True, death is not totally
alien to the romance spirit as it is to the comic; the tendencies of
these tales to spread out over several generations and to present
contests of good and evil raise the casualty count considerably.
But the principal characters lead charmed lives. Even Sidney's
Basileus, believed dead through many pages of the *Arcadia* and
theoretically dispensable as the father of grown-up heirs, reminds us of the stage resurrections when he awakes from his
drugged sleep just in time to stop his daughters' lovers from
being executed as his murderers. Time is as elastic in the romances as in the comedies, and other ordinarily fixed realities are
equally fluid and shifting. Characters assume disguises and new
roles at every point, highborn knights and ladies easily becom-
ing servants, shepherds, Moors, or army captains when the situation calls for it. Magic is omnipresent in the Spanish romances,
transforming people into animals and causing whole landscapes
to disappear. It is no wonder that Don Quixote, after his steady
diet of Amadises and Palmerins, suspected sorcerers at every
turn and ascribed even the most commonplace events to en-
chantment. In the world he knew best it was the only sensible
attitude. Variety of tone is not a feature of foreign romance, but
the English tradition occasionally finds room for unromantic
peasants next to its elegant principals: Doron and Carmela in
Greene's *Menaphon*, for example, and the Dametas-Miso-Mopsa
group in Sidney's *Arcadia*.

Familiarity with this romance world was not limited to the
well-bred and well-educated. If "silly gentlewomen" reveled in
Amadís and Palmerin,[28] so did shopkeepers and craftsmen. The
daily fare of Don Quixote, gentleman of La Mancha, is also that
of Ralph, grocer's apprentice of London in *The Knight of the
Burning Pestle* (1607). In *Eastward Ho* (1605) Gertrude, a gold-
smith's daughter, measures the behavior of her husband by that
of Lancelot, Tristram, and Palmerin of England.[29]

[28] Robert Burton, *The Anatomy of Melancholy*, ed. Floyd Dell and Paul
Jordan-Smith (New York, 1938), p. 700.
[29] There is plentiful evidence of the popular taste for romances and of the spe-

A WORLD ELSEWHERE   39

The comedies of Plautus and Terence, while hardly standard reading for apprentices, would have been familiar to anyone with a grammar-school education. Read or seen now, they seem far from the spirit of romantic comedy. The emphasis on intrigue and the everpresent cash nexus, with actions turning on sharp trading and the procurement of money, create a closed, hard, rather heartless atmosphere quite different from the expansive sentiment of the Elizabethans (the city comedy later popular on the Jacobean stage would be a different matter). Yet Madeleine Doran has cited Renaissance comment and book illustrations to demonstrate convincingly that readers of the time perceived the plays of Plautus and Terence as love stories leading to marriage by way of fortuitous revelations, happy coincidences, and newly discovered identities—in short, as essentially romantic.[30] If we look from this angle, paying attention to structure rather than to atmosphere, the links between Roman and Elizabethan comedy are clear enough. Love, or anyway sexual desire, sets in motion the plots of Plautus and Terence, and their journeys end in lovers' meetings. A good deal of manipulation and attempted manipulation goes on in between, sometimes by means of disguise and impersonation; and fortune cooperates to produce the happy ending, generally through the chance discovery that the desired slave-girl is freeborn after all and thus an acceptable bride for the hero. The comic law that favors lovers usually stretches coincidence even farther to provide her in the same revelation scene with a long-lost parent, and all of this happens just in time to prevent disaster. The inversion of male and female status which appears to have charmed the Elizabethans had no appeal for the Romans: heroines for the most part are passive objects. But Roman comedy overturns sanctified hierarchies of authority when the old surrender to the wishes of the young and the slaves lead and outwit their masters.

The Roman slaves are usually more involved in the action than their servant or rustic counterparts of the 1590s, but they

---

cial middle-class predilection for the Amadís and Palmerin cycles: see Henry Thomas, *Spanish and Portuguese Romances of Chivalry* (Cambridge, 1920), chap. 7; and Louis B. Wright, *Middle-Class Culture in Elizabethan England* (Chapel Hill, 1935), chaps. 4 and 11.

[30] Doran, *Endeavors of Art*, pp. 174-181.

40   A WORLD ELSEWHERE

are not too busy to establish a similar alternative perspective by
mocking their young masters' lovesickness and their old masters' high-minded speeches. Talkative, impudent, always hungry and thirsty, the Pseudoluses and Peniculuses could fit easily
enough into the taverns and pantries of Elizabethan comedy.
This variation in tone gets extra stress in Plautus's plays from
excursions into verbal play and exuberant abuse. Plautus often
creates another kind of dual perspective when his characters step
momentarily outside the play and call attention to its artificiality. Slaves regularly chat with the audience, announce their
plans, and tell what to watch for. Terence did not follow Plautus
in exploiting the gap between artificial play and real audience,
but his fondness for double plots makes for another sort of variety in perspective. While the plots are closely intertwined and do
not differ significantly in tone or social level as in Elizabethan
comedy, there is nevertheless more than one focus of attention.

The conventions established in the theater of the 1580s and
1590s and strengthened by parallel patterns and preoccupations
in narrative romance and classical comedy continued to flourish
in later Elizabethan and Jacobean drama, although the rise of
Jonsonian satiric comedy created a rival mode with, to some extent, a different set of conventions. Of the conventions we have
been considering, it is time to ask *why* this particular set
emerges, what they have to do with one another, what gives life
to this "significant form."

Shakespeare never advanced a particular theory of comedy in
his plays, nor does he seem to have paid much attention to those
current among critics in his day. In the absence of any personal
affirmations, we may return to the well-worn traditions of the
fourth-century grammarians Donatus, Evanthius, and Diomedes, which provide at least a starting place from which to probe
comic conventions. Comedy, say the theorists, conducts the
private affairs of citizens from a turbulent beginning through
vicissitudes without serious danger to a happy conclusion; while
tragedies draw their plots from history, comic plots are typically
fictions.[31] Even in this very rudimentary description, based on

---

[31] Doran, pp. 105-109; Marvin T. Herrick, *Comic Theory in the Sixteenth Century* (Urbana, Ill., 1950), pp. 58-60.

A WORLD ELSEWHERE

New Comedy and developed in part as an obverse to Aristotle's description of tragedy, there are the beginnings of a comic philosophy.

Take, for example, the premise that comedy ends happily and tragedy ends sadly. Inasmuch as all stories are about potential and realized trouble (else where would be the story?), this means that comedy evokes disaster only to avoid it, while tragedy evokes disaster as its destiny. Tragedy, as I have said in the Introduction, moves towards the inevitable, the chain of causality that denies or renders irrelevant all alternatives but one. Comedy always finds an alternative to break the chain. All its shifts and sleights can be seen as functions of an "evitability" principle, ways of creating new situations when the old ones become impossible. In real experience, death is the inevitable, no-alternative end of every human story—when we stop to think of it. Comedy gets around death, either by ignoring it completely or by presenting it as nonfinal, illusory.

It follows that comedy is less at home with "real experience" in this sense than is tragedy. The insistence of Evanthius and later Servius on the feigned plot as a distinctive feature of comedy is not completely accidental and arbitrary, any more than the prescription of historical plots for tragedy. The tragic writer works within the given limits of legend or history to express their significance as his hero must find *his* significance within the limits of inevitable failure and death. But the comic writer borrows from fictions and is as free to mold events as are his own magicians and manipulators.

Under the conventional rank and plot distinctions—the decisive acts of great ones for tragedy, the small change of common folk for comedy—can be discerned two opposite senses of life. I suggested in the Introduction that the conventions of tragedy could be related to a sense of one's own life as unique and never to be repeated, each decision and act consequential. Comedy's lesser stakes and its cast of more ordinary people reflect the obverse: life felt as common and ongoing, an endless stream in which we are participants but not the whole story. It is the contrast between Hamlet and the gravediggers, Cleopatra and the clown; between the sense of fateful moment and the relaxed, long-range view; between sharply defined identity and common

42   A WORLD ELSEWHERE

humanity (the gravediggers and the clown are not named). The dukes and even kings who people romantic comedy offer no serious qualification here. They are off-duty, so to speak, almost wholly engaged in wooings and cross-wooings. Life-and-death matters like war between England and Scotland or between Christians and Saracens merely provide a backdrop for the loves of James the Fourth and Orlando.

The commonplaces of classical and Renaissance comic theory, then, point to the intrinsic importance of evitability, freedom, and continuity of life in comedy. Those ideas came mainly out of examination of the ongoing New Comedy tradition. The commentaries are less valuable when they try to interpret that tradition in acceptable moral terms. Notions of strict didactic purpose, of holding a mirror to all manners and exposing the defective to ridicule and scorn, strike us as irrelevant to Elizabethan romantic comedy, and to much that went before it. Why, one wonders, should this edifying mirror of life be trained so relentlessly on courtship, doubtless a time of folly but one that after all occupies comparatively little time in the average human life? If moral instruction were essential rather than accidental to the comic playwright's aim, if it really dictated his principles of selection, surely we would expect to see many areas of life illuminated in turn, not this same one again and again. And why do certain characters and situations keep popping up while others never appear?

Two of these recurrent characters, the manipulator and the clown, have already received some attention. Often combined in the clever slave of Roman comedy, the two are distinct in figure and function on the Elizabethan stage. In terms of plot, the manipulator—magician, disguiser, clever heroine—acts out the natural law of comedy, the liberation from necessity and even probability that allows a harmonious ending to come out of a mess. But, as I noted earlier in this chapter, manipulators may operate around the edges of, and even in opposition to, the evolution toward a comic close. Looked at apart from plot promotion, simply as part of the comic milieu, the omnipresent manipulator constitutes an assertion of human power over environment and events, of the mind's power to change the intractable real into the wished-for. The clown, whose function in the plot is usually minor, is primarily a milieu-defining figure. His

A WORLD ELSEWHERE
43

principal value to romantic comedy, I have suggested, is to speak for the truth of animal needs and pleasures that is ignored in the truth of high romance—that is, to help meet comedy's need for alternatives of plot and philosophy.

Who else may be called permanent residents of the comic world? "Humours" of various sorts (pedants, braggarts, scolds, and so on), marriageable young men and women, and parents and other authority figures. The clown, preoccupied as he is with cakes and ale, is a kind of humour character, but he differs from the others in the wider scope of his comments and in his invincibility. The braggart or the pedant is usually introduced into the comic action in order to be worsted by it. The clown is rarely discomfited for long, and the play's end finds him confident and self-satisfied.

Young lovers also usually achieve their objective. Crosswooings are a staple of romantic comedy, and clearly not every lover can get the mate he or she wants at the start. But most lovers get *someone*. The real leftovers are few, generally minor characters like Thurio in *Two Gentlemen*. Comedy's whole trend is toward rewarding love, and if the love has been wrongly directed, sudden changes of heart can be contrived to guide each Jack to a suitable Jill.[32] In some cases suitability is not explored beyond the externals of rank and station; in others temperaments are matched—Berowne and Rosaline in *Love's Labour's Lost*, Petruchio and Kate in *Taming of the Shrew*. Tidy matching is carried to the point of parody in *Old Wives' Tale*, when ugly but gentle-tempered Celauta gets a blind husband and pretty but shrewish Zantippa a deaf one.

The fate of parents and dukes is more or less dependent upon their attitudes to the favored young lovers. If they have opposed young desires, they have to give in. Egeus's will is overborne, and even Theseus, who does the overbearing, simply represents the defeat of senior authority in a more gracious aspect. His own Athenian law is going by the boards as well as Egeus's tyrannical will. The two women of Abington arrive at their happy ending only by yielding to the initiative of their marriageable children:

---

[32] Both Fortunio in *Honest Man* and Ferdinand in *John of Bordeaux* end up without spouses in spite of their repentance. They have been guilty of attempted rape, but then so has Sempronio, who in fact gets the girl Fortunio wanted. One suspects here not a moral judgment but a shortage of available female characters.

44   A WORLD ELSEWHERE

Mall and Frank carry all before them. Fair Em's puzzled but loyal father is allowed to keep his dignity, which suggests that the old fare best as willing supporters of the young.

What determines winners and losers in comedy? While moral considerations may enter in peripherally, they cannot be central in a system that leaves foolish Thurio disconsolate but rewards vicious Proteus with Julia. Clowns are not better, morally speaking, than shrews or braggarts. Rather than virtue's conquest of vice, comedy gives us two other sorts of victory, of youth over age and of the comprehensive vision over the rigid and constraining humour. Both the typical characters and their typical disposition at the end point us back to the roots of comedy in ancient fertility rituals. One need not accept wholly F. M. Cornford's derivation of all characteristics of Old Comedy from Dionysiac ritual in order to find illumination in his discussion, especially of the spiritual links between the fertility rites and the scheme of winners and losers I have been examining. The rites invoke fertility and drive away death by a battle in which summer defeats winter, or by the displacement of an old king by a young one, or by the resurrection of a dead god, or by the expulsion of a scapegoat and the bringing in of green branches. Whatever form they take, they are about life, not virtue. The forms themselves show obvious links with romantic comedy's thrust toward mating and its insistence that the barren old fall back before the fertile young.

The downfall of the humour characters may be understood in terms of Cornford's discussion of the comic character types *eiron*, *alazon*, and *bomolochos*, and Northrop Frye's expansion on the theme in *Anatomy of Criticism*.[33] The central contrast is between eiron, the ironist who seems less than he is, and alazon, the imposter who pretends to be more than he is. At the heart of comedy is their contest, which always ends with the eiron victorious and the alazon cast out or shown up. The bomolochos, or buffoon, has no necessary role in this action but functions, as Frye says, to promote the festive mood.

[33] F. M. Cornford, *The Origin of Attic Comedy* (Cambridge, 1934), chaps. 7 and 8; Frye, *Anatomy*, pp. 171-175. The terms come from the *Tractatus Coisilianus*, a Greek outline treatise on comedy closely related to Aristotle's *Poetics*, *Ethics*, and *Rhetoric*.

A WORLD ELSEWHERE

Up to a point, these are useful categories for the characters we have been observing. It is easy to see the bomolochos in the Elizabethan clown; still easier to see the various humour characters as alazones, pretentious yet imprisoned in their own narrow self-images. The superior perception of the eiron certainly marks the manipulators, magicians, disguisers. There are problems, however. What are we to do with Kate, who is surely an alazon in her shrewishness and in the final scene is just as surely an eiron? The lovers who so consistently win their way to marriage ought all to be eirones, but does the term really fit Proteus in *Two Gentlemen*, Mall and Frank in *Two Angry Women*, or the whole quartet of lovers in *Midsummer Night's Dream*? Ironic awareness is not their strong suit. Frye's explanation, that the lover-hero "is an *eiron* figure because . . . the dramatist tends to play him down and make him rather neutral and unformed in character,"[34] is unconvincing. Perhaps the central terms serve best not to label characters but to define the basic conflict of comedy and explain its resolution. The eiron principle must win out over the alazon principle: that is, flexibility and superior knowledge of self must defeat—or transform—self-deception and the rigidity that results from it. Romantic lovers, even when they do not resort to disguise and are incapable of manipulation, nevertheless shift, improvise, adapt to new circumstances. This potential aligns them with the eiron, who has power in reserve, and against the alazon, whose vaunted power hides inner weakness. This is the potential which Petruchio awakens in Kate during her taming. Even the rather limp young men of *Midsummer Night's Dream* have it. Egeus the alazon, full of extreme threats in his role of heavy father, in action can only proclaim his will and stand fast. But Lysander and Demetrius adapt and act, one taking his girl to the woods to escape the law while the other reacts to this stealing of his presumptive bride by active pursuit.

The comic types may seem to have led us far away from affinities with fertility ritual in the invocation of life and the banishment of barrenness and death. Important connections exist, however. They are perhaps most apparent in the bomolochos, or clown, whose being is one long hymn to physical

[34] *Anatomy*, p. 173.

46   A WORLD ELSEWHERE

processes and whose departures from the plot into word-fun convey the purest kind of vitality, the kind that has no purpose beyond its own high spirits. One may also see in some versions of youth's victory over age the eiron-alazon opposition. Lysander, Demetrius, and Egeus are a case in point. But not all elders are alazones. *Midsummer Night's Dream* itself offers in addition to Egeus one authority figure, Oberon, who is clearly an eiron in his magical control of events, and another, Theseus, who, far from standing against life and fertility, is about to get married. What defines an alazon is not his age but his interference with ongoing life, his own life and that of others. He (or, of course, she) may stand in the way of a marriage, or may be overtly unfestive, like the revelry-hating Malvolio. In any case, the alazon is anti-life in his rigidity, his incapacity for change and expansion.

One might ask at this point why comedy rewards lovers for intransigent fidelity but punishes other kinds of intransigence? The answer, I suspect, is that lovers are stubborn in the cause of change and expansion. A lover's drive is beyond himself to union with another, while the Shylocks and Malvolios are preoccupied with their single selves and therefore trapped in them. Malvolio crystallizes the distinction. He thinks of himself as a lover, but in his daydream (*Twelfth Night* II.v) Olivia is not really a separate being at all: she is an adjunct, an adornment of his own self-image.

This look at the types and dispositions of stock comic characters has led us back once more to the principles adumbrated in the discussion of traditional definitions of comedy and of the omnipresent manipulators and clowns. Comedy celebrates the flexibility that ensures new life. In character relationships, in plot movement, and in perspective it rejects single necessity for multiple possibility. Readers familiar with Susanne Langer's brilliant exposition of comic rhythm will recognize in this eiron principle of flexibility and power in reserve something like her theme of survival through adaptation and "brainy opportunism." Starting from biology rather than literary theory, she sees the comic rhythm generated by the organism's impulse to survive and propagate, to respond to obstacles by varying its form and behavior and by exploiting whatever opportunities are at hand. For

A WORLD ELSEWHERE 47

man, this adaptation and exploitation are largely matters of mental agility.[35]

The eiron principle also helps us understand the persistent popularity of disguise in comedy. Disguise confers power. It may be an important manipulative power, like Rosalind's in *As You Like It*, as she sorts out the love affairs of Arden (including her own) by being both boy and girl. Even a disguise like Julia's in *Two Gentlemen*, which does not put her in control of events, nevertheless allows her to see and learn things that would be hidden from her in her normal role. At the least, the disguiser has the power of knowledge, the dual perspective that casts him as both participant and observer, simultaneously inside and outside the action. Such a dual perspective may bring embarrassment or even pain, but in the multifarious world of comedy a single perspective is dangerous. It is the quality of the alazon. Powerful disguiser-figures like Rosalind, and Portia in *Merchant of Venice*, show more strongly the liberating force of disguise. By dramatic convention it allows them to acquire, not just new trappings, but a new identity, without losing their own. Rosalind can be at once a girl in love and a boy scoffing at love; Portia becomes a learned doctor of laws without ceasing to be Portia. The limitations of the single self are transcended.

Other forms of this transcendence in comedy involve sequence rather than superimposition. *As You Like It* demonstrates the power of disguise, but even Rosalind's activities cannot achieve the entire comic resolution. The rest of it—the banished duke's reinstatement and the return of the happy couples to court—comes about because Duke Frederick, against all reasonable expectation, is suddenly converted from hardened tyrant to repentant eremite. Comedy is full of such unlikely transformations of character. Shrewish Kate becomes a docile though fun-loving wife, Proteus changes from faithful friend and lover to traitor, informer, and would-be rapist, and back again to friend and lover.[36] Critics used to complain that such quick and com-

[35] Langer, *Feeling and Form*, pp. 327-331.

[36] Even a change of sex is not ruled out. In Lyly's *Gallathea*, when two girls who have disguised themselves as boys fall in love with each other (each knowing herself to be female but thinking the other male), Venus straightens out a seemingly hopeless situation by changing one of them into a boy.

plete transformations were unconvincing, even ludicrous. More recently we have been taught to see them in terms of Elizabethan psychology or dramatic technique. Still, we may admit that Shakespeare's contemporaries tended to see passions as autonomous and that sudden repentance makes for exciting theater, and yet observe that these shifts are far more numerous and noticeable in comedy than in tragedy. This is no accident. Comedy's penchant for alternatives and multiple possibilities points naturally toward a flexible identity that may change in response to new situations, a self that is not fixed but alterable and even potentially plural. There is no such possibility in tragedy. The tragic protagonist may feel his identity disintegrating under siege—"Who is it that can tell me who I am?"—but no alternative identity is possible: "I am Duchess of Malfi still."

That Webster's heroine must be Duchess of Malfi *still* (that is, *always*) is part of her tragedy. But the contrary notion of an unfixed identity, liberating as it is, has its darker side as well. We have seen it in the panic of Hermia, the madness of Orlando. When hierarchies are overturned, when realities are transformed by magic or trickery, when even the self is not secure, chaos is a real threat. Comedy's audiences are protected by what I have called its natural law, which allows them to eat their cake and have it too. We want unrestricted liberty, but we fear the loss of security that goes along with that liberty. Comedy serves up alternatives, but it makes sure that the alternative will be better than what preceded it.

I have suggested earlier that this benevolent natural law is the only one comedy holds sacred. By now it is clear that comic lawlessness extends far beyond the silly oaths broken, the ridiculous laws overturned, even the servants and women who are cleverer than their master-males. Orthodox morality, we have seen, often fares no better than social law in comedy. Reason itself is challenged and put down when magic defies the usual laws of nature, when improbable coincidences bring about the happy ending, when mysterious forces draw men and women to each other against all prudence and good sense.

The word games, hyperboles, and digressions of comic speech flout reason in another way. Freud's analysis of jokes is

A WORLD ELSEWHERE

helpful here.[37] He saw wit as a mechanism of rebellion against civilization's restrictions, a use of psychic techniques to open up sources of pleasure normally inaccessible because of repression. The restrictions are moral and social (one must not engage in open sexual display, one must not vent hostility), but they also include reason itself. For adults in most situations, logic is the single accepted means of connecting word with word and idea with idea. Children play freely with other kinds of connection, especially that based on likeness in sound, but they lose this pleasure as they are trained in adult ways. Wit seeks that lost pleasure in a socially acceptable form. As in childhood, the mind uses play as an escape from reason's pressures, but the witticism is socially acceptable because by "making sense" on some level it appeases the demands of reason. Our pleasure, though, comes not from the sense but from the non-sense.

While Freud was interested mainly in the formal joke, his theory of psychic relief can be applied to our enjoyment of other forms of comic speech. Comic hyperbole delights by its rejection of rational possibility:

> What did he when thou saw'st him? What said he? How look'd he? Wherein went he? What makes he here? Did he ask for me? Where remains he? How parted he with thee? And when shalt thou see him again? Answer me in one word.
>
> (*AYL* iii.ii.204-209)

Rosalind's speech communicates something: she is wildly in love. But it communicates this by play rather than by statement. Still further removed from the workaday function of language is Feste's

> Bonos dies, Sir Toby; for as the old hermit of Prague, that never saw pen and ink, very wittily said to a niece of King Gorboduc 'That that is is'; so I, being Master Parson, am Master Parson; for what is 'that' but that, and 'is' but is?
>
> (*TN* iv.ii.12-16)

---

[37] *Wit and Its Relation to the Unconscious*, tr. A. A. Brill (London, n.d.); first published in German in 1905.

50   A WORLD ELSEWHERE

Feste's words communicate his temporary identity as doddery
Sir Topas, but they have no logical necessity in themselves. The
very unlikeliness of a meeting between the hermit of Prague
(whoever he was) and Gorboduc's niece, the extra inconsequence of the hermit's unlettered state—these please us, in the
way that holidays please us. Our language is released from strict
denotation and logic to play at will. There may even be a sense
in such passages, as W. H. Auden has suggested in regard to
comic rhymes, that language has escaped human control entirely, that the words have taken over the situation and on the
strength of their "auditory friendship" are dictating quite unreasonable and unlikely connections.[38]

For Freud wit was a way to attack powerful people and institutions with impunity, to say the forbidden thing. But just as
a joke must in some sense satisfy reason while evading it, so it
ultimately serves the society it is covertly attacking, in that it
gives a safe outlet for antisocial, antihierarchical impulses. The
process as he describes it makes an exact analogy with the traditional dynamic of comedy. Like the comic plot movement, wit
grows out of the conflict between natural drives, especially sexual ones, and the restraints imposed by society. It circumvents
these restraints through fantasy and play, and it concludes in
pleasurable relief. In our relief, as wit-makers and wit-enjoyers,
we are reintegrated with society, partly because hostility has
found a nondangerous release, and partly because wit is a necessarily social activity (there must be at least one hearer to respond
to the jokemaker) which draws people together in mutual pleasure. In this pattern there are places for all the elements of romantic comedy—the rigid society of the opening in which laws or

[38] Auden, "Notes on the Comic," *The Dyer's Hand and Other Essays* (New
York, 1962), p. 380. In the following passage from Jonson's *The Case is Altered*
(1597), the comic impulse to free words from the restraints of denotation is actually stated instead of merely being acted out:

> *Juniper*: . . . you mad *Hierogliphick*, when shal we swagger?
> *Valentine*: *Hieroglyphick*, what meanest thou by that?
> *Juniper*: Meane? Gods so, ist not a good word man? what? stand upon
> meaning with your freinds? Puh, *Absconde*.
>   (I.iv.6-10; Herford and Simpson ed.)

A WORLD ELSEWHERE 51

self-deceptions interfere with the forces of life; the topsy-turviness of the plot itself with its evasions of logic and its destruction of established forms; and the conclusion in a newly harmonious society symbolized in lovers' unions. Comedy shares with wit and with holiday festivity a therapeutic function. Its lawlessness, like theirs, results in better order. Again we touch on Langer's formulation of the comic rhythm, change achieving continuity.

Comic conventions, for all their diversity, do reveal common assumptions. The mode is too rich to enclose in any one formula, but the most pervasive principle is surely *the rejection of singleness*. The single self is seen as deficient, in more senses than one. We have already seen, underlying the comic victory of disguiser over impostor, self-knower over self-deluder, the sense that a single identity or perspective on things is imprisoning. And the conventional plot movement itself, toward marriage or, more usually, marriages, implies that twoness is better than oneness. Shakespeare's comedies in particular stress the uneasiness of isolation, whether self-imposed or not. Singleness is no more satisfying to Olivia in her bored mourning or to Kate in her tantrums than to the more approachable Rosalind or Portia. In this unquestioning, universal drive to pair off the young is not only nature's imperative—the world, as Benedick says, must be peopled—but also a sense that young individuals on their own are incomplete identities, like the hemispheres in Aristophanes' myth in the *Symposium*, which find rest and completion only by uniting with their opposite halves. The multiple marriages that conventionally end comedies operate as symbols for full participation in life.

Even a single shared reality is too limiting. The comedies' devotion to magic means, of course, that landscape and human shape are subject to change without notice; more than that, magic suggests another reality, largely unseen, coexisting with the one we know. It may be comical yet frightening like Friar Bacon's devils, or beautiful like the tiny society of Titania's elves. In any case it is *other*. Comedy must embrace more realities, more truths, than one. The single action, the single social level, the single perspective—these are not enough. Comedy

52 A WORLD ELSEWHERE

must open out to find the more comprehensive view, and so several plots are better than one, and clowns and malcontents must have their say as well as lovers. The audience may even be encouraged, by violations of the dramatic illusion or by references to stagecraft, to be conscious of its own reality coexisting with the fictive ones placed before it.

Delight in plurality informs comedy's witty speech as well. The various techniques of wit that Freud discerned and described[39] are all manipulations of duality. What he calls condensation, for example, creates wit by superimposing one idea on another or by finding a double application for the same word or phrase. Another technique is deviation, "displacing the psychic accent" by an unexpected shift from one perspective to another. Both of these tricks with word meaning have analogies in comedy's treatment of identity. The pun or portmanteau word superimposes one meaning on another, like disguise. Deviation works sequentially to produce a shift in psychic tone comparable to the unpredictable changes of personality brought about in comedy by love or remorse. The other techniques isolated by Freud also depend on twoness: unification of apparently separate things; representation through the opposite; representation through allusion, association, or comparison.

What is satisfying about the comic rejection of singleness? Surely no answer can leave out the unconscious, uncivilized self inside us that resists any restraint on gratification of its wishes. Time-urgency, cause and effect, inevitability, are all versions of singleness; and behind them all is the certainty of the single, inescapable end to each life. Comedy offers us vicarious escape into alternative realities, new roles, second chances. There is pleasure in throwing off these time constraints as there is in evading the social constraints that get in the way of gratification. The throwing-off is carefully limited, of course, both by simple time duration—the two hours' traffic of the stage—and by the comic conventions themselves. The limits are signaled not only by the comedy's coming to an end but by the nature of that end. Society regroups, order replaces anarchy, and journeys end not just in lovers' meetings but in socially sanctioned marriages.

[39] *Wit*, chap. 2.

A WORLD ELSEWHERE 53

Comedy offers conscious pleasures as well, intellectual pleasures that derive directly from its embrace of multiplicity. Empson's conclusions on the double plot give insight here:

> After you have made an imaginative response of one kind to a situation you satisfy more of what is included in your own nature, you are more completely interested in the play, if the chief other response possible is called out too. . . .
>
> . . . Also the device [double plot] sets your judgment free because you need not identify yourself firmly with any one of the characters.[40]

Empson might have linked these two notions more closely than he did, for one leads directly into the other. The first defines our pleasure in the juxtaposition of earthy clowns and lovelorn dukes as the pleasure of completeness. The antiromantic perspective of clown or cynic does not destroy romantic conventions for us, but it does allow us to see around them in a liberating way. That is, it leads to the freeing of the judgment. So it is in that scene in *Midsummer Night's Dream* where the audience participates momentarily in the panic of Hermia, alone in the woods. Dreaming that a serpent was eating her heart, she has awakened to find herself unaccountably deserted by her lover Lysander. She runs off, desperately vowing, "Either death or you I'll find immediately" (II.ii.156). But what do *we* find immediately? *Enter the clowns.* Their rehearsal of "Pyramus and Thisbe" evokes the love death again; but this time we see it differently, as part of an ill-managed fiction. Bottom and company do not believe in the passions they are representing. Much more real for them are the possibly ruffled sensibilities of the ducal court. This second perspective does not cancel out the first, but it frames it as a part of a larger pattern. We see around the edges of Hermia's despair.

We see. Hermia does not. This expansion of awareness is primarily an audience experience. Comedy tends to move its characters in the direction of greater awareness, and a few of them—Rosalind, for instance—embody a kind of ideal com-

---

[40] William Empson, *Some Versions of Pastoral* (London, 1950), pp. 53-54.

54   A WORLD ELSEWHERE

pleteness of vision; but generally we feel superior to the characters, we see more than they do. This too is part of the pleasure of multiple perception.

This, then, was the comic mode which Shakespeare helped to develop and which he had available as a point of reference in his tragic writing.[41] The world it presents is not real, yet it responds

[41] The romantic tradition continues in such plays of the later 1590s and early 1600s as *The Shoemaker's Holiday*, *The Merry Devil of Edmonton*, and *The Fair Maid of the Exchange*, as well as in Shakespeare's own later comedies. The critical or satiric mode being introduced by Jonson and Chapman was setting up its own conventional world, in some respects sharply at odds with that of romantic comedy, but one convention did not displace the other in Shakespeare's time. The romantic mode must have been alive and well in 1607, for example, if the mockery of *The Knight of the Burning Pestle* was to have any point.

In *Every Man Out of his Humour* (1599) Jonson himself shows how strongly the older comic tradition conditioned audience expectations even while he clarifies his own departures from it. He presents two onstage observers of the play, Mitis (mild, gentle) and Cordatus (sagacious). Mitis is a lover of romantic comedy who thinks "that the argument of his *Comœdie* might have beene of some other nature, as of a duke to be in love with a countesse, and that countesse to bee in love with the dukes sonne, and the sonne to love the ladies waiting maid: some such crosse wooing, with a clowne to their servingman, better then to be thus neere, and familiarly allied to the time" (III.vi.195-200; Herford and Simpson ed.). But Cordatus, identified in the Dramatis Personae as "the Authors friend," knows his Cicero: true comedy is not that at all, but "*Imitatio vitæ, Speculum consuetudinis, Imago veritatis*; a thing throughout pleasant, and ridiculous, and accommodated to the correction of manners" (206-209). The exchange, however it stacks the deck in Jonson's favor, brings out some important contrasts between his comedy and the romantic kind. He rejects the concentration on courtship for "manners" in general. Love in his plays is but one occasion for folly among many others: avarice, conceit, superstition, social pretension. And where romantic comedy indulges its lovers, too much indulgence would be out of place in comedies aimed at the *correction* of manners. Critical comedy, indeed, affirms the victory of eiron over alazon, but its emphasis is different. Shakespeare glorifies the eiron principle in his lovers and contrivers. Jonson has some notable eirons—Brainworm, for example—but his main interest is in exposing and discomfiting the hosts of alazon humours. James Feibleman's formula from *In Praise of Comedy* (London, 1939) that comedy "criticizes the finite for not being infinite" (p. 201) works for both kinds. But critical comedy shows up the shortcomings of the finite through satire, while romantic comedy, especially Shakespeare's, is a process of moving the finite toward the infinite, of breaking through the limitations of actuality.

In other ways, the comedies of Jonson, Chapman, and their followers carry on

A WORLD ELSEWHERE

to real human needs in its refusal of restraint and finitude. When Shakespeare addressed restraint and finitude as tragic necessities, he had at hand a developed "world elsewhere" that might be evoked to focus by contrast tragic effect. But for all its coherence the comic convention had its patches of thin ice, its latent strains and even contradictions. Comedy's force is so centrifugal that in its welter of possibilities the potential fragmentation of all form and meaning is never far off. Chaos is held in check only by comedy's arbitrary natural law, and perhaps those magicians and other manipulators were felt to be necessary as visible reassurance that things would finally not fall apart, that the center would hold. Comedy's world might thus be seen not as completely elsewhere but as a possible starting point, or a running accompaniment, or even a constituent element, of Shakespeare's tragic vision.

---

unchanged the conventions and assumptions of romantic comedy. Clever manipulators and disguisers still have their power, plots still multiply, servants are still hungry, and time out is still called for bouts of wit and verbal arabesques.

[2]

Beyond Comedy:
Romeo and Juliet and *Othello*

Both *Romeo and Juliet* and *Othello* use the world of romantic
comedy as a point of departure, though in different ways. In the
early play a well-developed comic movement is diverted into
tragedy by mischance. The change of direction is more or less
imposed on the young lovers, who therefore impress us primarily as victims. Othello and Desdemona are victims too, in one
sense, but in their tragedy destruction comes from within as
well, and comedy is one means by which Shakespeare probes
more deeply into his characters and their love. He gives us in the
early scenes a brief but complete comic structure and then develops his tragedy of love by exploiting the points of strain and
paradox within the system of comic assumptions that informs
that structure.

That these two plays are Shakespeare's only ventures into the
Italianate tragedy of love and intrigue is no coincidence. The
very features that distinguish this subgenre from the more dominant fall-of-the-mighty strain move it closer to comedy: its
sources are typically novelle rather than well-known histories,
its heroes are of lesser rank, its situations are private rather than
public, its main motive force is love. Madeleine Doran, whose
designation and description I follow for this kind of tragedy, has
pointed out its affinity with comedy: "We are in the region
where tragedy and comedy are cut out of the same cloth."[1] The

---

[1] *Endeavors of Art*, p. 137; Italianate intrigue tragedy is discussed on pp. 128-
142. Doran includes under this heading the revenge tragedies *Titus Andronicus*
and *Hamlet*; but these touch only peripherally on sexual love, and as she notes,
they also "cross the lines of the other big class, the tragedy of power" (p. 131).
On the other side, Leo Salingar distinguishes the four *comedies* based on
novelle—*Merchant of Venice*, *Much Ado*, *All's Well*, and *Measure for Measure*—as
verging on the tragic in somberness of mood and seriousness of issue, though

ROMEO AND JULIET, OTHELLO   57

source tales of *Romeo* and *Othello*[2] would, I think, suggest quite readily to Shakespeare the possibility of using comic convention as a springboard for tragedy.

The movement of *Romeo and Juliet* is unlike that of any other Shakespearean tragedy. It becomes, rather than is, tragic. Other tragedies have reversals, but here the reversal is so complete as to constitute a change of genre. Action and characters begin in the familiar comic mold and are then transformed, or discarded, to compose the shape of tragedy.[3] In this discussion I shall have to disregard much of the play's richness, especially of language and characterization, in order to isolate that shaping movement. But isolating it can reveal a good deal about *Romeo*, and may suggest why this early experimental tragedy has seemed to many to fall short of full tragic effect.

---

not in structure; see *Shakespeare and the Traditions of Comedy* (Cambridge, 1974), pp. 301-305.

[2] Arthur Brooke's *Tragical History of Romeus and Juliet* (1562) recounts a story that appears also in the novella collections of Bandello and Painter; another such collection, Giraldi Cinthio's *Hecatommithi* (1565), provided the source for *Othello*.

[3] Various critics have commented on the comic thrust of the early acts of *Romeo*, with interpretations ranging from H. A. Mason's somewhat lame and impotent conclusion, "Shakespeare decided that in a general way the play needed as much comedy as he could get in" (*Shakespeare's Tragedies of Love* [London, 1970], p. 29), to Harry Levin's well-argued contention that the play invokes the artifices of romantic comedy in order to transcend them ("Form and Formality in *Romeo and Juliet*," *Shakespeare Quarterly*, 11 [1960], 3-11). Levin's essay is illuminating on the play's style; he does not speculate on what the transcendence-of-artifice theme (admittedly already used by Shakespeare in a comedy, *Love's Labour's Lost*) has to do with tragic structure. Franklin Dickey deals at some length with *Romeo* as "comical tragedy" in *Not Wisely But Too Well*, pp. 63-88. But Dickey's treatment of comedy is nonorganic, dwelling on such features as the witty heroine, the motif of lovers' absurdity, the debate on love's nature, the elaborate patterning of language, and the *commedia dell'arte* type-characters. He does not deal with why Shakespeare would want to present a tragic story this way or how the large comic element shapes the play as a whole. To explain the presence of that element, Dickey invokes the conventional association of love with comedy. J. M. Nosworthy thinks the comic admixture a mistake and blames it on Shakespeare's immaturity, as well as on the influence of Porter's *Two Angry Women of Abington*. "The Two Angry Families of Verona," *Shakespeare Quarterly*, 3 (1952), 219-226.

58   BEYOND COMEDY

It was H. B. Charlton, concurring in this judgment, who classed the play as "experimental." According to Charlton, Shakespeare in his early history-based tragic plays failed to find a pattern of event and character that would make the dramatic outcome feel inevitable; in *Romeo* he took a whole new direction, that of the modern fiction-based tragedy advocated by the Italian critic Giraldi Cinthio.[4] Certainly dramatic thrust and necessity are unsolved problems in *Titus Andronicus* and *Richard III*, and perhaps in *Richard II* too. But one need not turn to Italian critical theory to explain the new direction of *Romeo*. Given the novella-source, full of marriageable young people and domestic concerns, it seems natural enough that Shakespeare would think of turning his own successful work in romantic comedy to account in his apprenticeship as a tragedian.

We have seen that comedy is based on a principle of "evitability." It endorses opportunistic shifts and realistic accommodations as means to new social health. It renders impotent the imperatives of time and law, either stretching them to suit the favored characters' needs or simply brushing them aside. In the tragic world, which is governed by inevitability and which finds its highest value in personal integrity, these imperatives have full force. Unlike the extrinsic, alterable laws of comedy, law in tragedy is inherent—in the protagonist's own nature and in the larger patterns, divine, natural, and social, with which that personal nature brings him into conflict. Tragic law cannot be altered, and tragic time cannot be suspended. The events of tragedy acquire urgency in their uniqueness and irrevocability: they will never happen again, and one by one they move the hero closer to the end of his own personal time.

Comedy is organized like a game. The ascendancy goes to the clever ones who can take advantage of sudden openings, contrive strategies, and adapt flexibly to an unexpected move from the other side. But luck and instinct win games as well as skill, and I have discussed in the preceding chapter the natural law of comedy that crowns lovers, whether clever or not, with final success. Romeo and Juliet, young and in love and defiant of obstacles, are attuned to the basic movement of the comic game toward marriage and social regeneration. But they do not win:

[4] Charlton, *"Romeo and Juliet" as an Experimental Tragedy*, British Academy Shakespeare Lecture, 1939 (London, 1940), pp. 8-12.

ROMEO AND JULIET, OTHELLO

the game turns into a sacrifice, and the favored lovers become victims of time and law. We can better understand this shift by looking at the two distinct worlds of the play and at some secondary characters who help to define them.

If we divide the play at Mercutio's death, the death that generates all those that follow, it becomes apparent that the play's movement up to this point is essentially comic. With the usual intrigues and go-betweens, the lovers overcome obstacles and unite in marriage. Their personal action is set in a broader social context, so that the marriage promises not only private satisfaction but renewed social unity:

> For this alliance may so happy prove
> To turn your households' rancour to pure love.
>
> (II.iii.91–92)

The households' rancor is set out in the play's first scene. This Verona of the Montague-Capulet feud is exactly the typical starting point of a comedy described by Frye—"a society controlled by habit, ritual bondage, arbitrary law and the older characters."[5] The scene's formal balletic structure, a series of matched representatives of the warring families entering neatly on cue, conveys the inflexibility of this society, the arbitrary barriers that limit freedom of action.

The feud itself seems more a matter of mechanical reflex than of deeply felt hatred. Charlton noted the comic tone of its presentation in this part of the play.[6] The "parents' rage" that sounded so ominous in the prologue becomes in representation an irascible humour: two old men claw at each other, only to be dragged back by their wives and scolded by their prince. Charlton found the play flawed by this failure to plant the seeds of tragedy; but the treatment of the feud makes good sense if Shakespeare is playing on *comic* expectations. At this point, the feud functions in *Romeo* very much as the various legal restraints do in Shakespearean comedy. Imposed from outside on the youthful lovers, who feel themselves no part of it, the feud is a barrier placed arbitrarily between them, like the Athenian law giving fathers the disposition of their daughters which stands be-

---

[5] *Anatomy*, p. 169. Although the younger generation participate in the feud, they have not created it; it is a habit bequeathed to them by their elders.

[6] *Experimental Tragedy*, pp. 36–40.

60   BEYOND COMEDY

tween Lysander and Hermia in *A Midsummer Night's Dream*—
something set up in order to be broken down.

Other aspects of this initial world of *Romeo* suggest comedy as
well. Its characters are the gentry and servants familiar in romantic comedies, and they are preoccupied, not with wars and the
fate of kingdoms, but with arranging marriages and managing
the kitchen. More important, it is a world of possibilities, with
Capulet's feast represented to more than one young man as a
field of choice. "Hear all, all see," says Capulet to Paris, "And
like her most whose merit most shall be" (i.ii.30-31). "Go
thither," Benvolio tells Romeo, who is disconsolate over
Rosaline, "and with unattainted eye / Compare her face with
some that I shall show" (85-86) and she will be forgotten for
some more approachable lady. Romeo rejects the words, of
course, but in action he soon displays a classic comic adaptability, switching from the impossible love to the possible.

Violence and disaster are not totally absent from this milieu,
but they are unrealized threats. The feast again provides a kind
of comic emblem, when Tybalt's proposed violence is rendered
harmless by Capulet's festive accommodation.

> Therefore be patient, take no note of him;
> It is my will; the which if thou respect,
> Show a fair presence and put off these frowns,
> An ill-beseeming semblance for a feast.
>
> (i.v.69-72)

This overruling of Tybalt is significant because Tybalt in his inflexibility is a potentially tragic character, indeed the only one in
the first part of the play. If we recognize in him an irascible
humour type, an alazon, we should also recognize that the tragic
hero is an alazon transposed.[7] Tybalt alone takes the feud really
seriously. It is his *inner* law, the propeller of his fiery nature. His
natural frame of reference is the heroic one of honor and death:

> What, dares the slave
> Come hither, cover'd with an antic face,

---

[7] Maynard Mack, "Engagement and Detachment in Shakespeare's Plays," in
Essays on Shakespeare and Elizabethan Drama in Honor of Hardin Craig, ed. Richard
Hosley (Columbia, Mo., 1962), pp. 287-291.

ROMEO AND JULIET, OTHELLO 61

To fleer and scorn at our solemnity?
Now, by the stock and honour of my kin,
To strike him dead I hold it not a sin.

(I.v.53-57)

Tybalt's single set of absolutes cuts him off from a whole range
of speech and action available to the other young men of the
play: lyric love, witty fooling, friendly conversation. Ironically,
his imperatives come to dominate the play's world only when he
himself departs from it. While he is alive, Tybalt is an alien.

In a similar way, the passing fears of calamity voiced at times
by Romeo, Juliet, and Friar Laurence are not allowed to dominate the atmosphere of the early acts. The love of Romeo and
Juliet is already imaged as a flash of light swallowed by darkness,
an image invoking inexorable natural law; but it is also expressed as a sea venture, which suggests luck and skill set against
natural hazards and chance seized joyously as an opportunity for
action. "Direct my sail," says Romeo to his captain Fortune.
Soon he feels himself in command:

I am no pilot; yet, wert thou as far
As that vast shore wash'd with the farthest sea,
I should adventure for such merchandise.[8]

The spirit is Bassanio's as he adventures for Portia, a Jason voy-
aging in quest of the Golden Fleece (*MV* I.i.167-172). Romeo is
ready for difficulties with a traditional lovers' stratagem, one
which Shakespeare had used before in *Two Gentlemen*: a rope
ladder, "cords made like a tackled stair; / Which to the high
top-gallant of my joy / Must be my convoy in the secret night"
(II.iv.183-185).

But before Romeo can mount his tackled stair, Mercutio's
death intervenes to cut off this world of exhilarating venture.
Shakespeare developed this character, who in the source is little
more than a name and a cold hand, into the very incarnation of
comic atmosphere. Mercutio is the clown of romantic comedy,
recast in more elegant mold but equally ready to take off from
the plot in verbal play and to challenge idealistic love with his
own brand of comic earthiness.

[8] I.iv.113; II.ii.82-84. Later Mercutio hails the lovers' go-between, the Nurse,
with "A sail, a sail!" (II.iv.98).

62   BEYOND COMEDY

Nay, I'll conjure too.
Romeo! humours! madman! passion! lover!
Appear thou in the likeness of a sigh;
Speak but one rhyme and I am satisfied;
Cry but 'Ay me!' pronounce but 'love' and 'dove';

.   .   .   .

I conjure thee by Rosaline's bright eyes,
By her high forehead and her scarlet lip,
By her fine foot, straight leg, and quivering thigh,
And the demesnes that there adjacent lie.

(II.i.6-20)

He is the best of game-players, endlessly inventive and full of
quick moves and countermoves. Speech for him is a constant
exercise in multiple possibilities: puns abound, roles are taken up
at whim (that of conjuror, for instance, in the passage just
quoted), and his Queen Mab brings dreams not only to lovers
like Romeo but to courtiers, lawyers, parsons, soldiers, maids.
These have nothing to do with the case at hand, which is
Romeo's premonition of trouble, but Mercutio is not bound by
events. They serve him merely as convenient launching pads for
his flights of wit. When all this vitality, which has till now ignored all urgencies, is cut off abruptly by Tybalt's sword, it
must come as a shock to a spectator unfamiliar with the play. In
Mercutio's sudden, violent end, Shakespeare makes the birth of
tragedy coincide exactly with the symbolic death of comedy.
The alternative view, the element of freedom and play, dies with
Mercutio. Where many courses were open before, now there
seems only one. Romeo sees at once that an irreversible process
has begun:

This day's black fate on moe days doth depend [hang
     over];
This but begins the woe others must end.

(III.i.116-117)

It is the first sign in the play's dialogue pointing unambiguously
to tragic necessity. Romeo's future is now determined: he *must*
kill Tybalt, he *must* run away, he is Fortune's fool.

This helplessness is the most striking feature of the second, tragic world of *Romeo*. The temper of this new world is largely a function of onrushing events. Under pressure of events, the feud turns from farce to fate; tit for tat becomes blood for blood. Lawless as it seems to Prince Escalus, the feud is dramatically "the law" in *Romeo*. Before, it was external and avoidable. Now it moves inside Romeo to be his personal law. This is why he takes over Tybalt's rhetoric of honor and death:

> Alive in triumph and Mercutio slain!
> Away to heaven respective lenity,
> And fire-ey'd fury be my conduct now!
> Now, Tybalt, take the 'villain' back again
> That late thou gav'st me.
>
> (III.i.119-123)

Even outside the main chain of vengeance, the world is suddenly full of imperatives. Others besides Romeo feel helpless. Against his will Friar John is detained at the monastery; against his will the Apothecary sells poison to Romeo. Urgency becomes the norm. Nights run into mornings, and the characters seem never to sleep. The new world finds its emblem not in the aborted attack but in the aborted feast. As Tybalt's violence was out of tune with the Capulet festivities in Act II, so in the changed world of Acts III and IV the projected wedding of Juliet and Paris is made grotesque when Shakespeare insistently links it with death.[9] Preparations for the wedding feast parallel those made for the party in the play's first part, so as to make more wrenching the contrast when Capulet must order,

> All things that we ordained festival
> Turn from their office to black funeral:
> Our instruments to melancholy bells,
> Our wedding cheer to a sad burial feast,
> Our solemn hymns to sullen dirges change.
>
> (IV.v.84-88)

The play's last scene shows how completely the comic movement has been reversed. It is inherent in that movement, as we have seen, that the young get their way at the expense of the old. The final tableau of comedy features young couples joined

[9] III.vi.23-28; III.v.201-202; IV.i.6-8, 77-85, 107-108, IV.v.35-39.

in love; parents and authority figures are there, if at all, to ratify with more or less good grace what has been accomplished against their wills. But here, the stage is strikingly full of elders—the Friar, the Prince, Capulet, Lady Capulet, Montague. Their power is not passed on. Indeed, there are no young to take over. If Benvolio survives somewhere offstage, we have long since forgotten this adjunct character. Romeo, Juliet, Tybalt, Mercutio, and Paris are all dead. In effect, the entire younger generation has been wiped out.

I have been treating these two worlds as separate, consistent wholes in order to bring out their opposition, but I do not wish to deny dramatic unity to *Romeo and Juliet*. Shakespeare was writing one play, not two; and in spite of the clearly marked turning point we are aware of premonitions of disaster before the death of Mercutio, and hopes for avoiding it continue until near the end of the play. Our full perception of the world-shift that converts Romeo and Juliet from instinctive winners into sacrificial victims thus comes gradually. In this connection the careers of two secondary characters, Friar Laurence and the Nurse, are instructive.

In being and action, these two belong to the comic vision. Friar Laurence is one of the tribe of manipulators, whose job it is to transform or otherwise get round seemingly intractable realities. If his herbs and potions are less spectacular than the paraphernalia of Friar Bacon or John a Kent, he nevertheless belongs to their brotherhood. Such figures abound in romantic comedy, as we have seen, but not in tragedy, where the future is not so manipulable. The Friar's aims are those implicit in the play's comic movement: an inviolable union for Romeo and Juliet and an end to the families' feud.

The Nurse's goal is less lofty but equally appropriate to comedy. She wants Juliet married—to anyone. Her preoccupation with bedding and breeding reminds us of comedy's ancient roots in fertility rites, and it is as indiscriminate as the life force itself. But she conveys no sense of urgency in all this. On the contrary, her garrulity assumes the limitless time of comedy. In this sense her circumlocutions and digressions are analogous to Mercutio's witty games and, for that matter, to Friar Laurence's counsels of patience. "Wisely and slow," the Friar cautions Romeo; "they

ROMEO AND JULIET, OTHELLO

stumble that run fast" (II.iii.94). The Nurse is not very wise, but she is slow. The leisurely time assumptions of both Friar and Nurse contrast with the lovers' impatience, to create first the normal counterpoint of comedy and later a radical split that points us, with the lovers, directly towards tragedy.

Friar Laurence and the Nurse have no place in the new world brought into being by Mercutio's death, the world of limited time, no effective choice, no escape. They define and sharpen the tragedy by their very failure to find a part in the dramatic progress, by their growing estrangement from the true springs of the action. "Be patient," is the Friar's advice to banished Romeo, "for the world is broad and wide" (III.iii.16). But the roominess he perceives in both time and space simply does not exist for Romeo. *His* time has been constricted into a chain of days working out a "black fate," and he sees no world outside the walls of Verona (17).

Comic adaptability again confronts tragic integrity when Juliet is forced to marry Paris—and turns to her Nurse for counsel, as Romeo has turned to Friar Laurence. In the Nurse's response comedy's traditional wisdom of accommodation is carried to an extreme. Romeo has been banished, and Paris is after all very presentable. In short, adjust to the new state of things.

> Then, since the case so stands as now it doth,
> I think it best you married with the County.
> O, he's a lovely gentleman!
> Romeo's a dishclout to him.
>
> (III.v.217-220)

She still speaks for the life force, against barrenness and death. Even if Juliet will not accept the dishclout comparison, an inferior husband is better than no husband at all: "Your first is dead, or 'twere as good he were / As living here and you no use of him" (225-226).

But her advice is irrelevant, even shocking, in this new context. There was no sense of jar when Benvolio, a spokesman for comic accommodation like the Nurse and the Friar, earlier advised Romeo to substitute a possible love for an impossible one. True, the Nurse here is urging Juliet to violate her marriage vows; but Romeo also felt himself sworn to Rosaline, and for

66 BEYOND COMEDY

Juliet the marriage vow is a seal on the integrity of her love for Romeo, not a separable issue. The parallel points up the move into tragedy, for while Benvolio's advice sounded sensible in Act I and was in fact unintentionally carried out by Romeo, the course of action that the Nurse proposes in Act III is unthinkable to the audience as well as to Juliet. The memory of the lovers' passionate dawn parting that began this scene is too strong. Juliet and her nurse no longer speak the same language, and estrangement is inevitable. "Thou and my bosom henceforth shall be twain," Juliet vows when the Nurse has left the stage.[10] Like the slaying of Mercutio, Juliet's rejection of her old confidante has symbolic overtones. The possibilities of comedy have again been presented only to be discarded.

Both Romeo and Juliet have now cast off their comic companions and the alternative modes of being that they represented. But there is one last hope for comedy. If the lovers will not adjust to the situation, perhaps the situation can be adjusted to the lovers. This is the usual comic way with obstinately faithful pairs, and we have at hand the usual manipulator figure to arrange it.

The Friar's failure to bring off that solution is the final definition of the tragic world of *Romeo and Juliet*. There is no villain, only chance and bad timing. In comedy chance creates that elastic time that allows last-minute rescues. But here, events at Mantua and at the Capulet tomb will simply happen—by chance—in the wrong sequence. The Friar does his best: he makes more than one plan to avert catastrophe. The first, predictably, is patience and a broader field of action. Romeo must go to Mantua and wait

> till we can find a time
> To blaze your marriage, reconcile your friends,
> Beg pardon of the Prince, and call thee back . . .
> (III.iii.150–152)

---

[10] III.v.241. In the potion scene Juliet's resolve weakens for a moment, but almost immediately she rejects the idea of companionship. The momentary wavering only emphasizes her aloneness: "I'll call them back again to comfort me. / Nurse!—What should she do here? / My dismal scene I needs must act alone" (IV.iii.17-19).

It is a good enough plan, for life if not for drama, but it depends on "finding a time." As it turns out, events move too quickly for the Friar. The hasty preparations for Juliet's marriage to Paris leave no time for cooling tempers and reconciliations.

His second plan is an attempt to *gain* time: he will create the necessary freedom by faking Juliet's death. This is, of course, a familiar comic formula. Shakespeare's later uses of it are all in comedies.[11] Indeed, the contrived "deaths" of Hero in *Much Ado*, Helena in *All's Well*, Claudio in *Measure for Measure*, and Hermione in *The Winter's Tale* are more ambitiously intended than Juliet's, aimed at bringing about a change of heart in other characters.[12] Time may be important, as it is in *Winter's Tale*, but only as it promotes repentance. Friar Laurence, more desperate than his fellow manipulators, does not hope that Juliet's death will dissolve the Montague-Capulet feud, but only that it will give Romeo a chance to come and carry her off. Time and chance, which in the other plays cooperate benevolently with the forces of regeneration and renewal, work against Friar Laurence. Romeo's man is quicker with the bad news of Juliet's death than poor Friar John with the good news that the death is only a pretense. Romeo himself beats Friar Laurence to the tomb of the Capulets. The onrushing tragic action quite literally outstrips the slower steps of accommodation before our eyes. The Friar arrives too late to prevent one half of the tragic conclusion, and his essential estrangement from the play's world is only emphasized when he seeks to avert the other half by sending Juliet to a nunnery. This last alternative means little to the audience or to Juliet, who spares only a line to reject the possibility of adjustment and continuing life: "Go, get thee hence, for I will not away" (v.iii.160).

The Nurse and the Friar show that one way comedy can operate in a tragedy is by its irrelevance. Tragedy is tuned to the extraordinary. *Romeo and Juliet* locates this extraordinariness not so much in the two youthful lovers as in the love itself, its intensity

[11] Or in the comic part of a history, in the case of Falstaff's pretended death on the battlefield at Shrewsbury.

[12] The same effect, if not intention, is apparent in the reported death of Imogen in *Cymbeline*.

68   BEYOND COMEDY

and integrity. As the play moves forward, our sense of this intensity and integrity is strengthened by the cumulative effect of the lovers' lyric encounters and the increasing urgency of events, but also by the growing irrelevance of the comic characters.

De Quincey saw in the knocking at the gate in *Macbeth* the resumption of normality after nightmare, "the re-establishment of the goings-on of the world in which we live, [which] first makes us profoundly sensible of the awful parenthesis that had suspended them."[13] I would say, rather, that the normal atmosphere of *Macbeth* has been and goes on being nightmarish, and that it is the knocking episode that turns out to be the contrasting parenthesis, but the notion of sharpened sensibility is important. As the presence of other paths makes us more conscious of the road we are in fact traveling, so the Nurse and the Friar make us more "profoundly sensible" of the love of Romeo and Juliet and its tragic direction.

The play offers another sort of experiment in mingled genres that is less successful, I think. It starts well, in iv.iv, with a striking juxtaposition of Capulet preparations for the wedding with Juliet's potion scene. On the one hand is the household group in a bustle over clothes, food, logs for the fire—the everyday necessaries and small change of life. On the other is Juliet's tense monologue of fear, madness, and death. It is fine dramatic counterpoint, and its effect is stronger in stage production, as Granville-Barker observed, when the curtained bed of Juliet is visible upstage during the cheerful domestic goings-on.[14] The counterpoint, of course, depends on the Capulets' ignorance of what is behind those curtains. It comes to an end when in scene v Nurse and the others find Juliet's body. But Shakespeare keeps the comic strain alive through the rest of the scene. The high-pitched, repetitive mourning of the Nurse, Paris, and the Capulets sounds more like Pyramus over the body of Thisbe than a serious tragic scene. Finally Peter has his comic turn with the musicians. What Shakespeare is attempting here is not counterpoint but the *fusion* of tragic and comic. It doesn't quite work. S. L. Bethell suggests that the mourners' rhetorical excesses di-

[13] "On the Knocking at the Gate in *Macbeth*," in *Shakespeare Criticism: A Selection*, ed. D. Nichol Smith (Oxford, 1916), p. 378.

[14] *Prefaces to Shakespeare* (London, 1963), iv, 62-63.

ROMEO AND JULIET, OTHELLO

rect the audience to remain detached and thus to reserve their
tears for the real death scene that will shortly follow.[15] This
makes good theatrical sense. It is also possible that the musicians' dialogue, modulating as it does from shock to professional
shop to dinner, was meant to set off the tragic action by project-
ing a sense of the ongoing, normal life that is denied to Romeo
and Juliet. Still, the scene tends to leave spectators uneasy—if, in
fact, they get to see it at all: often the mourning passages are cut
and the musicians' business dropped altogether.[16] Shakespeare's
hand is uncertain in this early essay at fusing tragic and comic.
Mastery was yet to come, first in the gravediggers' scene in
Hamlet and then more fully in *King Lear*.

The structural use of comic conventions does work. The result, however, is a particular kind of tragedy. Critics have often
remarked, neutrally or with disapproval, that external fate rather
than character is the principal determiner of the tragic ends of the
young lovers. For the mature Shakespeare, tragedy involves
both character and circumstances, a fatal interaction between
man and moment. But in *Romeo and Juliet*, although the central
characters have their weaknesses, their destruction does not
really stem from those weaknesses. We may agree with Friar
Laurence that Romeo is rash, but it is not rashness that propels
him into the tragic chain of events. Just the opposite, it would
seem. In the crucial duel between Mercutio and Tybalt, Romeo
is trying to keep the combatants apart, to make peace. Ironically,
this very intervention leads to Mercutio's death.

[15] *Shakespeare and the Popular Dramatic Tradition* (London and New York,
1944), p. 111. Charles B. Lower agrees and argues as well for the more doubtful
proposition that the audience needs to be reassured that Juliet is really still alive.
Lower convincingly defends the authenticity of a Ql stage direction, "*All at once
cry out and wring their hand* [*s*]," which, by requiring the laments of Lady Capulet,
the Nurse, Paris, and Capulet (IV.v.43-64) to be spoken simultaneously like an
opera quartet, would increase the scene's burlesque quality. "*Romeo and Juliet*,
IV.v: A Stage Direction and Purposeful Comedy," *Shakespeare Studies*, 8 (1975),
177-194.

[16] Granville-Barker wrote in 1930 that modern producers usually lowered the
curtain after the climactic potion scene and raised it next on Romeo in Mantua,
skipping the mourning and the musicians entirely. *Prefaces*, IV, 63-64. The most
notable production of more recent years, by Franco Zeffirelli, omitted the musicians. J. Russell Brown, *Shakespeare's Plays in Performance* (London, 1966),
p. 177.

Mer. Why the devil came you between us? I was hurt
under your arm.
Rom. I thought all for the best.

(III.i.99–101)

If Shakespeare had wanted to implicate Romeo's rash, overemo-
tional nature in his fate, he handled this scene with an ineptness
difficult to credit. Judging from the resultant effect, what he
wanted was something quite different: an ironic dissociation of
character from the direction of events.

Perhaps this same purpose lies behind the elaborate development of comic elements in the early acts before the characters are
pushed into the opposed conditions of tragedy. To stress milieu
in this way is necessarily to downgrade the importance of individual temperament and motivation. At the crucial moment
Romeo displays untypical prudence with the most upright of
intentions—and brings disaster on himself and Juliet. In this unusual Shakespearean tragedy, it is not what you are that counts,
but the world you live in.

Shakespeare may have been dissatisfied with his experiment. At
any rate, he wrote no more tragedy for several years, and he
never again returned to the comedy-into-tragedy structure. He
came closest to it in *Othello*, where comic success precedes tragic
catastrophe, but the effect is very different. Character and fate,
dissociated in *Romeo and Juliet*, are completely intertwined in this
mature tragedy of love. Once again a novella source, with its
love motive and deception plot, seems to have prompted the
dramatist to shape his material in ways that would remind his
audience of comic conventions. But here external forces do not
defeat the comic, as in *Romeo*; destruction comes from inside,
both inside Othello and inside the assumptions of romantic love.
Othello develops a tragic view of love by looking more penetrat-
ingly at some of those strains and contradictions I have pointed
out within the comic convention, a tragic view adumbrated already in some of Shakespeare's lyric poetry. The personalities
and situations of *Othello* are such as to put maximum pressure on
those areas of thin ice, until the ice breaks and the treacherous
currents below are released.

ROMEO AND JULIET, OTHELLO 71

To see how this is so, we need to look in more detail at the conventional comic treatment of love outlined in the preceding chapter, and at Shakespeare's own romantic comedies of the decade and more before he wrote *Othello*. What is pertinent is not the explicit themes of these plays but their common underlying assumptions about love.

The *value* of love and of its proper fruition, marriage, is a basic premise of all Shakespeare's comedies, which invariably present as all or part of their initial situation individuals in a single and unsatisfied state and direct them through plot complications toward appropriate parings-off at the end. Unanimous approval extends from supernatural Oberon to bumpkin Costard; Jaques is the only significant dissenter, and even he is made to bless the Arden marriages (one of which he actively promoted: *AYL* III.iii) before bowing out of society to brood in his hermitage. Indeed, Jaques' election to live permanently in the forest has a certain irony, for his real adversary in this debate is nature itself.

We have observed that in comedy, law and conventional morality generally must give way before nature. The "winners" in comedy are those in tune with the natural forces of life-renewal. Shakespeare is explicit about the naturalness of mating in some comedies (*Love's Labour's Lost*, for example); the notion is implicit in all of them. Those that promote release and resolution of conflicts by moving the characters to some out-of-bounds locale—described for us spatially by Frye's "green world" and temporally by Barber's "holiday"[17]—give structural reinforcement to this sense of nature as love's ally. For all of the artificial and magical elements in the forests of *Two Gentlemen*, *Midsummer Night's Dream*, and *As You Like It*, nature in those places is less trammeled and perverted than in the polite, treacherous court of Milan, or in Theseus's lawbound Athens, or in the dominions where Duke Frederick sets the ethical standard by crimes against his own kindred. Turned out or self-exiled from civilization, the lovers are righted and united in the woods.

Love is natural, then, as well as right. But comedy also affirms that love is irrational and arbitrary. "To say the truth," muses Bottom, "reason and love keep little company together now-a-days. The more the pity that some honest neighbours will not

---

[17] Frye, "The Argument of Comedy," *English Institute Essays 1948*; Barber, *Shakespeare's Festive Comedy*.

72   BEYOND COMEDY

make them friends" (*MND* iii.i.131-133). He speaks for comedy
in general, not just *Midsummer Night's Dream*. Oberon's potent
flower can be seen as an emblem for the unreasonable passions of
Titania, Lysander, and Demetrius, but also for those that immediately enslave Orlando to Rosalind (but not Celia), Oliver to
Celia (but not Rosalind), Navarre and his friends to the Princess
and *her* friends (with balletic tidiness), and, less fortunately,
Phebe to Rosalind, Proteus to Silvia, Olivia to Viola-Cesario. If
some of these sudden obsessions seem slightly less arbitrary than
those of, say, Ariosto's characters as they veer from one course
to another with each sip from the fountains of love and hate, it is
only that Shakespeare has provided for his *final* couplings an acceptable degree of compatibility in sex, rank, and temperament.
But there is no suggestion that this compatibility was reasonably
appraised by the lovers or that it influenced their decisions—if
they can be called that—at all.

   This insistence that anything so vital as the love-choice is totally beyond rational control does not bother comic characters.
Bottom is untroubled by his pronouncement, and by the fairy
queen's amazing dotage that provokes it. Lovers generally abandon what reason they have without a struggle, and this course
seems to be the approved one. When one of them attempts to
rationalize his new emotions, as Lysander does when the mis-
applied love-juice compels him to love Helena, the result fools
no one.

> *Lys.* Not Hermia but Helena I love:
> Who will not change a raven for a dove?
> The will of man is by his reason sway'd,
> And reason says you are the worthier maid.
> Things growing are not ripe until their season;
> So I, being young, till now ripe not to reason;
> And touching now the point of human skill,
> Reason becomes the marshal to my will,
> And leads me to your eyes . . .
>
> .   .   .   .
>
> *Hel.* Wherefore was I to this keen mockery born?[18]

---

[18] *MND* ii.ii.113-123. More reflective characters, like Helena in *All's Well* and
Viola in *Twelfth Night*, recognize that they love against all reason, but still irrational emotion prevails over self-awareness. They go right on loving.

ROMEO AND JULIET, OTHELLO

It is only in the security of comedy's natural law that we can dismiss with laughter Lysander's attempts to reconcile love with reason. Comedy provides no "honest neighbour" to make them truly friends.

The convention of ending comedies with marriage promised, or marriage celebrated, or marriage ratified emotionally and socially (*Taming of the Shrew*, *Merchant of Venice*, *All's Well*), has a further corollary. Comedies in this dominant pattern[19] by implication locate the important stresses and decisions of love in the courtship period. Their silence about shifts of direction after marriage suggests that there will be none, that once Jack has Jill, nought can go ill—or, if couples like Touchstone and Audrey seem headed for less than perfect harmony, at least that the "story" is over.

To sum up: Shakespeare's comic forms and conventions assume, first, the value of engagement with a mate, and second, the cooperation of forces beyond man, natural and otherwise, in achieving this mating and forestalling the consequences of human irrationality and malice, as well as plain bad luck. To call these "assumptions" does not, of course, mean that Shakespeare or his audiences accepted them as universally true. Rather, the dramatist's use of the comic formulas and the playgoers' familiarity with them directed which aspects of their diverse perception of experience should be brought forward—wish as well as belief—and which should be held in abeyance.

To the extent that Shakespeare allowed bad luck to defeat love in *Romeo and Juliet*, we may see him as questioning comic assumptions in that play, but the questioning does not go very deep. The lovers' relationship is presented as natural and right in itself. If it makes them irrationally impetuous, it is nevertheless not this rashness that precipitates the tragedy. In *Othello*, however, Shakespeare subjects the comic assumptions about the love union, nature, and reason to a radical reassessment, and in so doing exposes the roots of tragedy.

Just as such a scrutiny logically comes *after* the first unquestioning acceptance, so Othello's and Desdemona's story is deliberately set up as postcomic. Courtship and ratified marriage, the

---

[19] Only *Merry Wives* and *Comedy of Errors* depart from it to the extent of finding major plot material in postmarital strain as well as in courtship.

whole story of comedy, appear in *Othello* as a preliminary to tragedy. The play's action up until the reunion of Othello and Desdemona in Cyprus (II.i) is a perfect comic structure in miniature. The wooing that the two of them describe in the Venetian council scene (I.iii) has succeeded in spite of barriers of age, color, and condition of life; the machinations of villain and doltish rival have come to nothing; the blocking father has been overruled by the good duke; and nature has cooperated in the general movement with a storm that disperses the last external threat, the Turks, while preserving the favored lovers. Othello's reunion speech to Desdemona underlines this sense of a movement accomplished, a still point of happiness like the final scene of a comedy:

> If it were now to die,
> 'Twere now to be most happy; for I fear
> My soul hath her content so absolute
> That not another comfort like to this
> Succeeds in unknown fate.
>
> (II.i.187-191)

But at the same time that Othello celebrates his peak of joy so markedly, his invocations of death, fear, and unknown fate make us apprehensive about the postcomic future. Desdemona's equally negative mode of agreement ("The heavens forbid / But that our loves and comforts should increase . . .") indirectly reinforces this unease, and Iago's threat does so directly: "O, you are well tun'd now! / But I'll set down the pegs that make this music." In these few lines Shakespeare prepares us for tragedy, in part by announcing the end of comedy. The happy ending is completed, and Othello and Desdemona are left to go on from there.

If I am right to see the tragedy of *Othello* developing from a questioning of comic assumptions, then the initial comic movement ought to make us aware of unresolved tensions in this successful love. And it does, in various ways. Othello's account of their shy, story-telling courtship, however moving and beautiful, is in retrospect disturbing. "She lov'd me for the dangers I had pass'd; / And I lov'd her that she did pity them" (I.iii.167-168). Is it enough? Some critics have on this hint pro-

claimed the Moor totally self-centered, incapable of real love.
This is surely too severe. Nevertheless, in his summary their
love has a proxy quality. "The dangers I had pass'd" have served
as a counter between them, a substitute for direct engagement
or, at best, a preliminary to something not yet achieved. Twice
before, Shakespeare had used comedy to explore the inadequacies of romantic courtship, cursorily in *Taming of the
Shrew* and more thoroughly in *Much Ado*. In the latter play,
Claudio and Hero move through the paces of conventional
wooing, depending on rumors and go-betweens, without direct
exploration of each other's nature. Thus, Hero can be traduced
and Claudio can believe it, lacking as he does the knowledge of
the heart that should counteract the false certainty of the eyes.
Much Ado is a comedy, and thus the presiding deities give time
for Dogberry's muddled detective work and provide in the Friar
a benevolent countermanipulator against Don John. The love of
Othello and Desdemona has the same vulnerability, but no time
is given; and instead of Friar Francis, Iago is in charge.

Iago is the most obvious potential force for tragedy in the
early part of the play. We see him thwarted in his first plot
against Othello but already, at the end of Act I, planning the
next. His speech at this point suggests in both overt statement
and imagery the thrust beyond the comic, the germination out
of the first failure of a deeper evil:

> I ha't—it is engender'd. Hell and night
> Must bring this monstrous birth to the world's light.
>
> (I.iii.397-398)

It was Bradley, expanding on suggestions from Hazlitt and
Swinburne, who compared Iago in his first two soliloquies to a
playwright in the early stages of writing a new play—"drawing
at first only an outline, puzzled how to fix more than the main
idea, and gradually seeing it develop and clarify as he works
upon it or lets it work."[20] Bradley's parallel highlights the unexpected kinship between Iago and the magicians and friars of
comedy, who arrange "fond pageants" in which other characters play unaware the parts assigned to them, and who dispose

[20] A. C. Bradley, *Shakespearean Tragedy*, 2nd ed. (London, 1924), p. 231.

events toward the desired ending as a dramatist does. The implication that a single human being can control persons and change realities, exhilarating within the safe parameters of comedy, is sinister here.

So is the holiday from reason that comedy proclaims for romantic love. Iago is the most intelligent character in the play, and reason—or the appearance of reason—is his chief means of controlling others. The *power* of the rational view, in the comedies so easily dismissed with laughter or overruled by emotion, is grimly realized in Iago's accurate estimates of character

> The Moor is of a free and open nature
> That thinks men honest that but seem to be so;
> And will as tenderly be led by th' nose . . .
>
> (I.iii.393–395)

his telling arguments from experience

> In Venice they do let God see the pranks
> They dare not show their husbands . . .
>
> .   .   .   .
>
> She did deceive her father, marrying you
> (III.iii.206–210)

his plausible hypotheses

> That Cassio loves her, I do well believe it;
> That she loves him, 'tis apt and of great credit
> (II.i.280–281)

and his final triumph in converting Othello to the philosophy of "ocular proof" (III.iii.364). Against him the love of Othello and Desdemona is vulnerable, rooted as it is not in rational evaluation of empirical knowledge but in instinctive sympathy. The same scene that underlines how indirect was their courtship (I.iii) also brings out the peculiar strength of their love that is a weakness as well:

> *Des*. I saw Othello's visage in his mind.
> (252)

> *Oth*. My life upon her faith!
> (294)

ROMEO AND JULIET, OTHELLO 77

There is a core of power in this instinctive mutual recognition that survives Iago's rational poison and in a sense defeats it, but this victory comes only in death. In his posing of Iago against Othello and Desdemona, Shakespeare fully explores the conventional dichotomy between reason and love and uncovers its deeply tragic implications.[21]

If reason's opposition to love is traditional, nature in *Othello* appears to have changed sides. Love's ally is now love's enemy, partly because the angle of vision has changed: nature as instinctual rightness gives way to nature as abstract concept, susceptible like all concepts to distortion and misapplication. Brabantio, Iago, and finally Othello himself see the love between Othello and Desdemona as *un*natural—"nature erring from itself" (III.iii.231). But there is more to it than this. In key scenes of *Othello* a tension develops between two senses of *nature*, the general and the particular.

It is to general nature, the common experience and prejudice by which like calls only to like, that Brabantio appeals in the Venetian council scene. An attraction between the young white Venetian girl and the aging black foreigner, since it goes against this observed law of nature, could only have been "wrought" by unnatural means.

> She is abus'd, stol'n from me, and corrupted,
> By spells and medicines bought of mountebanks;
> For nature so preposterously to err,
> Being not deficient, blind, or lame of sense,
> Sans witchcraft could not.
>
> (I.iii.60-64)

The other sense of *nature* is particular and personal. What Iago means in his soliloquy at the end of this scene when he says the Moor "is of a free and open nature" is individual essence: the

---

[21] The irrationality of love in *Othello* has called forth some perceptive comment from critics, e.g., Winifred Nowottny, "Justice and Love in *Othello*," *University of Toronto Quarterly*, 21 (1952), 330-344; and Robert B. Heilman, *Magic in the Web* (Lexington, Ky., 1956), esp. the discussion of "wit" versus "witchcraft," pp. 219-229. Terence Hawkes explores the same opposition in "Iago's Use of Reason," *Studies in Philology*, 58 (1961), 160-169, using the concepts of *ratio inferior* and *ratio superior*.

78   BEYOND COMEDY

inscape of Othello. Brabantio tries to bring in this nature to support the other in his appeal against the marriage. He says that Desdemona is essentially timid, thus by nature (her own) cannot love the fearsome Moor.

> A maiden never bold,
> Of spirit so still and quiet that her motion
> Blush'd at herself; and she—in spite of nature,
> Of years, of country, credit, every thing—
> To fall in love with what she fear'd to look on!
> It is a judgment maim'd and most imperfect
> That will confess perfection so could err
> Against all rules of nature.
>
> (I.iii.94–101)

But this personal nature is the very ground of Desdemona's love. In her answer to her father and the Venetian Senate she tells how, penetrating through the blackness and strangeness, she saw Othello's true visage in his mind and subdued her heart to that essence, his "very quality."[22]

For Desdemona, then, nature as individual essence is not the enemy of love. But Iago has the last word in this scene, and his conclusion is ominous: Othello's very generosity and openness will make him take the appearance of honesty for the fact. That is, Othello will act instinctively according to the laws of his own nature rather than according to reasoned evaluation (which would perceive that most liars pretend to be telling the truth). This internal law of nature, then, implies the same vulnerability that we have seen in the instinctive, nonrational quality of Othello's and Desdemona's love.

Brabantio's general nature is implicitly reductive in that it derives rules for individuals from the behavior of the herd. Iago's is explicitly reductive. For him "the herd" is no metaphor, and the view he expounds to Roderigo has no place for human values or ethical norms. Natural law for Iago, as for Edmund in *King Lear*, is Hobbesian—a matter of animal appetites promoted by cleverness, with the strongest and the shrewdest winning out.[23]

---

[22] I.iii.250-252; Q1 has "utmost pleasure" for "very quality."

[23] See J. F. Danby, *Shakespeare's Doctrine of Nature* (London, 1949), pp. 31-43.

ROMEO AND JULIET, OTHELLO 79

Desdemona, he assures Roderigo, will tire of Othello because the appetite requires fresh stimuli:

> Her eye must be fed; and what delight shall she have to look on the devil? When the blood is made dull with the act of sport, there should be—again to inflame it, and to give satiety a fresh appetite—loveliness in favour, sympathy in years, manners, and beauties—all which the Moor is defective in. Now for want of these requir'd conveniences, her delicate tenderness will find itself abus'd, begin to heave the gorge, disrelish and abhor the Moor; very nature will instruct her in it, and compel her to some second choice.
>
> (II.i.221-233)

Compel her—here is yet another "law," generalized from the ways of animal nature. The context is wholly physical, as the persistent images of eating and disgorging keep reminding us. Iago has begun the discussion by prodding on the hesitant lover Roderigo with a bit of folk wisdom: "They say base men being in love have then a nobility in their natures more than is native to them" (212-214). But he does not pretend to believe it himself. Love is rather "a lust of the blood and a permission of the will"; Roderigo, in love or not, is a snipe; our natures are "blood and baseness."[24] In Iago's determined animalism there is another unexpected reminder of comedy, this time of the antiromantic servant or rustic whose imagination is bounded by the physical. It is perhaps because this view can be destructive when actually *acted out* against idealized love that the clowns of comedy are kept largely apart from the plot, as onlookers. Iago is a clown

---

[24] I.iii.333, 379, 327. E.A.J. Honigmann sees in Iago's soliloquy at the end of II.i another expression of his reductive generalizing. Since his plot against Othello depends on the universality of sexual appetite, he is lining up examples to prove a general "Law of Lust." That Cassio lusts for Desdemona is plausible; that Desdemona lusts for Cassio is not hard to believe; that Othello will go on lusting for Desdemona is likely; "and come to think of it, Iago continues, snatching another example out of the air, 'I do love her too!' (the unspoken thought being that this is reassuring, since it proves that the Law of Lust applies generally, therefore Desdemona and Cassio must 'love,' therefore Iago's plot will work)." *Shakespeare, Seven Tragedies: The Dramatist's Manipulation of Response* (New York, 1976), p. 87.

80   BEYOND COMEDY

without good humor and (what underlies that lack) without
self-sufficiency, who must therefore prove his theories on other
people. Interestingly, this transfer of the debunking low-life perspective to the service of active malevolence seems to have left
no function for the play's official clown. His feeble essays at
bawdry and wordplay have nothing conceptual to adhere to, and
after a second brief appearance in Act II he departs unmourned.

In Shakespeare's portrayal of Iago we can see a version of the
clash I have been describing. In spite of his reductive general
view, he can recognize the essential goodness of Othello ("free
and open nature," "constant, loving, noble nature") as well as
Desdemona's generosity and the daily beauty of Cassio's life.[25]
Critics have complained of the inconsistency, and if *Othello* were
naturalistic drama, they would be right to do so. But Iago is not
just an envious spoiler; he is the symbolic enemy of love itself.
The play's conception demands that the weapons of both "natures," like those of reason, be put in his hands.

In his great self-summation at the play's end, Othello says he
was "wrought" from his true nature, and so he was. His own
nature, noble and trusting, gave him an instinctive perception of
Desdemona's, a perception which breaks forth at the sight of her
even while Iago is poisoning his mind: "If she be false, O, then
heaven mocks itself! / I'll not believe it" (III.iii.282-283). But
Iago is able to undermine that trust with false rationality, the insistence that Desdemona's honor, which is "an essence that's not
seen," be made susceptible of ocular proof. He succeeds, where
Brabantio failed, in using both conceptions of nature against
Othello. The Moor's own generous nature, Iago suggests,
makes him an easy dupe. "I would not have your free and noble
nature / Out of self-bounty be abus'd; look to 't" (203-204).
Taught to look from the outside instead of trust from the inside,
Othello soon sees Desdemona's choice of him as an aberration,
nature erring from itself. Iago quickly advances the other nature,
the law of all things, to reinforce the idea:

> Ay, there's the point: as—to be bold with you—
> Not to affect many proposed matches
> Of her own clime, complexion, and degree,

[25] I.iii.393; II.i.283; II.iii.308-309; V.i.19-20.

ROMEO AND JULIET, OTHELLO

Whereto we see in all things nature tends—
Foh! one may smell in such a will most rank,
Foul disproportion, thoughts unnatural.

(232-237)

And so Othello violates his own peculiar essence and internalizes Iago's law of the many. Desdemona soon realizes uneasily that he is altered ("My lord is not my lord": III.iv.125) and, in an ironic reflection of Othello's confusion, seeks the explanation in a generalization about "men": "Men's natures wrangle with inferior things, / Though great ones are their object" (145-146). Later the Venetian visitors gaze horrified at the change in that nature that passion could not shake, as Othello strikes his wife and then exits mumbling of goats and monkeys. He has taken into himself Iago's reductive view of man as animal. In the next scene (IV.ii) he will see Desdemona in terms of toads coupling and maggots quickening in rotten meat.

The love that in comedies was a strength in *Othello* is vulnerable to attacks of reason, arguments from nature. More than that: vulnerability is its very essence. Before falling in love with Desdemona, Othello was self-sufficient, master of himself and of the battlefield. After he believes her to be false, his occupation is gone. Why? Because love has created a dependency, a yielding of the separate, sufficient self to incorporation with another. What comedy treated as a liberating completeness becomes in *Othello* the heart of tragedy. Even in the play's comic phase there are signs of this new and potentially dangerous vulnerability. Othello's images for his love-commitment are not of expansion but of narrowing and confining:

But that I love the gentle Desdemona,
I would not my unhoused free condition
Put into circumscription and confine
For the seas' worth.

(I.ii.25-28)

To love totally is to give up the freedom of self for the perils of union, and the expansive great world for an other-centered, contingent one. Othello makes a significant metaphor for Desdemona near the end of the play:

82   BEYOND COMEDY

> Nay, had she been true,
> If heaven would make me *such another world*
> Of one entire and perfect chrysolite,
> I'd not have sold her for it.[26]

"My life upon her faith" is literally true. Desdemona has become Othello's world.[27]

It is in this light, I think, that we can best understand why Othello reacts to Iago's insinuations about Desdemona by renouncing his profession. The great aria on military life invokes, not chaos and carnage, but *order*. War is individual passion subordinated to a larger plan, martial harmony, formal pageantry, imitation of divine judgment.

> O, now for ever
> Farewell the tranquil mind! farewell content!
> Farewell the plumed troops, and the big wars
> That makes ambition virtue! O, farewell!
> Farewell the neighing steed and the shrill trump,
> The spirit-stirring drum, th' ear-piercing fife,
> The royal banner, and all quality,
> Pride, pomp, and circumstance, of glorious war!
> And O ye mortal engines whose rude throats
> Th' immortal Jove's dread clamours counterfeit,
> Farewell! Othello's occupation's gone.
>
> (III.iii.351-361)

Stylistically and rhythmically, the formal catalogues and ritual repetitions strengthen this selective picture of war as majestic order. Earlier in this scene Othello has said that when he stops loving Desdemona, chaos will come again. Now it has happened. With his world thrown into chaos, his ordering generalship is gone.

Othello's disintegration of self is the dark side of comedy's re-

---

[26] v.ii.146-149; my italics. The idea of Desdemona as a world also animates "I had rather be a toad, / And live upon the vapour of a dungeon, / Than keep a corner in the thing I love / For others' uses" (III.iii.274-277) and "Methinks it should be now [at Desdemona's death] a huge eclipse" (v.ii.102).

[27] Theodore Spencer relates some of these speeches through the similar notion that Othello has *given* his world to Desdemona. *Shakespeare and the Nature of Man*, 2nd ed. (New York, 1961), pp. 129-130, 135.

ROMEO AND JULIET, OTHELLO 83

jection of singleness, its insistence on completing oneself with another. But Shakespeare goes deeper in his exploration of comic assumptions by showing that the desired merging of self and other is in any case impossible. The more or less schematized pairings-off of the comedies combine necessary opposition (male/female) with sympathies in age, background, temperament.[28] It is enough in comedy to suggest compatibility by outward signs and look no farther than the formal union. But in *Othello* Shakespeare has taken pains in several ways to emphasize the separateness of his lovers.

Cinthio's Moor in the source tale is handsome, apparently fairly young, and a longtime Venetian resident. Apart from sex, his only real difference from Desdemona is one of color, and Cinthio does not dwell on it much. Shakespeare dwells on it a great deal. Black-white oppositions weave themselves continually into the verbal fabric of *Othello*. Indeed, the blackness of Cinthio's hero may have been one of the story's main attractions for Shakespeare. Certainly he altered other details of the story to reinforce this paradigmatic separation into black and white, to increase Othello's alienness and widen the gulf between his experience and Desdemona's. Shakespeare's Moor is a stranger to Venice and to civil life in general; his entire career, except for the brief period in which he courted Desdemona, has been spent in camp and on the battlefield (I.iii.83-87). Even Othello's speech reminds us constantly, if subtly, of his apartness. It is hardly rude, as he claims to the Venetian Senate, but it is certainly different from theirs. His idiom naturally invokes Anthropophagi and Pontic seas, roots itself in the exotic rather than the everyday social life that is familiar to the others but not to him. He knows as little of Venetian ways as Desdemona knows of "antres vast and deserts idle," and he is given no time to learn. While Cinthio's Moor and his bride live for some time in Venice after their marriage, Othello and Desdemona must go at once to Cyprus—and not even in the same ship. No wonder that, when Iago generalizes about the habits of his countrywomen ("In Venice they do let God see the pranks / They dare not show their husbands' . . ."), Othello can only respond helplessly, "Dost

---

[28] See above, p. 43.

84   BEYOND COMEDY

thou say so?'' (III.iii.206-209). Shakespeare has deprived him of
any common ground with Desdemona on which he can stand to
fight back—not only to facilitate Iago's deception, but to
heighten the tragic paradox of human love, individuals dependent on each other but unalterably separate and mysterious to one
another in their separateness. The two great values of comic
convention—love and the fuller self—are seen as tragically incompatible.

To sharpen the contrast, Othello is made middle-aged, thick-
lipped—everything Desdemona is not. The image of black man
and white girl in conjunction, so repellent to some critics that
they had to invent a tawny or café-au-lait Moor, is at the center
of the play's conception of disjunction in love. It gives visual
focus to the other oppositions of war and peace, age and youth,
man and woman. This disjunction serves the plot: it assists
Iago's initial deception, and it provides most of the tension in the
period between the deception and the murder, as Desdemona
inopportunely pleads for Cassio, and Othello in turn can communicate his fears only indirectly, through insults and degrada-
tions. But beyond this plot function the disjunction constitutes a
tragic vision of love itself.

What I am suggesting is that the action of *Othello* moves us
not only as a chain of events involving particular people as initia-
tors and victims, but also as an acting out of the tragic implications in any love relationship. Iago is an envious, insecure
human being who functions as a perverted magician-manipu-
lator, cunningly altering reality for Othello. But he is also the
catalyst who activates destructive forces not of his own creation,
forces present in the love itself.[29] His announcement of the
"monstrous birth" quoted above (p. 75) has special significance
in this regard. Coming at the end of a resolved marriage scene, it
implies that the monster will be the product of the marriage.
Iago says, "It is engender'd," not "I have engendered it," be-

[29] In arriving at this conclusion I have been influenced by Kenneth Burke's
idea of the "agent/act ratio"; see especially his "*Othello*: An Essay to Illustrate a
Method," *Hudson Review*, 4 (1951), 165-203, in which he shows how the characters of Othello, Desdemona, and Iago are determined by their roles in the play's
central tension, which they actualize. My interpretation of that tension, however, differs from Burke's, which centers on love as exclusive ownership.

ROMEO AND JULIET, OTHELLO

cause he is not parent but midwife. "Hell and night," embodied in this demi-devil who works in the dark, will bring the monster forth, but it is the fruit of love itself.

Because *Othello* is a play, and a great one, tragic action and tragic situation are fully fused in it, and it would be pointless to try to separate them. But a look at some of Shakespeare's non-dramatic work may help clarify the paradoxical sense of love as both life and destruction that informs the events of this play. The sonnets present a range of attitudes to love, from joyous assurance to disgust and despair, but they return again and again to a certain kind of tension between lover and beloved. Sonnet 57 is one example.

> Being your slave, what should I do but tend
> Upon the hours and times of your desire?
> I have no precious time at all to spend,
> Nor services to do, till you require.
> Nor dare I chide the world-without-end hour,
> Whilst I, my sovereign, watch the clock for you,
> Nor think the bitterness of absence sour,
> When you have bid your servant once adieu;
> Nor dare I question with my jealous thought
> Where you may be, or your affairs suppose,
> But, like a sad slave, stay and think of nought
> Save where you are how happy you make those.
>> So true a fool is love that in your will,
>> Though you do anything, he thinks no ill.

This apparently positive statement belies its own assent to the terms of relationship by double-edged phrases like "no *precious* time" and "Nor *dare* I chide," and by the bitter wordplay of the couplet: "So true a fool" suggests the loyally loving innocent, but also "so absolutely a dupe." "Fool" completes the sonnet's identification of beloved as monarch and lover as slave. He is not just any kind of slave but the king's fool, a hanger-on who is valued for the occasional diversion he provides. The total effect is of a speaker pulled in contrary directions by need of his friend and esteem of himself.

In Sonnet 35, images and syntax convey the cost of commitment in love.

No more be griev'd at that which thou hast done:
Roses have thorns, and silver fountains mud;
Clouds and eclipses stain both moon and sun,
And loathsome canker lives in sweetest bud.
All men make faults, and even I in this,
Authorizing thy trespass with compare,
Myself corrupting, salving thy amiss,
Excusing thy sins more than thy sins are;
For to thy sensual fault I bring in sense—
Thy adverse party is thy advocate—
And 'gainst myself a lawful plea commence;
Such civil war is in my love and hate
    That I an accessary needs must be
    To that sweet thief which sourly robs from me.

The poem strives to repair the damaged relationship by creating a new equality between lover and beloved. It does indeed achieve this, but only at the cost of the speaker's own integrity. He manages to absolve his friend of fault by natural comparisons, nature having no moral dimension to justify blame, and then implicates himself in fault for making those very comparisons—authorizing the trespass with compare. The last part of the sonnet strains against the first quatrain, and in that strain lies its impact. Can we accept the absolution given in lines 1-4 if the mode of absolution turns out to be sinful? The images reinforce this sense of disjunction: those of the first quatrain are drawn exclusively from the natural world, and those of the remainder come from the civilized world of moral man, especially the law courts. "Civil war," finally overt in line 12, is implicit earlier in the like-sounding antitheses that shape lines 7-10 into a series of tensions. The couplet, its message of inner division supported by the difficult twisting of the last line, completes the violation of self that love has required.

The same kind of violation, expressed with less anguish and more wry acceptance, is the theme of Sonnet 138:

    When my love swears that she is made of truth,
    I do believe her, though I know she lies. . . .

Here is a comic response to the problem of integrity compromised by dependence on another, as *Othello* is a tragic re-

ROMEO AND JULIET, OTHELLO 87

sponse. In its mutual accommodation reached through lies and
pretenses, Sonnet 138 also stresses the other side of the paradox,
the necessary separateness of lovers. Even the more idealistic
sonnets never proclaim complete union. And the most idealistic
of all, Sonnet 116, presents quite an opposite picture, of love
persisting on its own in spite of the beloved's infidelity:

> Love is not love
> Which alters when it alteration finds,
> Or bends with the remover to remove.
>
> . . . .
>
> Love alters not with his brief hours and weeks,
> But bears it out even to the edge of doom.

This is selfless but ultimately single, more like God's love for
man than like any human relationship. Edward Hubler saw in
Sonnet 116 Shakespeare's affirmation of mutuality as the essence
of love.[30] It seems to me just the contrary, a recognition that if
love does depend on being requited it will be neither lasting nor
true. It must necessarily bend with the remover, meet defection
with defection.

Enduring mutuality does not seem to be a possibility in the
sonnets. When Shakespeare does address himself to the merging
of separate identities, the result is the rarefied allegory of "The
Phoenix and Turtle." Here the impossibility is even clearer. The
phoenix and the turtle dove are perfectly united, but they are
dead. Most of the poem is a dirge sung at their funeral, and it
ends in complete stasis—triplets with a single rhyme sound asserting that these lovers left no progeny, that what they represented is gone forever.

> Leaving no posterity—
> 'Twas not their infirmity,
> It was married chastity.
>
> Truth may seem, but cannot be;
> Beauty brag, but 'tis not she:
> Truth and beauty buried be.

What do we make of this? It has been argued that "The Phoenix
and Turtle" approaches "pure poetry" in being all vehicle with

[30] *The Sense of Shakespeare's Sonnets* (Princeton, 1952), pp. 92-93.

88 BEYOND COMEDY

no tenor. Certainly it is hard to relate these dead birds and their metaphysical-paradoxical union to the affairs of mortal men and women. Do phoenix and turtle die because annihilation is implicit in perfect union, or because their obliteration of distance, number, and individuality offends against natural law, or because such perfection is possible only outside of time? In any case, the poem makes it clear that the ideal will never again be realized on earth.

The dead-end quality of "The Phoenix and Turtle" illuminates tragic love in *Othello* in one way, as the sonnets' tensions and compromises do in another. The sonnets, indeed, provide the most succinct statement of the dilemma I have been exploring in *Othello*, in the opening lines of Sonnet 36:

> Let me confess that we two must be twain,
> Although our undivided loves are one.

In his comedies Shakespeare viewed the coming together of incomplete opposites from a certain intellectual distance. In *Othello* he struck a vein of tragedy by focusing on the contradiction within such a conception: denial of self-sufficiency combined with continued isolation in the self. The comic structure at the beginning of *Othello* does not, as in *Romeo and Juliet*, arouse comic expectations. The seeds of tragedy are already there, and Iago threatens in a way that Tybalt could not. Instead, the rather neat comic pattern, glossing over the vulnerabilities and ambiguities in Othello's and Desdemona's love and disposing too opportunely of the implacable forces represented by Iago, sets up a point of departure for what is to follow: the look beyond and beneath comedy.

In calling *Othello* a tragic statement about love in general I do not mean to deny the power and beauty of the relationship between Othello and Desdemona, which the play celebrates fully. The great worth of love is, after all, what makes its internal flaws so painful. Nor do I wish to turn this very human drama into an allegory. But I do suggest that the universal dimension, the wider reverberations that some critics have felt lacking in *Othello*,[31] emerge very clearly when the play is seen from this

[31] See Helen Gardner, "*Othello*: A Retrospect, 1900-67," *Shakespeare Survey*, 21 (1968), 1-3.

ROMEO AND JULIET, OTHELLO

perspective. We have perhaps spent too much time asking the traditional questions about this play: Is Othello culpable in succumbing to Iago's suggestions? What makes Iago do what he does? These are important questions, but it is also important to look beyond the individual events of *Othello*, the defeat of a more or less noble dupe by an obscurely motivated villain, to the tragic inadequacies and contradictions of love itself.[32]

Shakespeare's two Italianate tragedies offer companion pictures of the vulnerability of love, threatened from without in *Romeo and Juliet*, from within in *Othello*. It is this concentration on vulnerable *love* that distinguishes these plays from two others where love comes to grief, *Troilus and Cressida* and *Antony and Cleopatra*. Both of the latter present their romantic principals with considerable comic distancing and deflation; that is, their emphasis is on the vulnerability of the *lovers*. *Troilus* is so dominated by the debunking vein, which affects the warriors as well as the lovers, that no sense of the heroic survives in it. Confusion over its genre began in Shakespeare's own time—the quarto title pages called it a history, the author of the 1609 preface praised it as a comedy, the First Folio editors apparently planned to place it among the tragedies—and continues in our own. *Antony*, however, is tragic in form and effect. If I had included it in this study,[33] its proper place would have been between *Hamlet* and

---

[32] After I had arrived at my conclusions on *Othello*, I came across a similar emphasis in John Middleton Murry's *Shakespeare* (London, 1936). For Middleton Murry, *Othello* expresses "the pain and anguish and despair which true lovers must inevitably inflict upon one another, because they are one, and because they are not one" (pp. 316-317). Iago is central to the tragedy not merely as intriguer but as the embodiment of love's inevitable flaw. This reinforcement of my sense of the play is welcome, especially since Middleton Murry's starting point was quite different from mine. He began with the handkerchief, and the paradoxical fact that Desdemona forgets to be concerned for it because she is concerned over Othello's sudden illness. That is, she loses the love token because she loves (pp. 313-316).

The case is the reverse with another study read after my own discussion was first published, Leslie Fiedler's *The Stranger in Shakespeare* (New York, 1972). In his chapter on *Othello* ("The Moor as Stranger," pp. 139-196), Fiedler notes two of my own starting points—the one-act comedy at the play's beginning and the use of Othello's blackness as a symbol of cultural apartness rather than of racial inferiority—but moves from them to conclusions very different from mine.

[33] See above, pp. 6-7.

King Lear. Antony, like Hamlet, suffers from his own largeness of spirit and consequent inability to narrow down, choose, discard alternatives. Like Lear, he exemplifies a special version of the heroic which must justify itself in the face of direct comic attack, of intimations of absurdity. But even this attack is adumbrated in *Hamlet*, which looks forward as well as back in its rich exploitation of comic means for tragic ends.

[3]

The Tragedy
of Multiplicity: *Hamlet*

What has *Hamlet* to do with the comic world? A good deal, when one considers the gravediggers' grisly jokes, the intrusion of comic-garrulous Polonius and Osric into a sphere they do not understand, the Tweedledum-and-Tweedledee pair Rosencrantz and Guildenstern, Hamlet himself as role-player, manipulator, crafty madman, wit, and eiron. Nothing at all, when one sees that Hamlet's superior awareness brings not the liberation promised by comedy but frustration, and that the play transmutes the comic celebration of multiplicity into an existential nightmare of competing perceptions of reality. Yet even this complete inversion of comic values suggests that some patterns in the complex drama become more coherent when viewed from the vantage point of comedy.

The Prince himself shows us how the multiple perspective can create agony rather than assurance. Generations of critics have sought a consistent Hamlet, one whose conviction that he must take revenge is not really at odds with his reluctance to take that revenge. But Hamlet himself sees that they are at odds and tells us so, most clearly in the "O what a rogue and peasant slave" soliloquy that ends Act II. This speech demands close attention if we are to understand Hamlet's superawareness and the dilemma it creates for him as an avenger. Roused by the passioning of the Pyrrhus speech, Hamlet rages at himself for not having already acted against Claudius. The player who wept over Hecuba was moved by a mere fiction, but Hamlet feels himself impotent in the face of a real event, "a king / Upon whose property and most dear life / A damn'd defeat was made." From the first self-disgusted outburst, the speech builds to frenzy:

92   TRAGEDY OF MULTIPLICITY

> Bloody, bawdy villain!
> Remorseless, treacherous, lecherous, kindless villain!
> O, vengeance!

In all this swell of emotion there is self-questioning (am I a coward?) but no doubt whatsoever of Claudius's guilt and the rightness of revenge. Claudius is the worst of villains; he made the "damn'd defeat"; it can only be cowardice that has held back Hamlet's avenging hand. But a few lines later Hamlet is saying something quite different:

> The spirit that I have seen
> May be a devil; and the devil hath power
> T'assume a pleasing shape; yea, and perhaps
> Out of my weakness and my melancholy,
> As he is very potent with such spirits,
> Abuses me to damn me. I'll have grounds
> More relative than this.

In this new version of the situation, the Ghost's origins are not certain at all and so Claudius's guilt is not certain. The action indicated is not to denounce and kill the King out of hand but to force a public, confirming confession.

Bradley thought that Hamlet's doubt, opposing as it does his certainty in the first part of the soliloquy, was an "unconscious fiction." Other critics have followed him, or have believed in the doubt rather than the certainty.[1] But the conventions of Elizabethan soliloquy are against fictions in such circumstances, whether conscious or not.[2] The inconsistency is real. No ingenious analysis should be allowed to smooth away a contradiction that Shakespeare has made so prominent—especially since this is not an isolated instance but merely the most sharply focused of many such inconsistencies in Hamlet as he is shown to us in the

---

[1] Bradley, *Shakespearean Tragedy*, p. 131; on the other side see, for example, J. Dover Wilson, *What Happens in "Hamlet"*, 3rd ed. (Cambridge, 1951), pp. 73-75.

[2] See Bernard Spivack, *Shakespeare and the Allegory of Evil* (New York, 1958), pp. 24-27. Spivack supports Schücking's assertion, "It must be made a principle to deny that Shakespeare makes any character in a monologue state reasons for his actions that are not meant to be substantially correct and sufficient." Levin L. Schücking, *Character Problems in Shakespeare's Plays* (London, 1922), p. 212.

HAMLET
93

early part of the play. It is better to look where Shakespeare himself is directing our attention, to the contradiction itself. What makes a man feel and say one thing in all sincerity, and then in equal sincerity feel and say its very opposite?

The dynamic of the speech is instructive. It does not move directly from statement to contradiction but changes tone radically at two points. The first howl for vengeance is followed abruptly by "Why, what an ass am I!" Fully inside his passion one moment, Hamlet steps outside the next to view himself objectively: a man raging all by himself, unpacking his heart with words, is a ridiculous object. Rhythm and phrasing here become less broken and exclamatory than in the preceding denunciations of Claudius and himself, but the section ends with another short outburst—"Fie upon 't! foh!" Then there is another shift, into more formal, meditative verse. Emotional thought gives way to a more speculative sort. Significantly, the new mood is signaled by the words "About, my brains."

The dynamic, then, is a move from emotion to reason and from subjective commitment to objective detachment. It is this shift, with the two kinds of awareness it implies, that should command our attention. By this point in the play the audience badly needs some explanation of Hamlet's conduct. The conduct has been puzzling, both as we see it and as others describe it, ever since his wild and whirling words after encountering the Ghost; and the explanations Hamlet offers onstage are not to be trusted. Given its position and its portentous preface ("Now I am alone"), this soliloquy ought to provide the long-awaited insight into Hamlet's situation. And so it does. This is a man caught between subjective surety and his own awareness that it *is* subjective. He is both inside his emotional conviction and outside it looking on.

This is a position of power for a figure like Rosalind-Ganymede in *As You Like It*, where two views are better than one, more whole, and where the need to choose and act can be suspended in the free play of the mind. But Hamlet's situation calls for action, and coherent action is impossible while his two apprehensions remain separate and opposed. In its own way *Hamlet*, like its successor in the chronology of Shakespearean tragedy *Othello*, finds its tragic core in the comic assumptions.

94 TRAGEDY OF MULTIPLICITY

But the ways of these plays are as different as their heroes. To be sure, Othello sees the world subjectively, but he does not know he is seeing it subjectively—not until after the tragic decision is made and its consequences are before him. Like most tragic heroes he is very much the alazon, self-deceived and totally committed. As Bradley long ago pointed out, Othello could have handled Hamlet's problem.[3] It is Hamlet's peculiar tragedy to be flexible where flexibility is a drawback, to see beyond his own convictions, to be eiron as well as alazon in a situation that demands the single-minded alazon response.[4]

As Hamlet's awareness of subjective distortion is such a departure from the usual tragic pattern, it is not surprising that Shakespeare has called attention to it in smaller ways throughout the first two acts. Hamlet's comments to Rosencrantz and Guildenstern earlier in this same scene, for example, show his special way of perceiving things. "Denmark's a prison," the subjective view, is not allowed to stand unqualified. "*To me* it is a prison," he adds. The prison is real for Hamlet, but he knows it is not real for those who "think not so." The same double vision of the eiron informs his speech "I have of late—but wherefore I know not—lost all my mirth." The earth is goodly but seems "*to me*" a sterile promontory; the skies are excellent and majestic but "*to me*" foul vapors; man is creation's masterpiece, akin to gods and angels, yet "*to me*" the quintessence of dust. And lest we miss the general point, he supplies it directly: "There is nothing either good or bad, but thinking makes it so."[5]

Only an intellectual could be so conscious of the mind's tricks and deceptions. D. G. James reminds us that so far as we know Shakespeare was the first to give Hamlet a university background.[6] But if his condition is part of his intellectuality, it is nevertheless abnormal. Intellectuals are not inevitably caught in

[3] *Shakespearean Tragedy*, p. 175.

[4] Maynard Mack observes that, unlike the committed Othello, Hamlet is "partly an *eiron* figure," and that "disengagement is in a sense his problem." "Engagement and Detachment in Shakespeare's Plays," in *Essays on Shakespeare and Elizabethan Drama in Honor of Hardin Craig*, ed. Richard Hosley (Columbia, Mo., 1962), pp. 286-287.

[5] II.ii.242-250, 294-309; my italics.

[6] *The Dream of Learning* (Oxford, 1951), pp. 41-42.

HAMLET

95

impotence between knowing and not-knowing. How has it happened to Hamlet? Certainly unresolved grief has made him melancholy; and Rosalie Colie has observed with insight that in *Hamlet* Shakespeare has used the melancholic syndrome as "a medium for the character's own confusions" and as "an idiom which to some extent takes for granted the imbalance, the relativism, the insecurities implicit in any judgment."[7] Montaigne in the "Apology of Raymond Sebond" offers another perspective when he describes how the overthrow of one accepted belief calls all others into question, leaving the doubter nothing to rely on but his own lonely judgment.[8] Hamlet's basic belief was in the goodness of his parents and their relationship. Recent events have not only brought an emotional shock in the loss of his father but have overthrown established belief by the sudden revelation of his mother's fleshly weakness. This is the burden of his first soliloquy in Act I, scene ii, an important speech that is clearly meant to define Hamlet's condition of mind *before* he hears the Ghost, the condition out of which he will react to the Ghost's message.

Hamlet begins with his weary distaste for life—"O, that this too too solid flesh would melt"—and goes on to the cause of that distaste, which is not so much grief for his father as disillusion with his mother. Seemingly loving and good, she has betrayed her real nature by posting with wicked speed to incestuous sheets. Hamlet's disjointed words and memories keep coming back to that suddenly opened abyss between how he saw her and what she was. "Why, she would hang on him / *As if* increase of appetite had grown / By what it fed on. . . . / *Like* Niobe, all tears . . . / . . . most unrighteous tears" (my italics). Neither love nor grief was real in Gertrude. Her son is left with powerful emotions to stifle and no sureties to cling to.

The whole scene has been building toward this effect. Hamlet has come on mute and even when addressed by the King has only tossed him contemptuous one-liners without caring if Claudius hears them or not. What rouses him to passionate speech is Gertrude's "Why seems it so particular with thee?" For

[7] *Shakespeare's Living Art* (Princeton, 1974), p. 216.

[8] *Montaigne's Essays*, tr. John Florio, ed. J.I.M. Stewart (London, 1931), I, 646.

96 TRAGEDY OF MULTIPLICITY

reply he fires at her a hysterical diatribe against "seems," which we understand only later as a rebuke for those unrighteous tears she shed for her first husband. At the time, the outburst is puzzling to the audience, like everything else about this sullen young prince. It raises the question that he will answer when he is alone; and it is the first sign of the multiple awareness that lies underneath his obsession with seeming, delusion, and subjectivity.[9]

That obsession is apparent in some of Hamlet's other responses in Act I. In the meditation on the "dram of eale" (I.iv), for example, his mind is not on how things are but on how they *look*, how the image of the whole may be altered and distorted by a part. The dram and the humour growing beyond bounds relate loosely to the play's persistent imagery of spreading poison. Hamlet does not say, however, that heavy drinking corrupts Danish lives and morals. He says that the Danes' drinking habits have given them a generally bad name.

> This heavy-headed revel east and west
> Makes us *traduc'd and tax'd of other nations*;
> They *clepe* us drunkards, and with swinish *phrase*
> Soil our *addition*.

(my italics)

It is an odd turn for his thought to take, all the more so because he has passed up an opportunity for a direct slur on Claudius—who is, after all, doing the drinking. Instead of the sneer we expect, what comes through is Hamlet's preoccupation with seemings and distorted pictures. Even in his rage that soon follows, when the Ghost tells him what Claudius did, what does Hamlet single out for his tables of remembrance? That one may smile and smile, and yet be a villain. He is shaken, not so much by evil *per se* as by evil hidden under a masquerade of order, affection, good.

---

[9] Bernard McElroy similarly connects Hamlet's speech to his mother with the first soliloquy: see *Shakespeare's Mature Tragedies* (Princeton, 1973), pp. 48-49. Although his study of *Hamlet* takes a direction different from mine, McElroy also finds central Hamlet's multiple viewpoint, his capacity for "believing simultaneously two or more things which logically should cancel each other out" (p. 38).

HAMLET
97

The Ghost's accusation of Claudius gets Hamlet's immediate intuitive assent: "O my prophetic soul!" Yet he has become suspicious of all certainties, superconscious as he is of the distortions of the mind's eye. Believing the Ghost with his emotions and his prophetic soul, he is aware that his belief could be false. The Ghost has spoken to no one but himself. Hamlet knows he is melancholy, out of balance. And ghosts themselves are problematic beings, not always what they seem. So he knows and does not know.[10] A man in such a state cannot be a consistent character in the ordinary sense, because he can demonstrate the grip of subjectivity only by expressing beliefs with passionate conviction and the need for objectivity only by doubting or contradicting those beliefs.

Hamlet's later soliloquy "How all occasions do inform against me" (IV.iv) shows a similar jar between subjective sureness and objective wariness. Even as he berates himself for thinking too precisely on the event and resolves for blood, Hamlet knows simultaneously that his temporary model, Fortinbras, has no more grounds for *his* bloody course than a straw or an eggshell. This monologue, present only in the Second Quarto,[11] reflects more on the past situation than on the present one, for at the moment the well-guarded Hamlet hardly has "means" to kill Claudius, as he says he does. It is interesting that both the occasions that inform against Hamlet in this way, the player's speech in Act II and Fortinbras' expedition in Act IV, represent forms of

[10] Cf. Karl Jaspers on Hamlet, *Tragedy Is Not Enough*, tr. Harald A. T. Reiche, Harry T. Moore, and Karl W. Deutsch (London, 1953): "It is not his character that paralyzes him. Only the predicament of a man who knows—with a sovereign command of penetrating vision—yet does not know, makes him linger. . . . He is, as it were, caught up in his knowledge, and in the knowledge of his ignorance" (pp. 64–65).

[11] Wilson and Greg both thought that the Folio omission of "How all occasions" and its preamble represented playhouse practice. *The Manuscript of Shakespeare's "Hamlet"* (Cambridge, 1934), I, 30; and *The Editorial Problem in Shakespeare* (Oxford, 1942), p. 65. Empson suggests in "*Hamlet* When New" (*Sewanee Review*, 61 [1953], 41) that "How all occasions" was reserved as an encore speech, to use when the performance went well. In any case, the speech seems detachable from its situation in a way that other soliloquies are not detachable from theirs. Eleanor Prosser speculates that Shakespeare intended to use the speech earlier in the play, later found it redundant, tried it in IV.iv, and finally cut it completely. *Hamlet and Revenge* (Stanford, 1967), p. 206.

98　　　　TRAGEDY OF MULTIPLICITY

delusion. The player raves and weeps for a mythical queen; Fortinbras risks death for a fantasy and trick of fame. In both cases Hamlet feels his own motive to be more real, but the association—I should be like this actor, I should be like this seeker after fantasies—is nevertheless troubling. Even a third spur to action, the Ghost's reappearance in III.iv, is made ambiguous by Gertrude's failure to see and hear it. Hamlet's subjective mazes are not easy to escape.

The Ghost and Fortinbras can lead us further, to two ways in which Shakespeare manipulates the multiple possibilities dear to comedy for tragic tension in *Hamlet*. One, a series of open questions, involves us as spectators in the difficulty of choosing among possibilities; the other, a set of reflector characters, suggests the limitations of freedom and power inherent in any such choice. In this latter regard, it is clear that Fortinbras and the other young men who serve as foils for Hamlet do not suffer his conflict between the heart's convictions and the mind's doubts. Rather, each in his single awareness embodies one or the other term of that conflict. Fortinbras, Laertes, and Horatio are whole in a way that Hamlet is not; yet we see in them as well the limitations that inhere in the single view. Critics have long noted that Hamlet's situation as a son impelled to avenge a dead father is mirrored in the situations of Laertes and Fortinbras. Laertes leaps to his task with no hesitation. When he consigns "conscience" to the profoundest pit (IV.v.129), it is in both senses of the word: he rejects not only moral scruple but also full awareness and consideration. As for Fortinbras, while he might draw the line at poisoned foils, he is similarly bent on honor at the expense of justice. We have it not only from Claudius, whose word might be suspect, but also from the disinterested Horatio that Old Fortinbras' lands were fairly lost.[12] His son's expedition is diverted away from revenge against Denmark, but Fortinbras in his Polish exploit is no more thoughtful than Laertes. The large discourse that looks before and after is foreign to both of them. And Fortinbras' unthinking action, however Hamlet may envy it, is as fruitless in its way as Laertes'. His conquest in Poland means nothing, and he gains the lands he really wants by *not* fighting for them.

[12] I.ii.23-25; I.i.80-95.

HAMLET

While Laertes and Fortinbras act out Hamlet's subjective side and show its insufficiency as a guide for action, we have for the objective side Horatio, the man that is not passion's slave. Horatio gets high praise from Hamlet (as indeed do Fortinbras and Laertes), but he is finally as insufficient as they. In Horatio, Hamlet says admiringly, blood and judgment are well commingled. Actually, from what we see of him, Horatio's "blood" is so well subdued to judgment as to be almost nonexistent. Significantly, Hamlet sees as the happy result of this commingling not decisive action but a kind of stoicism.[13] Horatio's capacity for detached endurance, however admirable in the abstract, answers Hamlet's own case no better than the emotional rashness of Fortinbras and Laertes. Horatio is an adviser, a go-between, an explainer, but not a doer. We should not forget that the one action in the play that he initiates on his own, although he is not allowed to carry it out, is suicide.

In short, to consider any of these partial reflectors by the side of Hamlet is to become aware of the diminution involved in narrowing down from multiple possibilities to one actuality. In tragedy the eiron retains his superiority to others even while his greater capacities are the cause of his torment.

Horatio illuminates Hamlet's conflict of perceptions in another way. He is the validator, called on first to test the apparition seen by the sentries and then, more centrally, to give objective confirmation of Claudius's guilt. The context of Hamlet's praise of his detachment is the Prince's desperate need of that calm vision to confirm his own apprehension, or to correct its distortion. Directly after his tribute to Horatio he explains:

> There is a play to-night before the King;
> One scene of it comes near the circumstance
> Which I have told thee of my father's death.
> I prithee, when thou seest that act afoot,
> Even with the very comment of thy soul
> Observe my uncle. If his occulted guilt

---

[13] For thou hast been
   As one, in suff'ring all, that suffers nothing;
   A man that Fortune's buffets and rewards
   Hast ta'en with equal thanks.

(III.ii.63-66)

100 TRAGEDY OF MULTIPLICITY

Do not itself unkennel in one speech,
It is a damned ghost that we have seen,
And my imaginations are as foul
As Vulcan's stithy. Give him heedful note;
For I mine eyes will rivet to his face;
And, after, we will both our judgments join
In censure of his seeming.

(III.ii.73–85)

It is usually assumed that Hamlet gets the reassurance he wants
when he and Horatio talk after the play has broken off and the
King and court have left the stage. But what does Horatio really
say?

Ham. O good Horatio, I'll take the ghost's word for a
thousand pound. Didst perceive?
Hor. Very well, my lord.
Ham. Upon the talk of the poisoning.
Hor. I did very well note him.
Ham. Ah, ha!

(III.ii.280–285)

What did Horatio perceive and note? Claudius has not unken-
neled his guilt in words; he has only gone off in some agitation.
Hamlet has told us himself that powerful dramatic speech would
"appal the free" as well as "make mad the guilty."[14] None of the
courtiers seems to suspect anything (except, perhaps, that Hamlet himself is madder and more dangerous than ever). Possibly
Horatio is trying to temper Hamlet's excitement with his own
moderation, but why withhold a simple yes? He is strangely
noncommittal, even ambiguous.[15] Yet Horatio is not habitually
indefinite: at various points in the action he warns Hamlet not to
follow the Ghost, advises Gertrude to see Ophelia, counsels
Hamlet to forgo the duel with Laertes, all with admirable clarity. It would seem that what Shakespeare wanted in this exchange, onstage at least, was something short of decisive con-

[14] Harold Skulsky makes this point in considering Claudius's less than clear
reaction to the Mousetrap. " 'I Know My Course': Hamlet's Confidence,"
PMLA, 89 (1974), 484.
[15] Horatio's opinion is no less ambiguous in the briefer exchange of Q1: he
says only, "The king is moved, my lord."

HAMLET

101

firmation. (The theater audience does not doubt any longer, I think; but they have already heard Claudius's guilty aside in III.i.) Horatio is still not sure, and Hamlet must go off to his fateful encounters with the King and Queen once again subjectively certain but with no clearly validated course of action. Not until Act V, when he is faced with the undisputable evidence of Claudius's murderous move against his nephew, does Horatio condemn the King. By that time, as we shall see, the dilemma has been resolved another way, and his confirmation has no importance.

As validator, then, Horatio functions by not functioning. He calls attention to Hamlet's problem of knowledge by refusing to confirm or deny. The same could be said of Shakespeare himself, who in this tragedy of competing realities introduces an unusual number of open questions and resolves as few of them as possible.

The most obvious of these, as I suggested above, is the Ghost. What is he and where does he come from? Dover Wilson has shown that there was no single accepted contemporary view about ghosts. For some they were actual spirits of the dead whose commands had to be obeyed, while others saw them as devils assuming familiar shapes to work evil on men, and still another opinion refused them any existence at all except as delusions of the mind.[16] All three possibilities are raised in *Hamlet*. Horatio speaks to the apparition as the dead king's spirit which must be pacified ("If there be any good thing to be done, / That may to thee do ease . . .") but also as a hallucination ("Stay, illusion") and as an imposter:

> What art thou that usurp'st this time of night
> Together with that fair and warlike form
> In which the majesty of buried Denmark
> Did sometimes march?[17]

The sentries show similar confusion about "this thing." Hamlet himself does not know how to react when the Ghost appears to him. Is it a spirit of health or a goblin damned? Even after he has heard the Ghost's story, his response is not unambiguous: "O all you host of heaven! O earth! What else? / And shall I couple

---

[16] *What Happens in "Hamlet"*, pp. 52–86.   [17] I.i.130–131, 127, 46–49.

TRAGEDY OF MULTIPLICITY

hell?"[18] It seems clear that Shakespeare is trying to leave the question of the Ghost's provenance wide open, unsettling any individual spectator's convictions by introducing the other possibilities. The audience is not allowed to part company with Hamlet, to rest secure in certainty while he hesitates and doubts. The technique indeed, as Wilson says, justifies Hamlet's unsureness, but it does more: it involves the audience experientially in that unsureness.[19]

The Ghost is far from the only open question in the play. Is the marriage of Claudius and Gertrude incestuous? Is Hamlet the rightful heir to the Danish throne, cheated out of his inheritance by a usurper? Practitioners of historical criticism have sought to establish definitively how the average Elizabethan would have answered these questions. Wilson, for example, offers a well-researched, unequivocal yes to both.[20] But on these points, which should be very clear if their proper interpretation is as important as Wilson says it is, Shakespeare is noticeably equivocal. The council of state has approved the royal marriage (I.ii.14-16), and no one except Hamlet seems to feel uneasy about it. Perhaps, as critics often assume, the Danish court is corrupt from the beginning. But where is the evidence? Polonius is commonplace but not vicious. Hamlet, indeed, calls the marriage incestuous, and so does the Ghost. Once again we are made not just to see Hamlet's dilemma but to share it, feeling on the one side his sureness of wrongdoing and on the other the disturbing absence of external confirmation. And once again Shakespeare is exploiting an already existing ambiguity of attitude in his society. To marry one's brother's widow was normally forbidden, but the marriage of a widowed queen ("imperial jointress") to the new king could nevertheless be approved

[18] I.v.92-93. Wilson sees "And shall I couple hell?" as a returning doubt about the Ghost's origin, immediately stifled in a self-rebuking "O, fie!" *Hamlet*, New Cambridge ed. (Cambridge, 1936), p. lii.

[19] In his British Academy Shakespeare Lecture *Hamlet: The Prince or the Poem* (London, 1942), pp. 11-12, C. S. Lewis describes well this sense of the Ghost as "permanently ambiguous." His statement that Hamlet is convinced when in the Ghost's presence and doubtful in its absence brings out an important element in the situation but does not account for assertions of certainty when the Ghost is not there, such as the first part of "O what a rogue."

[20] *What Happens in "Hamlet"*, pp. 26-44.

HAMLET

as wise policy. Advantages in terms of resolving dynastic rivalries could overrule the usual sanctions against incest.[21]

The question of Hamlet's succession raises the same possibility of more "truths" than one. Wilson may be right in asserting that Shakespeare's audience would think of the Danish constitution in terms of what they were used to, the English system of inherited rule. Not until Act v is it made clear that the Danish monarchy is elective rather than hereditary. On the other hand, the audience has heard very early in the play about a nearby kingdom, Norway, in which the crown has passed to the dead king's brother rather than to his son, apparently in the normal course of things.[22] In any case, we must be less than certain about Hamlet's rights to the throne simply because so little is made of them in the play. Council and court say nothing. Do we assume Claudius has bribed them all? Gertrude says nothing. Yet her other reactions assure us that her love for Claudius has not canceled out her love and concern for Hamlet. If a major injustice has been done to him, would she not be aware of it? Horatio says nothing. Even that politically minded pair Rosencrantz and Guildenstern, while they hint that Hamlet is ambitious, never suggest that he has a real claim to the throne. Hamlet himself flirts with the ambition motive in various contexts of deception, but in soliloquy he says not a word of being cheated out of a crown. When he denounces Claudius to Gertrude as "cutpurse of the empire" (III.iv.99), he may mean that his uncle stole the throne from the legitimate heir—or he may mean simply that Claudius won the kingdom by treacherous murder rather than by merit or open conquest. His only direct reference to the choice of king, which comes very late in the play (v.ii.65), implies that he himself was a likely candidate for the throne, though by no means the undoubted successor. Claudius popped in between the election and his *hopes*, not his rights. With so little

[21] Marriage to the brother's widow was proposed for Charles IX of France and Mary Queen of Scots after the death of Mary's husband François II. And, of course, it was carried out in the case of Henry VIII and Catherine of Aragon, widow of Henry's elder brother Arthur.

[22] J. P. Malleson, *Times Literary Supplement*, 4 January 1936, p. 15, and 25 January 1936, p. 75; cf. E.A.J. Honigmann, "The Politics in *Hamlet* and 'The World of the Play,' " in *Hamlet*, ed. J. Russell Brown and Bernard Harris, Stratford-upon-Avon Studies, 5 (London, 1963), pp. 129-147.

TRAGEDY OF MULTIPLICITY

support for its instinctive reaction based on familiar rules of primogeniture, the audience is left in a state of uncertainty that must color response to many scenes. In I.ii, for example, Claudius's careful deference to Polonius and the council and his naming of Hamlet as his chosen successor to the throne may be seen as signs of a shaky title, but they may just as well be seen as a new king's attempts at magnanimity and good government. We simply do not know, and by not knowing we re-create in ourselves another version of Hamlet's dilemma of conflicting perceptions.

Shakespeare raises these questions in *Hamlet* in such a way as to forestall any easy resolution, going to some pains to nurture rather than dispel ambiguity. The germs of ambiguity are already there, in that more than one defensible view existed on each issue. The point, again and again, is not one or the other "right" answer but the doubt. Other questions reinforce these. How guilty is Gertrude? Is Hamlet's grief natural or excessive? Even the central question—did Claudius in fact murder his brother?—is left in doubt until the third act. This last uncertainty is the most difficult for us to re-create in our experience of *Hamlet*. Everyone knows the end of the story. It is rare to find a student who is unfamiliar with the outlines of the plot, even if he has never read or seen the play. When, some years ago, I did come across one who had somehow escaped foreknowledge, I was intrigued when he reported that up to the moment in the prayer scene when Claudius's own words condemned him, he had thought the King might be innocent. My student was a little ashamed, thinking that his late enlightenment showed him unperceptive. But in fact his experience probably came closer to Shakespeare's intention than that of his knowing classmates.[23]

---

[23] It might be argued that at least some of the audience would have known the Hamlet story through an earlier version—that of Saxo Grammaticus, Belleforest, or the old play—and thus could not have doubted the Ghost's authenticity and Claudius's guilt. It is possible; but the likeliest source of their expectation, the Ur-*Hamlet*, is not extant, and we know nothing about it except that it featured a ghost and the tag line "Hamlet, revenge!" Compared with the sources available, Shakespeare's play consistently makes the clear unclear. In the Latin and French narratives, the characters know from the start who killed the king, no problematic ghost troubles the night, and there is no question about the incestuous nature of the new king's marriage. With these certainties muddled into

HAMLET

Hamlet should be, but too rarely is, in Stephen Booth's phrase, "the tragedy of an audience that cannot make up its mind."[24]

For both Hamlet and the audience the eiron state of awareness is uncomfortable. To perceive more truths than one is to be sure of no truth. Nevertheless, it is still a position of superiority. The other characters take up a good part of the play's action demonstrating that to be sure, alazon-fashion, is generally to be wrong.

In this connection the nature of the initiating event, the murder, is very important, as is the kind of imagery it generates. The Ghost tells Hamlet that after the poison entered his ear "a most instant tetter bark'd about, / Most lazar-like, with vile and loathsome crust, / All my smooth body" (I.v.71-73). The symptoms were everywhere, but the source and working of the poison were concealed. So it is with Denmark, where Claudius has not only polluted the springs of public and private health (lawful monarchy, ties of blood) but has set himself up as a counterfeit spring of health: false father, false king. His crime has bred not only corruption but confusion about that corruption. As Maurice Charney says, refining on the general disease motif stressed by Wolfgang Clemen, "If there is indeed a leitmotif of disease imagery stemming from the Ghost's narration, it does not refer merely to disease in general, but to the hidden disease, the disease that is deliberately concealed."[25] Thus, its ramifications take in not only the painted harlot's cheek, the ulcer filmed over while rank corruption infects unseen, and the secret disease feeding on the pith of life, but also the hidden corpse of Polonius that will announce its presence eventually by the stench of decay. This last implies directly what the others imply indirectly, that the concealed evil will at some time come to light. "Foul deeds will rise, / Though all the earth o'erwhelm them, to men's eyes." And so it happens in the last scene, when the ulcer breaks open and its poison is finally exposed by Laertes' shout "The King, the King's to blame."[26]

---

ambiguities—the murder secret, the Ghost suspect, etc.—even a spectator who knew the old story could not be sure it would proceed in the usual way.

[24] "On the Value of *Hamlet*," in *Reinterpretations of Elizabethan Drama*, ed. Norman Rabkin (New York, 1969), p. 152.

[25] *Style in "Hamlet"* (Princeton, 1969), p. 36; see Charney's discussion following, pp. 36-39.

[26] III.i.51; III.iv.147-149; IV.i.21-23; IV.iii.35-37; I.ii.256-257; V.ii.312.

106   TRAGEDY OF MULTIPLICITY

But through the early acts we see the symptoms rather than the cause. Something is rotten, and the whole early movement is toward finding out what that thing is. Diverse ways of seeing the action *become* the action. The question What is wrong with Denmark? is defined by most of the characters as What is wrong with Hamlet? The answers they give prove that Hamlet the eiron has good reason to suspect the single, subjective truth, for they are all inadvertent self-definitions. The impulse to interpret Hamlet according to the interpreter's own concerns and fears, so noticeable in Coleridge and Freud, Stephen Dedalus and J. Alfred Prufrock, begins inside the play itself.[27]

Each of the interpreting characters could well say with Hamlet, "By the image of my cause I see / The portraiture of his" (v.ii.77-78). Gertrude, uneasy about her own conduct, sees at the root of Hamlet's trouble her husband's death and her "o'erhasty" marriage (II.ii.56-57). Claudius, conscious of his own hidden guilt, thinks Hamlet must harbor a corresponding dangerous secret:

> There's something in his soul
> O'er which his melancholy sits on brood;

[27] Coleridge's image of Hamlet comes through most clearly in the 1818 *Lectures* ("a great, an almost enormous, intellectual activity, and a proportionate aversion to real action") and in the *Table Talk* comment of 24 June 1827 ("Hamlet's character is the prevalence of the abstracting and generalizing habit over the practical. . . . I have a smack of Hamlet myself"). Quoted in *Hamlet: A Casebook*, ed. John Jump (London, 1968), pp. 30-31. Freud's attribution of Hamlet's troubles to an unresolved Oedipus complex appeared at the height of his interest in that pattern, in *The Interpretation of Dreams* (first published 1900). *Basic Writings of Sigmund Freud*, tr. A. A. Brill (New York, 1938), pp. 309-310. In the library scene of Joyce's *Ulysses*, Stephen Dedalus interprets *Hamlet* in terms of his own dilemmas as son and artist. *Ulysses* (New York, 1934), pp. 182-215. For Eliot's Prufrock, Hamlet is not a projection of himself but rather everything he wishes he were and fears to be. This Hamlet, quite opposite to that of Coleridge, is active and powerful like the other Renaissance figures in the poem, but Prufrock himself is "not Prince Hamlet, nor was meant to be." Instead he identifies with the supporting character, an "attendant lord" who is a composite of Polonius, Osric, Horatio, Rosencrantz and Guildenstern.

In *Some Shakespearean Themes* (London, 1959), L. C. Knights points out how consistently Shakespeare's plays of this period concern themselves with subjective illusion. In addition to *Hamlet*, he cites *Troilus and Cressida, Much Ado, Othello*, and *Julius Caesar*: "In all these plays . . . we find we are pondering questions of a kind that are prompted by Blake's dictum, 'As a man is, so he sees' " (p. 171).

HAMLET
107

And I do doubt the hatch and the disclose
Will be some danger.

(III.i.164-167)

Others offer different but equally self-revealing interpretations.
And here another, more direct use of comedy in *Hamlet* for
tragic effect becomes apparent. Comedy's tendency is expansive
and inclusive, but like any genre or convention it is ultimately
defined by the limits within which it treats the human condition.
In the case of the opposed modes of comedy and tragedy, these
limits operate not so much on subject matter as on point of view:
love and jealousy are perceived tragically in *Othello*, while death
itself becomes comic in *The Old Wives' Tale*. Thus, if the tragic
focus is to be on attitudes and limited perceptions, as in *Hamlet*,
the perspectives evoked by comic convention can be especially
useful as misinterpreters. This is a particular application of the
"irrelevance" function already observed in the Friar and the
Nurse in *Romeo and Juliet*. Here, it is clearest in Polonius and
Osric.

Polonius naturally sees Hamlet's derangement as "the very
ecstasy of love" (II.i.102) because his spiritual home is comedy.
Like the clown, he is in love with words. He has all the inconse-
quential garrulity of Juliet's Nurse and is forever attempting,
though not achieving, the verbal brilliance of Mercutio. Insofar
as Polonius can be envisioned apart from the grim events of
Claudius's Denmark, he would not be out of place in *Love's
Labour's Lost*, chewing on the scraps of language with Armado
and Holofernes. Busy as he is, he always has time to crack the
wind of a phrase, to make up a fine metaphor and then kindly
translate it into plain language lest he go over the heads of his
audience. He cannot express an opinion without his own brand
of wit, however urgently his hearers may wish for more matter,
with less art. As a connoisseur of words, Polonius is, inevitably,
a literary critic. "Beautified Ophelia," he thinks, is a vile phrase,
but "mobled queen" is good. In spite of this blessing on adjecti-
val obscurity, however, he is impatient at the length of the
player's Pyrrhus speech; and Hamlet dismisses him, significantly
enough, as one who cares only for comedy: "Prithee say on.
He's for a jig, or a tale of bawdry, or he sleeps" (II.ii.493-494).
Poor Polonius, who fancies himself the complete critic and can
parade before us all the dramatic kinds! His pastoral-comicals

TRAGEDY OF MULTIPLICITY

and tragical-historicals proliferate irrelevantly for their own sake and of their own accord, words outrunning meaning in the manner of the comic monologue.

The same is true of his aphorisms and *sententiae*, although what Polonius trots out as verbal decoration sometimes has ironic applications quite concealed from the complacent speaker. He counsels prudence, caution, and high-minded integrity to Laertes, more as a pleasing form of words than as an order he expects Laertes to follow (or why send Reynaldo to spy?). But Laertes' failure in just these qualities will lead to his downfall. Arranging Ophelia in a holy pose for less than holy purposes, Polonius cannot resist the facile moral: "We are oft to blame in this: / 'Tis too much prov'd, that with devotion's visage / And pious action we do sugar o'er / The devil himself" (iii.i.46-49). What is just another cliché for him pierces to the core of Claudius's sick conscience. Here as elsewhere Polonius's words reverberate suddenly through the play's deep waters while he, all unaware, bobs on the surface like a cork.

From the beginning right up to his death, Polonius behaves as if he were in a comedy. Suspicious of his children, spying on Laertes and interfering in Ophelia's love affair, he casts himself first as the traditional obstructive father. But like Bottom in "Pyramus and Thisbe," Polonius would like to play all the parts. Having brought about the comic impasse, Hamlet's supposed love madness, he switches to a manipulator role, the better to contrive a happy ending.[28] What he has in mind we are not told, but we can be sure that Polonius would not mind being father-in-law to the next king of Denmark. And so he would be, if *Hamlet* were in fact a romantic comedy.

Even after hearing Hamlet revile Ophelia, Polonius holds stubbornly to his belief that the Prince is mad for love and advises that the Queen question Hamlet in private before he is sent to England. Presumably the distraught lover would be more likely to confess his romantic problems to a sympathetic mother than to his stepfather or to the father of the lady in question.

[28] Frye (*Anatomy*, pp. 174-175) links Polonius with another comic type, the older authority figure who retreats from the action to see how the young will behave in his absence. Other examples are Knowell in *Every Man in His Humour* and Duke Vincentio in *Measure for Measure*.

HAMLET   109

Such a suggestion, if we are meant to infer it, enhances the terrible irony in that last attempt to soften Hamlet, for we know that he thinks of his mother with tormented disgust, as an adulteress driven by lust to connive at murder. Instead of pouring out love confidences the son will beat his mother to her knees with rebukes of her own gross appetites. And by that time Polonius will be dead.

Polonius has always been right before, as he makes Claudius admit, and he has verbally staked his life on being right this time (ii.ii.152-155). He loses. It is not a comedy after all, and the bustling intriguer finds at last that in this tense, shadowy world, to be busy is some danger. He dies because he is where he should not be, in the place of a greater figure. Thrust in among the affairs of the mighty, he is like the clown Hamlet earlier described to the players, irrelevant to the "necessary question."[29]

Polonius's complete consistency as a comic character creates a cumulative irony. Beyond such immediate effects as that inadvertent catching of the King's conscience, there is the larger irony of a subjective vision, coherent but quite distorted, seeing what we see but getting it all wrong. His total unawareness exacerbates our awareness. Most ironic of all, it is the death of this irrelevant intruder that sets the play unalterably on course to the final catastrophe. Out of the murder of Polonius come Ophelia's madness and suicide; Laertes' rage for revenge and the King's poison plot; and the deaths of Laertes, Gertrude, Claudius, and Hamlet himself. Hamlet's grim joke—"This man shall set me packing"—is all too prophetic. In some ways, Polonius's death is the structural equivalent of Mercutio's in *Romeo and Juliet*, but the differences are important. Mercutio embodies the comic possibilities available to the characters until the middle of the play. When he dies, these possibilities disappear before our eyes, and a potential comedy becomes a tragedy. Polonius never offered Hamlet any valid escape from his dictated course of revenge, although in his pretensions to wit and literary taste he is a parodic reminder of

---

[29] iii.ii.36-42. Hamlet's epitaph of "fool" for Polonius anticipates Antony's for one of Polonius's direct descendants: "Fool Lepidus!" (*Ant.* iii.v.17). Like Polonius a commonplace, well-meaning go-between, Lepidus too is caught in the conflict of mighty opposites, "half to half the world oppos'd" (iii.xiii.9). When he gets in the way, he is eliminated from the arena of power as irrelevant.

110   TRAGEDY OF MULTIPLICITY

the wide world of intellectual interests that was open to Hamlet
before Denmark closed in around him like a prison. For all that,
Polonius's longing for a central role in the action is finally fulfilled: not in the comedy he imagined but in the tragedy that is,
not as the lively manipulator but as the last of the play's fathers
to be killed and the first to be avenged.

For the family affairs of Polonius, Laertes, and Ophelia are
similarly drawn into the tragic orbit from outside. At first, as
Francis Fergusson observes, they function as a kind of domestic
comedy, related to the main action through contrasts of tone and
depth. We see one world in which Hamlet is trying to evade a
stepfather he despises and to bear a terrible burden of revenge
imposed on him by his own father from beyond the grave. Jux-
taposed is a smaller, safer world in which Laertes evades *his* omnipresent father by retreating to Paris and Polonius tries to reach
him, not across the abyss of eternity but over the measurable distance between Denmark and France, not with dread commands
but with "assays of bias" and "slight sullies."[30] But when
Polonius becomes relevant by dying, so to speak, his children
follow him into tragic roles, roles which have already been
adumbrated by Hamlet himself: distracted mourner and suicide,
rebel and avenger.

After Polonius becomes part of the tragedy in death, his comic
function is carried on by Osric. Even more remote from the true
springs of the action than Polonius, Osric has all his elder's chat-
tering inconsequence and delight in fashionable jargon. Like
Polonius he is a born go-between—busy, anxious to please—and
like him he knows nothing of the people he goes between. In the
middle of Hamlet's solemn discourse of death and providence,
soon after he has described his struggle with Claudius as "the
pass and fell incensed points / Of mighty opposites," comes
young Osric to invite Hamlet to a friendly duel arranged by
Claudius. The "young" is itself significant. Usually Shakespeare
puts it before a name to avoid confusion with the senior bearer
of that name, as in the case of Young Siward in *Macbeth* and occasionally "young Hamlet" and "young Fortinbras" in this play.
There is, however, no Old Osric in *Hamlet*. Osric is labeled

---

[30] Fergusson, *The Idea of a Theatre* (Princeton, 1949), pp. 108-109.

HAMLET

"young," by Shakespeare in the Folio stage direction and then by the King and the attendant lord, to emphasize for us his ignorance of what is going on around him. Here again he recalls Polonius, "that great baby" (II.ii.377). They are both children among adults, playing with toys while the world collapses above their heads.

Like Laertes, Fortinbras, and Horatio, Polonius and Osric in their limitations serve as partial reflectors for the multifaceted Hamlet. In their case the limitations are so drastic as to effect not just conventional measurement of greatness but comic parody. Osric is obviously setting up as the next glass of fashion and mold of form at the Danish court. His painfully elegant manners and strained vocabulary are a comic distortion of the Prince's easy grace and wit. The whole Osric encounter affords one last display of Hamlet's mastery, as he shifts with disconcerting suddenness from the blunt to the exaggeratedly foppish: "Put your bonnet to his right use; 'tis for the head. . . . The concernancy, sir? Why do we wrap the gentleman in our more rawer breath?" (v.ii.93, 121-122). Osric has taken over a corollary function of Polonius, as butt.

Polonius presents a comic version of Hamlet's intellectual side. A university man himself, he has studied logic and recognizes it when he sees it.

> *Pol.* Will you walk out of the air, my lord?
> *Ham.* Into my grave?
> *Pol.* Indeed, that's out of the air. [*Aside*] How pregnant sometimes his replies are!
>
> (II.ii.205-207)

What he sees, though, is only the superficial connection. The tragic logic of Hamlet's obsession with death escapes him. Polonius and Hamlet are both amateurs of the theater, but Polonius's parade of dramatic jargon only sets off Hamlet's true sense of the play and its power. Hamlet gives detailed instructions to the players on their art, stages and interprets a play himself, acts a variety of roles throughout the action as he penetrates the disguises of others. When Polonius played a role it was, inevitably, that of a victim—Julius Caesar.

The parallel between Polonius and Osric is clearest in the fol-

112   TRAGEDY OF MULTIPLICITY

lowing passages, where Shakespeare uses the same device to make the same comic point:

> *Ham.* Do you see yonder cloud that's almost in the shape of a camel?
> *Pol.* By th' mass, and 'tis like a camel indeed.
> *Ham.* Methinks it is like a weasel.
> *Pol.* It is back'd like a weasel.
> *Ham.* Or like a whale?
> *Pol.* Very like a whale.
>
> (III.ii.366–372)
>
> *Osr.* I thank your lordship; it is very hot.
> *Ham.* No, believe me, 'tis very cold; the wind is northerly.
> *Osr.* It is indifferent cold, my lord, indeed.
> *Ham.* But yet methinks it is very sultry and hot for my complexion.
> *Osr.* Exceedingly, my lord; it is very sultry, as 'twere—I cannot tell how.
>
> (v.ii.94–100)

It is not just that Polonius and Osric lack firm convictions and defer to the Prince. They have the herd instinct. Their shifts from weasels to whales and cold to hot are exaggerated forms of comic accommodation, the opposite of tragic integrity.

Two of Hamlet's other butts, Rosencrantz and Guildenstern, carry out the herd motif in a different way. It would be pleasingly tidy if these two represented a parody of the soldier Hamlet to parallel Osric's of the courtier and Polonius's of the scholar. Unfortunately, there is no evidence of anything of the kind, except insofar as soldiers may be more politically minded than courtiers (which is doubtful) or scholars. The main comic function of Rosencrantz and Guildenstern is to operate visually and aurally as a pair.

Anyone who teaches *Hamlet* finds that students tend to mix up the two names and talk of Rosenstern and Guildencrantz. There is, in fact, no good reason to keep them straight, for these two answer perfectly the demand of Giraudoux's Président for an assembly-line humanity with interchangeable parts.[31] Their

---

[31] *La folle de Chaillot*, ed. Mary E. Storer (New York, 1955), p. 20.

HAMLET   113

names are a perfect metrical match, which Shakespeare takes
care to emphasize:

> King. Thanks, Rosencrantz and gentle Guildenstern.
> Queen. Thanks, Guildenstern and gentle Rosencrantz.
>   (II.ii.33-34)

Also exactly matched, as Harry Levin has noted, are their opening speeches in this scene: a half line, two full lines, and another
half line for each, in the same rhythm.[32] Often they speak turn-
about, dividing a continued account between them. One never
appears without the other. No one ever speaks of Rosencrantz
without Guildenstern—or, of course, vice versa. The two may
differ externally in feature or dress, but inside they are indistin-
guishable, perversions of those identical twins in which comedy
delights. Bergson's notion of comedy as human beings sub-
merging their individuality in mechanical repetition helps us see
the comic foil effect of their perpetual twoness as they flank
Hamlet, revealing his loneliness as well as his greatness. In
Rosencrantz and Guildenstern it becomes apparent that there is a
sinister side to the submergence of the individual which comedy
ratifies by its drive toward pairing and social harmony, as there
is a sinister side to many of the other comic assumptions. Non-
persons, they reject personal responsibility.[33] If they were ac-
cused of betraying their friend, their answer might be that of
another notable pair in Shakespearean tragedy, the tribunes in
Coriolanus: "We do it not alone."[34] Behind one there is always
the other, and behind both there is society at large, the state.

For these good citizens Rosencrantz and Guildenstern, a dilemma like Hamlet's is impossible. The state must be served.
And to serve the state is to serve the King, "that spirit upon
whose weal depends and rests / The lives of many" (III.iii.14-
15). Not for them the torments of plural consciousness, the fear

---

[32] The Question of "Hamlet" (New York, 1959), pp. 51-52.

[33] For Thomas McFarland, Rosencrantz and Guildenstern lose their identities
because they reject the responsibilities of Existenz—in this case friendship. Tragic
Meanings in Shakespeare (New York, 1966), pp. 40-41.

[34] Cor. II.i.31. Against the political, accommodating we of Brutus and Sicinius
is set the heroic, individual I of Coriolanus: "If you have writ your annals true,
'tis there / That, like an eagle in a dove-cote, I / Flutter'd your Volscians in
Corioli. / Alone I did it" (v.vi.114-117).

114 TRAGEDY OF MULTIPLICITY

of subjective distortion. If the King's weal is the ultimate good, then to do right they have only to carry out the King's wishes.

Unaware of any questions that cannot be dealt with in political terms, Rosencrantz and Guildenstern naturally misinterpret Hamlet's problem as frustrated ambition. Denmark feels too narrow to him, hints Rosencrantz, because Claudius and not Hamlet is its king.[35] Later, when they ask him directly what is wrong and Hamlet replies, "Sir, I lack advancement," there is no question in Rosencrantz's mind how he should interpret this general remark. "How can that be, when you have the voice of the King himself for your succession in Denmark?" (III.ii.331-333). But the political interpretation defines only the narrow perceptions of Rosencrantz and Guildenstern, not the heart of Hamlet's mystery. Like Polonius they guess wrong, and like Polonius they suffer for it. The death (one singular noun will do for both) of these two does not incorporate them into the tragedy in the way that Polonius's did, but it has its own irony. Their respect for the royal seal, the emblem of majesty, causes them to deliver their own death warrant to England. Obedient ciphers to the end, they "go to 't," casualties in a war they did not understand.

Unconscious of the issues at stake, relentlessly ordinary in the face of the extraordinary, these four (three?) characters—Polonius, Osric, Rosencrantz and Guildenstern—function somewhat as the porter does in *Macbeth* or the clown in *Antony and Cleopatra*, to throw into relief the tragic shape of events and to measure the protagonist's stature. But they are also a part of the action, interwoven in it as the one-appearance porter and clown are not, because the generic anomalies they call into play comment directly on the nature of Hamlet's tragedy. As misinterpreters they make us aware, as Hamlet himself is painfully aware, that men see only what they can and want to see, not necessarily what is there. Yet it is also true that, for all their limitations and ultimate futility, the viewpoints these characters introduce into the play remind us that there are "worlds else-

---

[35] "Why then, your ambition makes it one; 'tis too narrow for your mind" (II.ii.251-252). Both Wilson in the New Cambridge edition and Kittredge in his annotated *Hamlet* (Boston, 1940) see in these lines a veiled reference to the fact that Hamlet has not succeeded his father as king.

HAMLET 115

where," alternative ways of life governed by premises other than the confining one of revenge. That is, they illuminate both sides of this unusual tragic hero, who is both eiron and alazon. Where the usual movement of tragedy is constriction, narrowing into a no-alternative course, it is exactly Hamlet's tragic situation that he must resist such constriction and the resistance renders him impotent. By having Polonius and the others act out their comic-social preoccupations, Shakespeare creates a certain sense of various possibility—especially when Hamlet takes up the diversions these people offer him and plays with them on their own terms. At the same time, the element of parody and the gulf between any of these perspectives and what we would wish for Hamlet denies validity to them as real possibilities. Shakespeare thus presents a play world that is at once claustrophobic and expansive, to keep us attuned to Hamlet's own division between the subjective thrust toward violent action (alazon) and the objective awareness of more than one reality (eiron).

The physical play world reinforces this effect of variety without real alternatives. The stage action never leaves Denmark, almost never leaves Elsinore, so that the audience can share Hamlet's sense of being closed in. Yet we are also made conscious of the wide arena that is available to other young men, if not to Hamlet. The disparate, unfocused journeys in the play's background—Fortinbras threatening from Norway, then traveling to Poland and finally to Elsinore; Horatio coming from Wittenberg; Laertes going off to Paris—all these may be untidy, as Goethe's Wilhelm Meister complained,[36] but it is a functional untidiness. Those trips here and there keep us aware that mobility and adventure are the norm for young men in *Hamlet*. Only Hamlet himself, the most receptive to new possibilities, must stay cooped up in his private prison. Getting away is the first action he attempts in the play. But Claudius will not let him escape to Wittenberg, and the journey planned for him later is to his death in England.

That never-completed trip turns out to be fated, for it does eventually lead to his death. But it is also freeing, for when he

---

[36] *Wilhelm Meisters Lehrjahre*, Book 5, cited in the New Variorum *Hamlet*, ed. H. H. Furness, reissue (New York, 1965), II, 274.

116 TRAGEDY OF MULTIPLICITY

returns, he has got beyond the old dilemma of the eiron. New experience—the pirate adventure and the discovery and reversal of the death warrant—brings new knowledge, and this time the knowledge is not crippling but enabling. The offstage voyage is the setting for this change, allows it through the chances of the sea, in a way even *means* it, as the unsettling forests of Shakespeare's romantic comedies came to signify new directions for their protagonists.

But in the first part of the play Hamlet's multiple awareness brings him only anguish at his constriction and unsureness about his cause. His torment illuminates that element in the tragic described by Karl Jaspers: "Man's mind fails and breaks down in the very wealth of its potentialities."[37] Yet somewhere behind Hamlet's inaction is the sense, also adumbrated by Jaspers, that *any* act cuts off possibilities and denies the perfection sought for. This is the dark side of the eiron principle and the rejection of singleness, the values of romantic comedy. In *Hamlet* they are still values, but they are placed in mortal conflict with the imperatives of filial duty, moral judgment, even self-definition. To choose and actualize only one potential is to deny wholeness. But not to choose and actualize threatens sanity itself.

Johnson assures us that among his contemporaries "the pretended madness of Hamlet causes much mirth."[38] Is it only because modern productions usually play down the zany side of Hamlet's antic disposition that our laughter in the "mad" scenes is tinged with unease? That straightforward mirth of the eighteenth century requires that the audience be certain that Hamlet's madness *is* entirely pretended; but this certainty, like so many others, the play denies us. Hamlet is a trapped eiron. Insofar as the antic disposition is a role he can consciously put on and off, it offers an escape of sorts from the constrictions that press in so heavily on him. Like the comic disguise, it allows a certain freedom—in this case the freedom of the fool who cannot be held accountable for his jibes at the mighty.[39] We should remember, though, that in comedy a disguise "put on" like a costume often goes beyond simple deception to call up in the dis-

[37] *Tragedy Is Not Enough*, p. 42.   [38] *Johnson on Shakespeare*, VIII, 1011.
[39] See Levin's discussion of the "antic disposition" in *Question of "Hamlet"* pp. 111-128.

guiser an alternate identity. When Rosalind poses as a page, she does more than conceal her sex. She becomes a new creature, Rosalind-Ganymede. On several occasions Hamlet's mad pose similarly seems to acquire a life of its own, pushing him into extravagant railing irrelevant to his auditor, as in his tirade to Ophelia against "you" painted, lisping wantons (III.i.142-145), or into obsessive repetitions: "You cannot, sir, take from me anything that I will more willingly part withal—except my life, except my life, except my life" (II.ii.214-216). But madness cannot fill out and complete a personality the way Ganymede completes Rosalind. Unworkable, through its lack of structure, as an alternate self, the antic disposition instead points to the ultimate in conflicting, unresolved possibilities. "Man's mind breaks down . . ."

The graveyard scene requires separate treatment. It uses comedy in a quite distinctive way, as an element within the tragic vision rather than as a contrasting ethos or a value to be turned inside out. As its impact is best approached through dramatic structure, we must at this point step back to survey the dynamics that lead up to the graveside encounter between Hamlet and the nameless clown. Of the many ways that one can look at structure in *Hamlet*, three are useful here: as fluctuation, as deflection, and as the quest for pattern.

Fluctuation dominates the early acts, with Hamlet pulled back and forth between what I have called his Horatio side and his Laertes side. He is torn in the struggle between "conscience," in the sense of consciousness, and the inner compulsions of disgust, hatred, and wounded honor. At times he allies himself with conscience, looking before and after, wishing to see his act whole, wishing to be sure. At other times reason and doubt are submerged in the need for passionate action. We have seen in the "O, what a rogue" soliloquy not only the two contrary states but the actual movement from one to the other, from bloodthirsty images of Claudius fatting the kites to "grounds more relative than this." The pattern has in fact begun much earlier, as soon as the Ghost has laid his command on Hamlet. I have already suggested that *Hamlet* departs from the usual tragic pattern of alternatives denied and possibilities narrowed into a single inevitable course, that here the tragic point is the hero's inability to achieve such narrowing even though he wants to and swears to. The desire is clear in his first response to the Ghost: "Haste me to know 't, that I, with wings as swift / As meditation or the thoughts of love, / May sweep to my revenge" (I.v.29-31). What until now have been his chief preoccupations—philosophical reflection and courtship—he immediately reduces to metaphors for his new devotion. Later he vows to forget everything but the Ghost's command (97-104). Yet immediately afterward this committed hero is suddenly diverging into mad comedy, "wild and whirling words," and quite literally running away from the omnipresent Ghost. The whole cellarage business is very slenderly motivated in terms of plot. There needs no ghost come from the grave to persuade Horatio and Marcellus to swear secrecy. Rather, the Ghost is reintroduced so that we may see Hamlet seeking to escape the commitment he has just made, physically backing off from the spirit to whom he has made it, and trying with comic nicknames to put distance between himself and that "hic et ubique" presence.

Fluctuation continues through Act II and the first part of Act III, the poles getting stronger and the struggle more intense. The Mousetrap scene stretches Hamlet's inner tension almost to the breaking point: it seals his emotional conviction of Claudius's guilt while denying him the desired objective confirmation of that guilt. The scene points to crisis in other ways. Hamlet and Claudius confront each other directly for the first time since I.ii, and from this ominous start tension rises as the Gonzago action comes closer and closer to the actual murder and Hamlet's commentary reveals his own mounting excitement. The dramatic peak, Claudius's disordered exit, is striking but ambiguous. We expect something more definitive structurally, and we get it in the double climax that follows: Hamlet's two meetings, an unplanned one with the King and a planned one with the Queen.

In the prayer scene Hamlet acts out his Horatio side in its fullest implications. Presented by accident with the chance for unimpeded, perhaps even unperilous revenge, Hamlet nevertheless rejects the act because he wants to see and control all its ramifica-

HAMLET   119

tions and consequences, even into the next world. Looking before and after, he recalls his father's unsanctified death, considers the King at his prayers, calculates the future, and concludes that a murderer who may be in a state of grace is not adequate payment for a good man condemned to purgatory for his unexpiated sins. And so he takes no action. "Conscience" is triumphant—not in the ethical sense, certainly, for Hamlet's desire to make sure of Claudius's damnation is appallingly savage—but in the sense of superawareness, of thinking too precisely on the event.

Perhaps because of what has just happened, or has not happened, Hamlet soon acts all too quickly. Excitedly rebuking his mother, he hears a noise behind the arras, strikes without making sure ("Is it the King?")—and kills the wrong man. Rashness in the style of Laertes and Fortinbras has followed Horatian hesitation, and neither has worked. Narrowing to one possibility for action or nonaction has been no more effective than trying to cope with all possibilities.[40] Polonius is dead and Claudius is not. These two facts will determine the play's tragic conclusion.

After these climactic scenes the fluctuation pattern ceases to dominate, although Hamlet's "How all occasions" soliloquy in IV.iv looks back at it in the manner of a musical reprise. Hamlet himself is offstage for much of Act IV, and when he returns in Act V, the inner conflict is no longer evident. To understand its disappearance we must turn to the other aspects of structure that I have called deflection and the quest for pattern. The climactic scenes just examined provide a useful focus for these two related movements. Both event and nonevent will ultimately be decisive, the killing of Polonius and the not-killing of Claudius, but at the time they seem meaningless. Hamlet's revenge against his mighty opposite is mistakenly, absurdly deflected onto the irrelevant Polonius. There is in fact an order into which these things fit, but between happening and meaning intervenes the large-scale deflection of Act IV. The whole thrust of the first three acts, Hamlet's dilemma and the resulting fluctuations, is dropped; he himself is apparently deflected from his purpose by

---

[40] "If Hamlet spares Claudius because he considers the matter too closely, he stabs Polonius because he does not consider the matter at all." McElroy, *Mature Tragedies*, p. 77.

120   TRAGEDY OF MULTIPLICITY

being ordered off to England; and he physically leaves the action
after scene iv. For the rest of the act, our attention is preempted
by the pathos of Ophelia, the rebellion of Laertes, the new
schemes of Claudius. Of Hamlet we learn only that he is returning, after some strange experiences. What they have to do with
his earlier state we must wait for Act v to reveal.

Various critics have in one way or another singled out deflection as a *theme* of the play and have shown how the general
course of the action is illuminated by such statements as
Ophelia's "Lord, we know what we are, but know not what we
may be" (IV.v.41-42), Claudius's reflections on goodness dying
in its own too-much (IV.vii.114-118), and most of all the Player
King's conclusion:

> But, orderly to end where I begun,
> Our wills and fates do so contrary run
> That our devices still are overthrown;
> Our thoughts are ours, their ends none of our own.
> (III.ii.205-208)

What has not been emphasized is how thoroughly the structure
of *Hamlet* embodies this notion of deflection: something always
intervenes between purpose and act, expectation and result.

"Deflection" in this sense may describe the same process that I
have called "fluctuation," in this case thought of in terms of line
and deviation rather than of pendulum swings back and forth. It
also applies to the series of attempted escapes that begins with
Hamlet's request to leave Elsinore for Wittenberg and continues
through his consideration of suicide, his wild and whirling
words in the cellarage scene, and the antic disposition itself.
From one point of view, indeed, the whole play is a form of deflection, between the imposition of the revenge task in I.v and its
final accomplishment in v.ii. Deflection is also the key to the ordering of parts, notably in II.ii and III.i. In the First Quarto
memorial reconstruction, the order of events is as follows:

1. Polonius announces his theory that Hamlet is mad for love;
   he and Claudius plan to test the theory by eavesdropping
   on an encounter between Hamlet and Ophelia.
2. Hamlet enters and speaks his "To be or not to be" soliloquy; the Ophelia encounter follows.

HAMLET

3. Rosencrantz and Guildenstern seek the cause of Hamlet's madness.
4. The players arrive, one performs the Pyrrhus speech, and Hamlet plans the Mousetrap.
5. Rosencrantz and Guildenstern report their failure but announce that Hamlet wants a play performed.
6. The play is performed.

This is a simpler ordering than that of the Second Quarto and the Folio, and a more "natural" one: plots are conceived and then carried out without delay. This is the way one might mistake the sequence of events in memory, or simplify it for provincial performance.[41] In the authoritative texts, however, some break *always* comes between plan and execution. Claudius's first plot to spy out Hamlet's mystery, which will employ Rosencrantz and Guildenstern, is followed by a second plot based on Polonius's theory of frustrated love, which will involve the "loosing" of Ophelia. Then the first plan is enacted, after which the players come on and Hamlet initiates a plan of his own. Before we see it executed, Claudius's second plot is put into action and found unsatisfactory ("Love! His affections do not that way tend"), and he proposes yet another one, dispatching Hamlet to England. Only then is Hamlet's own plot fulfilled in the Mousetrap scene. Always there is that intervention, like Eliot's "Shadow" that falls "between the idea / And the reality / Between the motion / And the Act."[42]

The unexpected break between cause and result is akin to the evitability of comedy. But in this case as with multiple truths and the superiority of the eiron, the comic notion serves tragic ends. Outside the safely bounded comic universe, discontinuous structure is not so much freeing as unsettling. It suggests a kind of cosmic irrelevance that interferes with expected patterns.

[41] Chambers argues for memorial reconstruction (*William Shakespeare: A Study of Facts and Problems* [Oxford, 1930], pp. 415-420); Greg prefers the provincial performance theory (*Editorial Problem*, p. 67).

[42] "The Hollow Men" (1925). Here, as in *Hamlet*, form expresses meaning: in each phrase, beginning is separated from conclusion by a line ending, and in each stanza a second phrase intervenes before we are given the result of the first.

Michael Goldman also finds the Q1 ordering unsatisfactory on the grounds that "the break in our expectations, the resistance to interpretation, is vital." *Shakespeare and the Energies of Drama* (Princeton, 1972), pp. 87-88.

122 TRAGEDY OF MULTIPLICITY

Each plan in this sequence does work out, to be sure, but never very definitively. Instead, one scheme gives way to another, and the sense of displacement persists. In his chapter on *Hamlet* in *Shakespeare and the Energies of Drama*, Michael Goldman has shown several ways in which "we are regularly invited to complete an action—to consider what it means, to anticipate where it may lead—only to have our response blocked, distracted, or diverted, compromised in some way."[43] Booth remarks that all through the play "the audience gets information or sees action it once wanted only after a new interest has superseded the old."[44] But Booth, unlike Goldman, sees even in the ending of *Hamlet* "an impossible coherence of truths that are both undeniably incompatible and undeniably coexistent."[45] Does this in fact match our experience at the end of *Hamlet*? In my view Shakespeare is being more directive than Booth will allow, first creating in the audience a need to find purpose and pattern in events and then satisfying that need in the play's final phase.

We arrive thus at my third structural approach to the comic encounter of Hamlet and the gravedigger in Act v. Although the formula "quest for a pattern" mainly describes the way an audience experiences the action of *Hamlet*, that quest also enters into the action itself. Various interpreting characters, as I have noted, shape the events they see to fit their own subjective reality. Meanwhile Hamlet tries to find the stance that will permit him, like the magician-manipulators of comedy, to set fully to rights his out-of-joint time. The interpretations of Polonius and the others are tried and found wanting. Hamlet himself in larger style tries both the Horatian withholder from action and the Laertean rash doer, only to find both inadequate. He does indeed set up a show in the manipulator tradition, but without the traditional results. The Mousetrap fails to provide the public clarifica-

[43] *Shakespeare and the Energies of Drama*, pp. 76-88.

[44] "On the Value of *Hamlet*," p. 143.

[45] Ibid., p. 171. Norman Rabkin in the stimulating discussion of *Hamlet* that opens his *Shakespeare and the Common Understanding* (New York, 1967) takes a similar position: "The experience of *Hamlet*, then, culminates in a set of questions to which there are no answers" (p. 9). Tillyard's parallel conclusion, reached by a different path, that *Hamlet* presents problems rather than solutions and significant ordering, led him to place it with the problem plays rather than with the tragedies. *Shakespeare's Problem Plays* (London, 1950), p. 31.

HAMLET

tion for which it was designed. Claudius, no mean manipulator himself, refuses the role of pawn in that he does not let loose his occulted guilt on cue, "in one speech." Nor does Claudius in the following scene conform any better to Hamlet's master-pattern, which requires that revenge be taken when the usurper is found in some characteristic grossness, not in prayer. And the next scene finds Polonius, yet another would-be manipulator, where Claudius ought to be. Claudius in fact is back in the manipulator-position, ordering an unfree Hamlet on a journey to England apparently irrelevant to any princely pattern of revenge. The order Hamlet tries to impose thus fails, short-circuited by rival craft and the waywardness of events.

When he returns from the abortive journey to England, his goal is no longer governing control. What he seeks now, and finds, is readiness as an agent, as part of a pattern he may perceive but did not create: "If it be now, 'tis not to come; if it be not to come, it will be now; if it be not now, yet it will come—the readiness is all" (v.ii.212-215). The returned prince is changed, as many critics have observed. While the nature of the change is subject for debate, most see in him a new calmness, an acceptance of life and death. Certainly there is no further expression of the struggle I have seen as informing the early part of the play, between emotional conviction and the need for external validation. Even when Hamlet seems to appeal once more for Horatio's confirmation ("Does it not, think thee, stand me now upon . . . / . . . is't not perfect conscience / To quit him with this arm?"), the question is really rhetorical. Hamlet is not asking any more; he is telling.[46]

What has happened to Hamlet at sea? By a chance indiscretion he discovered that Rosencrantz and Guildenstern carried a warrant for his execution. He responded by substituting a new order commanding the death of his former friends instead, and by another chance he had with him his father's signet to imprint the royal seal. The next day chance intervened again when pirates attacked the ship. Hamlet led the defense, was taken prisoner, found his new captors more accommodating than the old, and

---

[46] v.ii.63-68. Cf. A.J.A. Waldock, *"Hamlet": A Study in Critical Method* (Cambridge, 1931), p. 26: "Horatio does not answer the question, simply because he knows that Hamlet is not seriously asking it."

124   TRAGEDY OF MULTIPLICITY

returned to Denmark. That is, to this man who felt impelled to impose significant moral order on his own time but was unable to manipulate people and events to his own pattern, comes a series of events which he has not initiated but which displays the kind of clarity and sureness of effect he had lacked before. His friends have betrayed him, and so he is given the opportunity to serve them in the same way. His duel with Claudius is unfinished, and so circumstances cut off his journey to England and bring him back to Denmark. In telling this tale, Hamlet keeps interpreting it in terms of providential order: "Our indiscretion sometime serves us well, / When our deep plots do pall . . . / There's a divinity that shapes our ends"; "even in that was heaven ordinant" (v.ii.8-10, 48). It is this perception of what *has* happened that decides his approach to what *will*. In spite of his "gaingiving" about the projected duel, he defies augury and trusts in the special providence that governs even the fall of the sparrow (v.ii.210-211). He has found an objective truth outside himself, a pattern not subject to his distortion, with which the subjective element cooperates, knowingly or not. This order of things has saved his life and brought him home; he trusts it to bring about the final movement of his destiny.

The terms in which Hamlet describes this order have Christian resonance—divinity, heaven, the fall of a sparrow—but I doubt that they are meant to evoke Christian values full force. Such an emphasis would completely skew our view of Hamlet's duty of revenge, which the play never really questions.[47] Shakespeare used these Christian references, I suspect, because in their familiarity they would most easily call up for his audience the general sense of a plan in human existence. Those who see only a "desperate stoicism" in Hamlet's words before the duel miss this all-important conviction of purpose and pattern. The phrase belongs to Donald Stauffer, who concludes: "Augury is defied, destiny is bitterly acknowledged, and a passive readiness is all."[48] But in the context of Hamlet's positive affirmations that

[47] See below, n. 57.
[48] Stauffer, *Shakespeare's World of Images* (New York, 1949), p. 126. Cf. Bradley, *Shakespearean Tragedy*, p. 145; Schücking, *The Meaning of "Hamlet"* (London, 1937), p. 167; H. B. Charlton, *Shakespearian Tragedy* (Cambridge, 1944), p. 103.

HAMLET

125

heaven is ordinant and divinity shapes our ends, why should his acknowledgment be bitter? And his readiness is passive only in that he will respond to opportunity rather than create it—respond actively, as he has already done with Rosencrantz and Guildenstern and the pirates.

Nevertheless, before Hamlet tells us that the universe, however mysterious, is not without plan, we have the graveyard scene suggesting something quite different. The reader may think I have taken much too long to arrive at it, but I hope that as Shakespeare's deflections of plot ultimately justify their place in the play's dynamic, so my own windlasses and assays will allow a fuller interpretation of this strange venture into radical comedy. The graveyard scene is the last and most striking of the play's displacements. As in the earlier movement of plot and counterplot, the order of scenes and their revelations is significant here. In IV.vi, Hamlet's return is signaled by a letter to Horatio which, while it alludes to the events that brought about his new vision, says nothing of what that vision is. He raises expectations with "I have words to speak in thine ear . . . too light for the bore of the matter" (IV.vi.21-23). The words, however, are not spoken until V.ii. In between, the last scene of Act IV keeps Hamlet's unexplained return in our minds, with more hints in his letter to Claudius of revelations to come ; but the dramatic emphasis passes back to Claudius himself as he plans his most deadly plot against Hamlet. It seems like a reprise of the structural pattern of Acts II and III. We would expect, when Hamlet finally does appear, to find him plotting in his turn, or in any case making the great disclosures prepared for by his letters. Instead we get a pair of clowns digging a grave and Hamlet's long conversation with one of them, which is quite apart from his supposed preoccupations. There is a link, indeed, for the grave is Ophelia's; but Hamlet does not know it.

Structurally, though not tonally, the graveyard scene is the counterpart of Hamlet's "To be or not to be" soliloquy. There, too, against expectation, we step aside from the turmoil of plot and counterplot into a kind of reflective middle distance, where the hero speculates in general terms on the human condition. Before that entrance in III.i, Hamlet has been asking questions about his immediate problem—Am I a coward? Is the Ghost

126   TRAGEDY OF MULTIPLICITY

really a devil?—but now the questioning extends to everything: Why live? Why not die? The speech gives no real answer. Even the negative one Hamlet had advanced in his first soliloquy, God's prohibition of self-slaughter, fades into uncertainty here. Is there perhaps a divine tribunal that rewards and punishes, and thus makes sense out of life's grinding indignities and inequities? Hamlet's doubt comes through in his phrasing: "*perchance* to dream," "*something* after death." The shadowy sanction against suicide, even if it exists, imparts no positive meaning to the mortal coil. It simply paralyzes men in the action of shuffling it off. The soliloquy breaks off on a note indeterminate and ironic, as Hamlet hails Ophelia and her "orisons," which we know are not real prayers but window dressing for spying. The questions hang unresolved. What if there is no justice in the undiscovered country, after all? What if there is no undiscovered country? What if the fear of it exists only to prevent us from the one negatively significant act of ending life? In such a void, where is the validity of revenge or of anything else?

For a few moments Hamlet's anxiety is that of the modern existentialist, seeking a direction in life and finding only fear of the unknown and hints of absurdity. Caught up again in the climactic action of Act III, he moves into other moods, but the note struck here anticipates the graveyard meditations. The substance of those meditations is also anticipated, verbally at least, by Hamlet's preoccupation with Polonius's corpse.

> *Ham.* A certain convocation of politic worms are e'en at him. Your worm is your only emperor for diet: we fat all creatures else to fat us, and we fat ourselves for maggots; your fat king and your lean beggar is but variable service—two dishes, but to one table. That's the end.
>
> *King.* Alas, alas!
>
> *Ham.* A man may fish with the worm that hath eat of a king, and eat of the fish that hath fed of that worm.
>
> *King.* What dost thou mean by this?
>
> *Ham.* Nothing but to show you how a king may go a progress through the guts of a beggar.
>
> (IV.iii.20–31)

HAMLET

127

At this point, Hamlet's image of worms reducing royalty to the level of beggary is mainly a thrust at Claudius, the bloat king. Yet death works in the same way on the good as on the guilty, on princes as well as on kings. Among the graves, accepting the cheerful impersonality of the gravedigger, Hamlet will have to include himself and all men in the vision of universal decay.

What we have not been prepared for is the peculiar tone of the graveyard scene, the spirit of *play* that infuses its contemplation of death. The two gravediggers in their discussion of Ophelia's doubtful death strike a note of comic questioning that does not change with the entrance of the tragic hero. The clown who remains to gossip with the incognito Prince is not the usual "other voice" of tragedy introduced to challenge but ultimately ratify the heroic posture. Here it is rather the hero who seems to be ratifying the clown's view of things. Mack notes that the case the gravedigger makes for the "bread and cheese" of common life is not overborne by Hamlet.[49] We are, I think, invited to go further than this, to feel a whole new impact of the comic in a serious context as it bores to the heart of the tragic vision and questions the very notion of the heroic, irreplaceable self. Their talk is not of common life but of common death, which comes not only to the ordinary butts of satire like politicians and fine ladies but to Alexander and Caesar. It is all one to the clown and to the figure that looms behind him, Death the Leveler casting down indifferently the skull of a jester and the dust of an emperor. In this setting human choice seems no more than a bad joke. If Caesar ends up patching a wall, why strive to be Caesar? He is just as dead as Yorick. The equation of fool and world conqueror pushes us to the limits of comic relativism. No person or thing has any more value than any other. Points of honor have no more meaning than the niceties of the law which are here reduced to absurdity in the clowns' discussion of suicide. Ophelia is dead, whether "se offendendo" or not. Death is the only reality here. In the "To be or not to be" soliloquy it was at least a significant reality, at once fearsome and desirable. Now the comic perspective calls even that significance into question. Death just comes, whether you suffer nobly or take arms against

[49] "The Jacobean Shakespeare," in *Jacobean Theatre*, ed. J. Russell Brown and Bernard Harris (London, 1960), p. 22.

128   TRAGEDY OF MULTIPLICITY

your troubles; it is the end of life that makes every life equally
absurd.

In that earlier soliloquy Hamlet asked his own questions about
life's meaning or lack of it. Here he becomes part of the question
put to the audience, which is posed through his own musings
and, most tellingly, by the persistent use of comedy's alien perspective in this place of death. It is not just the jokes and incongruities, though these are plentiful: Alexander stops up a beer
barrel, Hamlet's madness will not be noticed in England where
everyone is as mad as he. It is Hamlet's satiric wit playing freely
with the futile activities of politicians and lawyers, piling up
puns and "quillets" in a burst of linguistic vitality, and the
clown's cheerful literalism: "A tanner will last you nine year"
(163). The clown has the habit of his comic brotherhood of reducing everything, including death, to the physical. The question for him is not whether the individual self survives death but
how long the bodily remains will last in the earth. Nor do the
great events of Claudius's Denmark take up much space on this
man's broad horizon. He, after all, looks all the way back to
Adam, the first gentleman, and forward to the end of the world,
when his graves will open. Specifically, he recalls the day Hamlet was born, and almost in the next breath prophesies that Hamlet's dead body will not last in the ground more than eight or
nine years. Perhaps the references to Adam and Doomsday
bring in some notion of a great sequence in the universe, but the
dominant sense is just that men have been getting born and
dying through countless ages and will go on doing so. This is
the matter-of-fact comic voice: there will always be more bodies
to bury. Shakespeare has in earlier plays pictured Death as an
"antic," laughing heroes and kings to scorn.[50] Yet even this image, which suggests malice directed at a specific individual
("scoffing *his* state and grinning at *his* pomp" in the imagination
of Richard II), is a less radical threat to the irreplaceable "I" of
tragedy than the gravedigger's good-humored impartiality. He
and his milieu make a direct address to the tragic fact of death,
but an address that emphasizes its *commonness* rather than the
quenching of a unique spirit. Hamlet's life is a mere "one" in a

[50] In *I Henry VI* iv.vii.18, the two heroic Talbots, father and son, are mocked.
Richard II sees Death as a jester at the King's court (*Richard II* iii.ii.160–170).

HAMLET

long panorama. The whole tendency of the play, in which the other comic characters have participated, has been to set Hamlet off from and above the mass of common humanity. Now, for a time, that movement is reversed.

It is in terms of this comic-absurd challenge to heroic individuality that we should see the actions that conclude this scene. As in III.i, the entrance of Ophelia returns Hamlet from his meditative distance. Reduced from roselike beauty to rotting flesh, she might well call forth some wry speculation in the vein of "imperious Caesar." Instead, Hamlet hurls himself into a series of self-affirmations.

> This is I,
> Hamlet the Dane
>
> .   .   .   .
>
> Why, I will fight with him upon this theme
> Until my eyelids will no longer wag.
>
> .   .   .   .
>
> I lov'd Ophelia: forty thousand brothers
> Could not, with all their quantity of love,
> Make up my sum. . . .
>
> .   .   .   .
>
> I lov'd you ever.
>
> (v.i.251-284)

In all this, as in his dramatic leap to (or into) the grave, there is a strong element of hyperbole. The contest of grief with Laertes feels overdone: Hamlet himself says, "I'll rant as well as thou" (278). But this extra assertive force is dramatically justified if Hamlet is defying not just Laertes but the whole foregoing perception of a senseless universe. Against that threat and his own acquiescence in it, his affirmations and commitments have a special dimension of the heroic, suggesting a willed self-creation out of nothingness rather than a simple return to tragic hyperbole. It is an important effect to grasp, especially for those readers and spectators who find the Hamlet of the next scene diminished by his willingness to give up the initiative, to be a mere pawn and not the master-manipulator. The unsupported, self-engendered heroism here should condition our reaction to

130 TRAGEDY OF MULTIPLICITY

the state Hamlet achieves at the last and prevent us from seeing in it no more than passive fatalism.

It is important that we are made to confront absurdity here only to learn in the next scene that Hamlet has in fact found a meaning and pattern in human existence. Why have Hamlet accede to the gravedigger rather than counter him with newfound apprehensions of providential plan? Why have the graveyard conversation at all, troubling the audience with nihilistic intimations when the problem has "already" been solved for the hero? The point, I think, is that we do not know about that "already" until afterwards, in retrospect. Shakespeare exploits this gap between logical time and stage time, between happening and revelation, to pursue his theme of multiple possibility right to the edge of the void. In terms of Hamlet's own consciousness, we can see in retrospect that the ordering of scenes—IV.vi and vii and v.ii surrounding v.i on either side—has contained uncertainty in certainty. But the audience is made to apprehend in time, to experience the extremest need for pattern by contemplating the complete absence of it, and thus to find special satisfaction in Hamlet's self-definition and his subsequent assertions of the divinity that shapes our ends.

Hamlet's words, of course, are not enough by themselves to create a sense of pattern. The whole ending does that. By the time Fortinbras arrives, the stage is littered with bodies, yet the deaths are handled so as to suggest order rather than senseless carnage. Each seems to define the life it ends in some significant way. Sometimes the significance is stated for us, as in Laertes' "I am justly kill'd with mine own treachery" (v.ii.299). Laertes also comments on Claudius after Hamlet has returned both poisons, of foil and of cup, back to the source of all poison: "He is justly serv'd" (319). There is a richer, though more indirect comment in Hamlet's furious pun on "union."

> Here, thou incestuous, murd'rous, damned Dane,
> Drink off this potion. Is thy union here?
> Follow my mother.
>
> (317-319)

The union, as Bradley pointed out, is at once the rich pearl that Claudius said he was throwing into the cup, the poison that he

HAMLET 131

did throw, and the incestuous marriage "which must not be broken by his remaining alive now that his partner is dead."[51] It thus subsumes everything Claudius could not let go ("my crown, mine own ambition, and my queen"), now turned to poison and choking him to death. It has already killed Gertrude. But while this death from the same cup alludes to her guilty union with Claudius, it also defines Gertrude's peculiar tragic position, caught between love for her husband and love for her son: she drinks in defiance of Claudius, to honor Hamlet.

Seen from this vantage point, the earlier deaths also show a defining fitness. Polonius mistook and was mistaken. The destruction of Rosencrantz and Guildenstern "[did] by their own insinuation grow" (v.ii.59). All three were still acting out their partial perspectives in death, Polonius caught in the classic comic role of eavesdropper and Rosencrantz and Guildenstern respecting the royal seal. Even poor Ophelia finds an appropriate death in pliant water, weighed down by the garments of convention.[52]

Hamlet's own life, as it has unfolded before us in this hero-centered play, is far too complex to receive any satisfying definition in his death. Certainly it is fitting that Claudius should be the prime mover and Laertes the instrument, that Hamlet's end should stem both from the "original sin" of the play, the murder of King Hamlet, and from his own disastrous plunge into action, the murder of Polonius. It accords with our dual perception of Hamlet as one who both suffers evil and causes it.[53] Beyond this, Shakespeare wisely attempts no further explanation. Instead of the summings-up that accompany the other deaths, we have only hints at insights never spoken: "Had I but time, as this fell sergeant Death / Is strict in his arrest, O, I could tell you— / But let it be. . . . / . . . the rest is silence."

Hamlet, the play as well as the hero, has been asking persistently, "What is real?" Act v responds to the question in two ways:

[51] *Shakespearean Tragedy*, p. 151.

[52] Maynard Mack, Jr., comments: "At first her clothes, trappings of the court, hold her up, like her obedience to Polonius, but before long the same courtly trappings pull her to her death." *Killing the King* (New Haven and London, 1973), p. 99.

[53] "He, like the others, is inevitably engulfed by the evil that has been set in motion. . . . he himself becomes the cause of further ruin." H.D.F. Kitto, *Form and Meaning in Drama* (London, 1956), p. 330.

132   TRAGEDY OF MULTIPLICITY

it brings Claudius's villainy into the open, and it adumbrates some order in human affairs. The double response is more effective than a single one—the exposure of Claudius—which would simply conduct Hamlet to his delayed revenge without illuminating the larger effects of the King's crime. Shakespeare has not, of course, solved the mystery of existence in *Hamlet*. Dramatic rather than philosophical means achieve the sense of pattern at the play's end, and its truth is one of emotions, not metaphysics.[54] It must be emphasized again that the providence Hamlet acknowledges has little to do with nicely adjusted rewards and punishments. The deaths of the major figures link character and deed to final end, but they are not weighted according to moral culpability. Ophelia suffers as much as Claudius. If we feel a principle of poetic justice operating in them, it is with a very heavy accent on *poetic*.

Comedy in *Hamlet* is at once more obvious and more deeply embedded than in *Romeo and Juliet* and *Othello*. Once again, as in *Romeo*, our awareness of a tragic situation is sharpened by the presence of characters who do not understand it. Polonius and Osric, all cheerful bustle, are good examples of what I have called the principle of irrelevance. They direct us to dark and depth by their bright, ordinary unawareness. So, in a lesser way, do Rosencrantz and Guildenstern, by their demonstration of the complete political creature. All of these characters present some version of the antitragic view, only to be discredited. Like other idealized modes, tragedy is the more compelling if it can incorporate and somehow disarm emotions and attitudes outside its realm rather than ignore them completely. In *Romeo* the Nurse's earthy practicality and Mercutio's mockery express two perspectives antithetical to the absolutes of love, but the Nurse is undercut through exaggeration and Mercutio is silenced. Emilia in *Othello* objectifies our potential for cynicism but then discredits

---

[54] Janet Adelman reaches a similar conclusion after observing that, like Hamlet at sea, the audience in Act v is "taken over by events, by the plot itself. Like Hamlet, we lose the leisure for questions and seem to be guided by something outside ourselves. . . . All the earlier questions of will and purpose that are posed intellectually are now answered, but not intellectually; in place of conceptual answers, we are given the *feeling* that they have been answered by the very movement of the plot." *The Common Liar*, p. 8.

HAMLET 133

it by her death, in which she chooses truth and loyalty over the pragmatic self-interest she once defended. With Polonius and Osric, Rosencrantz and Guildenstern, the point is made not so much through death, though three of the four do die, as through their whole stage existence: little, limited, constantly bested by the hero, they at once present and denigrate a possible critique of Hamlet's hyperawareness.

Below this level, Shakespeare projects a special kind of tragic disillusion in *Hamlet* by bringing into play an extraordinary amount of comic machinery only to subvert it. In *Romeo* the borrowings from comedy included a manipulator, the kind of friar-healer who had traditionally acted as an agent of comedy's natural law and had saved the situation by his cleverness and magic skill. Friar Laurence failed, caught in the tragic acceleration of time, but we were not invited to blame him or to question his assumption of control. In *Hamlet*, however, the comic devices of manipulation—the deceptions, masks, espials, diversions, plots, and play-acting of Hamlet himself and of Claudius and Polonius—beg basic questions about human power and benevolence. All three characters fail as manipulators because they are *not* above human passion and blindness and because, often concealed behind the apparently erratic relation between purpose and result, a slow process is working out the poison of Denmark according to its own inexorable rules. However satisfying in some ways is Hamlet's final submission to the dimly perceived larger order, there is nonetheless an accompanying sense of human impotence. *Hamlet* is like Shakespeare's other plays of this period (the early years of the new century) in its pessimism about man's ability to alter events by his mind and will. It is not simply a matter of genre. *All's Well* and *Measure for Measure* have the traditional happy endings of comedy, but their erring, unattractive heroes have to be dragged into grace against their wills, and the successful manipulating of Helena and Duke Vincentio carries strong overtones of miracle and power beyond the human. When left to their purely human devices, as in *Troilus and Cressida*, men achieve only their own devaluation and destruction. It is this disheartening vision that links the so-called problem plays, I think; and it is a vision that affects *Hamlet* and *Othello* as well, for all the magnetic force of their central figures.

134   TRAGEDY OF MULTIPLICITY

Othello offers the stronger countering affirmation, but the transmutation of the manipulator-figure into Iago is a tragic comment on the disjunction of goodness and power.

In Iago the awareness of the eiron, his traditional source of power in the comedies, is put in the service of destruction; in *Hamlet* that awareness itself threatens self-destruction. Multiple being, after all, is very close to nonbeing. Well before Shakespeare, in Erasmus's masterpiece of multiple vision, Folly had joked that wisdom's full awareness would get in the way of any action at all—except suicide.[55] In our own time, Jaspers has seen in Folly's paradox the essence of Hamlet's tragedy.

> All life-force stems from blindness. It grows from imagined knowledge, in myth taken for faith, and in the substitute myths; in unquestioning acceptance, and in mind-narrowing untruths. Within the human predicament the quest for truth presents an impossible task.
>
> If totally manifest, truth paralyzes. . . . Reflective thought—rational consciousness—enfeebles man, unless the unbroken drive of a personality gathers even more strength in the clear light of knowledge. But such a drive consumes itself without concrete fulfillment, leaving an impression of greatness superhuman—not inhuman—in its failure.[56]

The uncommitted life is no life, for human beings define, even create themselves by choice; yet any choice represents the closing off of other alternatives, an inevitable narrowing as multiple possibility gives way to a single commitment. This tragic fact emerges in almost every aspect of *Hamlet*: the play's unusual variety that Johnson noted, Hamlet's brilliantly versatile address to the world, his peculiar anguish under the Ghost's command, his attempted escapes, the balancing of Horatio against Laertes and Fortinbras, the paired, opposing climaxes of Act III, the revenge motive itself. Any proposed action may be seen as tragic in that it cuts off other possibilities and reduces multiple selves into one, yet a revenge plot offers a specially dramatic example. The significant action is difficult and dangerous, a matter solely

[55] *The Praise of Folly*, tr. Leonard Dean (Chicago, 1946), pp. 61-69.
[56] *Tragedy Is Not Enough*, pp. 70-71.

HAMLET   135

of individual initiative apart from the normal supports of law and society, and it is also imperative, dictated by the closest human tie: "If thou didst ever thy dear father love. . . ."[57]

So comprehensive is Hamlet's consciousness of plural meanings that it finally takes in even the absence of meaning. In the graveyard scene comedy approaches the tragic hero in a radical new way, not as contrast to his fate or material for his diversion but as a potential *part* of his fate, joining him at least hypothetically to his own butts Polonius, Rosencrantz and Guildenstern, as the object of a cosmic joke. In the gravediggers' matter-of-fact, undifferentiating view no individual is irreplaceable, no commitment more significant than any other. Horatio acts the foil role for the last time when he fails to see the full joke of Alexander stopping a beer-barrel: " 'Twere to consider too curiously to consider so." It is Hamlet's peculiar heroism that he can see the joke very clearly indeed and still in the face of absurdity assert the meaning of his own life, as lover, friend, son of the

---

[57] It has been argued that revenge was *not* an obligation. But assertions that Shakespeare, or Hamlet, or both, found revenge ethically repugnant cannot be supported from the play, which never invokes the Christian sanction against private vengeance. If Shakespeare wanted to make a central issue of the morality of revenge, he has done very strangely never to bring it out in Hamlet's self-questionings or in his talks with Horatio—that is, never to place it before us dramatically. Whatever evidence scholars may amass from other documents to show that Elizabethans were taught to repudiate revenge as a great sin, we must still trust to the guidance of the text in determining what issues are significant in *Hamlet*. Shakespeare's audience was as used to the heroic values of folk tale and legend as to the Christian ones of the catechism. Like audiences of today, they could hold in abeyance a moral reaction or bring it forth as directed by the playwright. Indeed, the success of either tragedy or comedy depends to some extent on the audience's willing suspension of a specifically Christian point of view.

Of course, in accepting the revenge obligation as a *donné*, we need not view the Ghost as a divine agent or give unqualified approval to every speech and action of Hamlet. Such black-and-white moral distinctions have no place in Shakespearean tragedy. Both of these corollaries seem to be assumed in Eleanor Prosser's *Hamlet and Revenge*. This is the most thorough and intelligent presentation of the case against revenge. But even Prosser, searching for dramatic expressions of the issue in the play, must resort to some indirect allusion, a very strained reading of "To be or not to be," and such dubious critical propositions as this: "The moral issue is implicit throughout the ["O what a rogue"] soliloquy, and . . . it is so subtly treated only because Shakespeare felt no need to make it explicit" (p. 155).

royal line. In the revelations about the voyage to England that follow the graveyard scene, we may feel that Hamlet has not simply been given his intuition of providential pattern, he has earned it.

Nevertheless, that intuition does follow and thus enclose safely the brief vision of absurdity in *Hamlet*. When Shakespeare next mingled comic with tragic in this radical way, he observed no such bounds of safety. *King Lear* is in a way the obverse of *Hamlet*, for there, order is enclosed in chaos and moral pattern in amoral patternlessness.

[4]

Between the Divine
and the Absurd: *King Lear*

The exploration of comic conventions in Chapter 1 brought us more than once up against the paradox that comedy promotes both order and chaos. It is Oberon's natural home, and also Puck's. Comic action moves from rigidity and false values, through a series of unsettling, painful experiences that break down the barriers to growth, to a new integration of characters and attitudes. The outline is orderly, but on the way to the happy ending identities come loose, words escape from the logic of plot or even of rational communication, cherished values are mocked and turned on their heads. In *King Lear*, Shakespeare makes his most radical use yet of comedy in tragedy. He sets comic order side by side with comic chaos, and out of the dislocation that results he develops a special, devastating tragic effect.

An exchange between Lear and Poor Tom on the heath will serve as an emblem of this process. The obsessed, suffering king speaks, and the Bedlam answers—or rather doesn't answer. It is, in little, the mode of the whole play: pattern jarring against patternlessness, both of them rooted in comedy.

> *Lear.* Is it the fashion that discarded fathers
> Should have thus little mercy on their flesh?
> Judicious punishment! 'twas this flesh begot
> Those pelican daughters.
> *Edg.* Pillicock sat on Pillicock-hill.
> Alow, alow, loo, loo!
>
> (III.iv.71-76)

At some point in this dialogue, sense gives way to nonsense. A modern spectator without much knowledge of Shakespeare's times would probably feel the dislocation at the unexpected, in-

138   DIVINE AND ABSURD

congruous image of women—Goneril and Regan rather than
Tom's mythical daughters—as pelicans. His Jacobean counterpart, on the other hand, would have had associations for the
pelican aside from its comical shape. He would know that the
pelican was a common type of selflessness, the bird that sac-
rifices its own flesh and blood to feed its offspring.[1] Such a spectator might well have reacted here to suffering age torn apart and
devoured by youth. *His* displacement would come with the
abrupt shift from "pelican," full of pain and moral significance,
to "pillicock," which is possibly a lewd transposition of Lear's
solemnities on flesh and begetting (*pillicock* may mean "penis")
or possibly sheer nonsense. In any case, sound has taken over
from sense to produce comic irrelevance.

Wilson Knight first called attention to the grotesque element
in juxtapositions like this one, deviations from the heroic norm
so jolting that they seem to call the norm itself into question and
hint at "the very absence of tragic purpose."[2] What happens in
the sideways shift from pelican to pillicock? By a chance
association—Auden's "auditory friendship"[3]—we are deflected
from tragic meaning to the very long, flattening-out view of
comedy that makes nonsense of the heroic posture and of any
individual who takes himself too seriously. Remember Hamlet,
who chanced into a graveyard and found noble Alexander stopping a bunghole.

This is one kind of comedy in *Lear*. In this exchange it directly
confronts the other kind. For although Lear is using the pelican
symbolism negatively, with stress on the rapacious young rather
than on the selfless parent, it nevertheless can call up a whole
familiar pattern of creative suffering, abasement as part of a
movement toward greater good. Its archetype is the divine comedy of redemption through the sacrifice of Christ, whom Dante
called "nostro pellicano."[4] That divine comedy is the ultimate
frame of reference for many of the conventions of comedy dis-

---

[1] See Kenneth Muir's note on this passage in *King Lear*, New Arden ed.
(Cambridge, Mass., 1952); and Russell Fraser, *Shakespeare's Poetics in Relation to
"King Lear"* (London, 1962), pp. 91-92.

[2] *The Wheel of Fire*, 4th ed. (London, 1949), p. 175.

[3] See above, p. 50.   [4] *Paradiso* xxv.113.

KING LEAR
139

cussed in the first chapter. It blots out death with love, and directs human beings from bondage to freedom not through a causal chain of works and rewards but through humiliation, self-dislocation, and the transforming faith that makes a new reality. Shakespeare's *Lear* is resolutely pre-Christian, but human analogues of the divine comedy inform it so persistently that many critics have more or less agreed with Bradley to subtitle the play "the redemption of King Lear."[5] How can such a positive, purposeful order of redemptive suffering coexist with the grotesque comedy of the Fool, of Lear himself as childish, impotent *senex iratus*, of Gloucester tumbling on his nose instead of to his death off Dover cliff? And why, with this notable reliance on comic perspectives, is *Lear* nevertheless overwhelmingly tragic, not only in its terrible conclusion but in its total emotional effect? To answer the first question is, I think, to go a long way toward answering the second.

King Lear has had a curious literary history. It is a tragedy preceded and followed by comedies. By "preceded" I mean that, for *Lear* alone among the tragedies, Shakespeare worked from a comedic source. Although Harbage and Schoenbaum classify the old play of *King Leir* as legendary history, that history is cast in the mold of comedy-romance, the familiar movement from folly through tribulation and testing to reconciliation and renewed social health. Like all other versions of the legend of Lear and his three daughters, it ends with Lear triumphantly reinstated as king. Shakespeare not only made a complex tragic character out of the passive, patient Leir, but he gave a new ending to the well-known story by killing off Cordelia and finally Lear. More striking still, the generations following Shakespeare's rejected that ending as disturbing and inappropriate. His play was displaced from the stage for almost a century and a half by Nahum Tate's version, which ends with Lear restored to the throne and Cordelia betrothed to Edgar. In this regard, too, *Lear* is unique. No other Shakespearean tragedy, however painful, was felt to be so in need of revision that critics and public could

[5] *Shakespearean Tragedy*, p. 285. W. R. Elton surveys optimistic readings of *Lear*, with which he does not agree, in *"King Lear" and the Gods* (San Marino, Calif., 1966), pp. 3-6.

140 DIVINE AND ABSURD

accept an alternate version for so long, with so little objection. Even Johnson preferred Tate's ending.[6]

So *King Lear* derives from one comedy and gives place to another. In itself the first fact suggests only that many members of Shakespeare's original audiences would have been expecting a happy ending. Of course, Shakespeare was perfectly capable of reconceiving the Lear story in orthodox tragic terms and molding events toward inevitable catastrophe, if he had wanted to. But did he want to? The murder of Cordelia, which brings about Lear's own death from grief and exhaustion, is anything but inevitable. It is not just that the downfall of persecuted virtue violates our sense of justice, as Johnson complained; Cordelia is not the first innocent to die on Shakespeare's tragic stage. But the play presents her murder as a senseless mistake rather than an unavoidable consequence—"Great thing of us forgot!" And the long preeminence of Tate's alterations, whatever else it may say about eighteenth-century taste, suggests that his version met some ordinary esthetic demand that Shakespeare had spurned.

It is clear that the spurning was deliberate. *King Lear* is full of the structures, motifs, and devices of comedy. It has a double plot and a developed Fool; it is concerned, like many comedies, with the passing of power from old to young; two of its characters are disguised through most of the play, one of them in a series of *personae* that allow him to manipulate other characters; the protagonists are forced out from society into educative confrontations in a natural setting and then return to society again; and this process is accompanied by the traditional disorder of comedy—social hierarchies turned upside down, logic and even sanity violated. The plot disregards probability as flagrantly as any romantic comedy, from the love test that sets it in motion to the conclusion of the Gloucester action in chivalric challenge, triumph of disguised hero over villain, deathbed repentance of villain.[7]

[6] *Johnson on Shakespeare*, VIII, 704. *Romeo and Juliet* was given a happy ending by James Howard in the Restoration period, but even this version (which has not survived) was played alternately with the tragic one. George C. Odell, *Shakespeare from Betterton to Irving* (London, 1921), I, 37. The versions of Otway, Cibber, and Garrick which dominated the eighteenth-century stage all ended with the lovers' deaths.

[7] Maynard Mack in *"King Lear" in Our Time* (Berkeley and Los Angeles,

KING LEAR   141

These constant appeals to the world of romantic comedy function in a complex way. They are often twisted to serve, and intensify, the immediate tragic effect. Yet they simultaneously
allow for a long-range hope, based on the well-established assumptions of comedy, that all the confusion and pain is leading
to a positive conclusion.

The double plot is a good example. In comedy, multiple actions permit the audience to escape confinement within a single
set of problems and relationships by shifting from one world to
another—court to country, nobles to common folk. As it gets
going in I.ii, the Gloucester plot seems to promise just this sort
of variety. The new initiator is a dashing young social outcast
instead of an old king. The focus shifts from state to domestic
matters, the style from ritual formality to racy colloquialism.
But events bring the two plots into closer and closer symmetry.
Edgar is cast out like Cordelia; Goneril and Regan take over the
initiative to line up with Edmund; and the two fathers suffer an-
tiphonally, find forgiveness and love with their good children,
and finally die. This is not to deny the differences of scale and
emphasis between the Lear plot and the Gloucester one, but
rather to recognize that the promise of escape was a trick. There
is no contrasting realm of action which operates by rules different from Lear's.[8] By introducing a potential contrast and then
dissolving it in dreadful parallelism, Shakespeare converts the
double plot from its usual freeing function to the service of
tragic claustrophobia.

Nevertheless, the shape of both actions suggests comedy, and
the repetition of one by the other makes us more aware of a
comic movement toward regeneration. Furthermore, the more
direct statements and more comprehensible actions of the

1965), pp. 63-66, and David Young in *The Heart's Forest: A Study of Shakespeare's
Pastoral Plays* (New Haven and London, 1972), pp. 76-78, have commented on
the romance features of *King Lear*. Michael Long's outline in *The Unnatural Scene*
(London, 1976) of the play's correspondences with the structure of festive com-
edy (pp. 162-164) informs his whole discussion of the rejuvenation of culture in
Lear.

[8] Schlegel observed long ago that the paralleling of plots removes Lear's situation from the area of individual misfortune, suggesting rather "a great commo-
tion in the moral world." *Lectures on Dramatic Art and Literature*, tr. J. Black, 2nd
ed. (London, 1886), p. 412.

142   DIVINE AND ABSURD

Gloucester plot help us to understand the complex orchestration
of the Lear plot, especially in Act IV, where the idea of education
through suffering is made explicit in Edgar's tutelage of his
father. We are thus given some retrospective clarification of
what has been happening to Lear in the confused meetings and
monologues on the heath, a direction to see growth of spirit in
those mad questionings and flashes of insight as well as in
Gloucester's quieter meditations. The paralleling of plots, then,
has a paradoxical effect: it cuts off easy escapes from involvement in pain, but it also brings out the larger outlines of the action more clearly, to hint that the pain is part of a necessary
order and is *leading* somewhere.

The heath itself and the rugged Dover countryside generate
the same ambivalence. Certainly they are harsh and dangerous,
tonally distant from the accommodating green worlds where the
characters of *A Midsummer Night's Dream* and *As You Like It*
work out their difficulties. *Lear* allows no easy pastoral idealism,
as David Young insists: "*King Lear* employs the pastoral pattern
in order to negate it; . . . it denies its characters and audience the
consolations supposed to accompany poverty, isolation, and
humiliation, . . . it suggests that renunciation is no insurance
against suffering. . . . *Lear* drives on to challenge [pastoral's]
basic assumption about the essential harmony of man and nature."[9] Still, if poverty and humiliation do not carry the conventional consolations of pastoral, they do awaken in Lear and
Gloucester some measure of fellow-feeling with the poor naked
wretches of this world. While renunciation does not indeed in-
sure against suffering, it is also true that the suffering jolts these
two out of their self-centered complacency:

> Lear.   They told me I was everything; 'tis a lie—I am not
>   ague-proof.
>
> (IV.vi.104–105)
>
> Lear.   I am a very foolish fond old man.
>
> (IV.vii.60)
>
> Glo.   I stumbled when I saw.
>
> (IV.i.20)

[9] Young, *The Heart's Forest*, p. 93.

KING LEAR   143

These revelations come at a terrible cost, but we should not deny their value. In its savage way the heath is not totally unlike comedy's green world. Its wild elementalism shows up the flatteries and the veiled verbal cruelties of Lear's, Goneril's, and Gloucester's castles. It provides a new point of view: Edgar as Poor Tom is for most purposes a new character who offers to Lear the image he requires of natural man ("the thing itself") and to both Lear and Gloucester the oblique tutelage of destitution and madness. In *Lear* no less than in *As You Like It*, the natural setting is a place where desires and needs can be acted out. Lear summons Goneril and Regan to judgment; Gloucester goes through the motions of suicide.

Even the rhythm of this section of the play is more like comedy than tragedy. Goneril and Regan are plotting against the old king's life, to be sure, and surrounding characters like Kent feel the need to move on at once. Yet the mad Lear is himself oblivious to outside dangers. So is the Fool, who sees only the natural discomforts, and so is Edgar in his guise of half-wit. In spite of the quick moves of Goneril and Regan, the advancing invasion, and the relentless pull of the characters toward Dover, the middle of *King Lear* lacks the forward thrust of events typical of Shakespeare's other tragedies. Compare this third act with others. Where Othello is tempted, falls, and sets his mind to vengeance; where Hamlet presents his play, confronts his mother, and kills Polonius instead of Claudius—Lear rails in the storm, seeks philosophy from Poor Tom, and conducts an imaginary trial of his absent daughters. Different as it is from *As You Like It* in tone, *Lear* is more like that comedy than like the other tragedies in the way it suspends the urgencies of plot, at least for the protagonist, and allows time for philosophical discussion, role-playing, and the expanding of perspectives.[10]

The double plot is a structural device borrowed from comedy; the sojourn in a natural setting is another structural device, which carries thematic significance as well. Another thematic convention of comedy operating in *King Lear*, though with a different effect, is the challenge of youth to age. We have seen

[10] Mack discusses affinities between *Lear* and *As You Like It* in *"King Lear" in Our Time*, pp. 64–65.

144   DIVINE AND ABSURD

that in comedy the young characteristically get their way at the
expense of fathers and dukes, whose authority is set up in various laws and pronouncements only to be overturned. The passing of power and centrality of position from parents to children
implies freedom, but it implies continuity as well. The society,
delivered from the rigidified customs of seniority, is reenergized
by the vitality of the next generation. Our satisfaction in such a
movement depends very much on the dramatist's maintaining
for us a wide and suitably detached perspective in which individual fates are submerged in the larger patterns of social renewal. Since it is the parents whose feelings will necessarily suffer, the writer of comedy must take care that parents evoke little
sympathy. The conventional *senex iratus* is a logical consequence. He storms and threatens; he is vain, stupid, easily duped
by his children, and often blind to their true natures. This is, in
fact, a good description of Lear at the beginning of the play. Indeed, he goes on for quite a while in this mode; but we cannot
respond as we do to the *senex* because we are painfully inside his
confusion and impotence, not outside looking on.

This invocation of comedy, unlike the double plot and the
green world, brings with it no hope of renewed life. Rather, it is
another of those reexaminations of comic assumption that we
have seen already in *Othello* and *Hamlet*. We are made to regard
the traditional yielding up of power through the eyes of the old,
and to feel the consequent frustration and humiliation. Experi-
enced from within, this is clearly part of the archtragedy, in that
it marks definitively the beginning of the irreversible descent
into death. Lear and Gloucester lose their powers and titles and
never regain them. How much Shakespeare changed the focus of
the action is apparent if we compare his play with *King Leir*,
which is as much about the daughters as about the father. The
older play is shaped by the contrast between Gonorill's and Ra-
gan's selfish sexuality and Cordella's romantic courtship, between their materialism and her grace. In these contrasts Leir
plays stereotyped roles as victim for the elder sisters and heavy
father for the youngest. While Shakespeare kept these patterns
and even added a second father-and-children action, he placed
the fathers firmly at stage center.[11]

[11] McElroy (*Mature Tragedies*, pp. 153-155) shows how Shakespeare high-

KING LEAR

145

Another departure from the old *Leir* follows from this one. Given his new tragic focus, Shakespeare needed some concrete sign to define the process of stripping away authority and even identity from the old. The source play offered nothing useful, but he could find in other versions of the story Lear's train of knights. Geoffrey of Monmouth, and John Higgins in the *Mirror for Magistrates* give the number as sixty, but Shakespeare made it a hundred. As director Grigori Kozintsev perceived, this is a magic number, symbolic like the knights themselves. "The number one hundred," he rightly says, "isn't a quantity, but a specific quality. . . . One hundred isn't a hundred times one. In this case the number one, as a single unit, doesn't exist." That is, the knights have no individual being. Kozintsev discovered, when he tried to find a basis in the text for separate characterizations, that Shakespeare had supplied none. The knights were not meant to be differentiated, he concluded; they are "not people, but a representation of a way of life."[12] They have only a brief, shadowy stage existence as anonymous "gentlemen," but as a corporate presence offstage they function freely in the audience's imagination as projections of Lear's royal self. The quarrel with Goneril and Regan is really a quarrel about his own autonomous identity. In defending his knights—"My train are men of choice and rarest parts / . . . And in the most exact regard support / The worships of their name"(I.iv.263-266)—Lear asserts his own worth as a person. His daughters chip away at that worth, the worship of his name, by reducing his train, which they naturally regard as a dangerous nuisance. The knights have no practical function, except perhaps to stir up trouble in the new regime as Goneril fears (I.iv.324-327). Lear does not *need* them, any more than an old woman sent off to a nursing home needs her own chair, her rug, and her pictures. But without them she feels her self diminished. "Allow not nature more than nature needs, / Man's life is cheap as beast's" (II.iv.265-266).

---

lights the conflict of generations in *Lear* by making almost all the major characters either very old or very young; "there is none of the balanced gradation of ages we find not only in real life but also in the worlds of *Hamlet*, *Othello*, and *Macbeth*" (p. 155).

[12] Kozintsev, "*Hamlet* and *King Lear*: Stage and Film," in *Shakespeare 1971*, ed. Clifford Leech and J.M.R. Margeson (Toronto, 1972), p. 197.

146   DIVINE AND ABSURD

Goneril and Regan can tolerate a father only if he is totally dependent on them. When, with bitter irony, Lear kneels before
Regan to beg for the necessaries of life, she rejects the gesture as
an "unsightly trick." But this is a response to the irony rather
than to the gesture itself, which in fact expresses the relationship
she wants: Lear as helpless child and herself as instructing and
chastising parent.

> You should be rul'd and led
> By some discretion that discerns your state
> Better than you yourself.
>
> (II.iv.146–148)

Mother knows best. Should Lear refuse to be ruled and led, he
will have to learn the hard way, from his own mistakes. "To
wilful men," moralizes Regan, "The injuries that they themselves procure / Must be their schoolmasters." Goneril agrees
contemptuously that old fools are babes again. It is left for the
Fool to spell out the moral for Lear in the crudest terms: "Thou
mad'st thy daughters thy mothers . . . thou gav'st them the rod,
and put'st down thine own breeches."[13] In the subplot Edmund
ascribes to Edgar the similar notion that aged fathers should be
put in the guardianship of their sons. Of course it is Edmund
himself who comes to see clearly, like Goneril and Regan, how
the young must rise at the expense of the old.[14] His first aim is
only to displace Edgar as Gloucester's heir. Before long he has
pulled down his father as well and taken over his earldom and
revenues.

Fathers may well become children in this world of upside-
downs where madmen counsel kings and servants lead their
masters (or defy them, like Cornwall's servant at the blinding of
Gloucester), and where women are better soldiers than their
husbands. Here are the typical inverted hierarchies of comedy,
but few of them give any joy. Even the most militant feminist
cannot cheer Goneril's cold defiance of Albany. Her threat to
"change arms at home, and give the distaff / Into my husband's
hands" (IV.ii.17–18) conveys, not holiday freedom, but malevolence throwing over all restraints of decency.

[13] II.iv.301–303; I.iii.20; I.iv.171–173.   [14] I.ii.68–71; III.iii.25.

KING LEAR
147

Goneril's supremacy over her husband offers no prospect of good, and the servants' rebellion only an ambiguous one—Cornwall dies, but so does the good servant. The central upsidedown motif of old men as children, however, points in a more positive direction. Children can learn. "Better is a poor and wise youth than an old and foolish king, who will no longer take advice."[15] In his humiliation Lear asks questions he had not asked before, and discovers that his maturity was a lie: "They flatter'd me like a dog, and told me I had white hairs in my beard ere the black ones were there" (IV.vi.96-97). Also, Lear and Gloucester have good successors in the next generation as well as bad ones. A second-childhood subordination to the good promises a kind of rebirth. Unlike Edmund, Edgar *is* a fit guardian for Gloucester. His role as moral instructor to his father has irritated some critics, but Gloucester himself accepts his lessons humbly:

> I do remember now. Henceforth I'll bear
> Affliction. . . .
>
> (IV.vi.75-76)

Edg. What, in ill thoughts again? Men must endure
Their going hence, even as their coming hither:
Ripeness is all. . . .

Glo.   And that's true too.

(v.ii.9-11)

And while his elder daughters' destructive domination drives him to madness, Lear marks his return to sanity by kneeling to the youngest, Cordelia, in the classic posture of the penitent child. It is a gesture as right as kneeling to Regan was wrong.

In Shakespeare's culture, the most familiar type of the repentant child was the biblical Prodigal Son (Luke 15:11-32). I have suggested elsewhere that this parable was in Shakespeare's mind when he was writing *Lear*.[16] In outline it resembles what

---

[15] Eccl. 4:13, Revised Standard Version. (The Geneva translation, widely used in Shakespeare's time, has "child" for "youth.") Thomas Carter applied this text to *Lear* in *Shakespeare and Holy Scripture* (London, 1905), p. 434.

[16] "*King Lear* and the Prodigal Son," *Shakespeare Quarterly*, 17 (1966), 361-369. Some time after this article was published I found I had been anticipated in part by Roy W. Battenhouse, who noted several parallels between *Lear* and the Prodigal Son parable, including Cordelia's image of her father hoveling with

148   DIVINE AND ABSURD

he found in his sources, a story of portions prematurely granted and a central character who starts by rejecting the one who loves him most and then pursues a reckless course that brings him eventually to suffering and want. When Cordelia imagines her father hoveling with swine (IV.vii.39), she seems to superimpose the Prodigal's career directly onto Lear's: it was not Lear who was reduced to living among the swine and sharing their husks, but the Prodigal. Recognizing Lear as a spiritual Prodigal reinforces the comic thrust of the plot, for the main point of the parable is its happy ending. The biblical father is so ready to forgive that he runs out to meet his son. Similarly, Cordelia sends soldiers to "search every acre in the high-grown field, / And bring him to our eye" (IV.iv.7-8). She receives the broken Lear as the father in the parable received his son, not with the expected reproach but with music, fresh garments, and a kiss. In both parable and play, reconciliation is rebirth. Lear is, in his own description, raised from the grave. The Prodigal's father rejoices that "this my son was dead, and is alive again."

I have noted earlier in this chapter some characters in *Lear* who have roots in comedy: the Fool and the disguisers, notably Edgar. The Fool, whose worm's-eye view of great events as well as his formal office links him to comic clowns and fools, belongs mostly to the play's grotesque comedy and will be discussed later in that context. But he does have a role in the other comedy of redemptive learning, as one of Lear's teachers. D. J. Enright has pointed out how paradoxical is his double function, first to joke the king into awareness of his folly and then to joke away the pain caused by that awareness, to avert madness and destruction.[17] This is the way comedy itself should operate. It must open the eyes of the self-deceived through exposure and mockery and yet prevent dire consequences. From this point of view, the Fool's failure at the second part of his mission (he cannot keep Lear from suffering and going mad) and his disappearance in the middle of the play may seem ominous, an anticipa-

---

swine. Battenhouse compares Cordelia to the wise child of Luke 49, and finds her attitude in the play evolving from that of the elder brother in the parable to that of the father. "Shakespearean Tragedy: A Christian Interpretation," in *The Tragic Vision and the Christian Faith*, ed. Nathan A. Scott, Jr. (New York, 1957), pp. 85–86.

[17] *Shakespeare and the Students* (London, 1970), p. 31.

KING LEAR   149

tion of the play's inability to avert tragic catastrophe. On the other hand, the Fool's disappearance may instead signify the end of one stage of Lear's education, which will be continued by Poor Tom. Or it may point to Lear's internalization of the Fool, his alter ego, as he grows in self-knowledge.[18] Either way, it is a sign of progress that the Fool is no longer needed.

Of the two disguisers Kent is the simpler, and his ties to comedy are more superficial. Shakespeare apparently invented Kent's disguise, borrowing from comedy the notion of serving the loved one incognito.[19] The closest parallel in his own work is Julia in *Two Gentlemen of Verona*. Kent has affinities as well with another conventional comic type, the father in disguise protecting his child.[20] He thus joins Cordelia and the others as a parent figure for the child-Lear and reinforces the sense of hierarchies overturned, both as earl turned servant and as servant protecting master.

Interestingly, Kent as Caius shows traces of the traditional comic freedom granted by disguise, mainly in his scenes with Oswald. His bluntness is his own; but the flights of virtuoso abuse in II.ii—"I'll carbonado your shanks," "Thou whoreson zed!" "three-suited, hundred-pound, filthy, worsted-stocking knave"—these belong to his *persona*. So do the parody of court language in this same scene and the slapstick tripping-up of Oswald in I.iv. Kent appears to take pleasure in shedding the dignity of an earl, pleasure the audience delightedly shares. The Oswald encounters, however, are only comic parentheses in his devoted attendance on Lear. For the most part, Kent in disguise is still himself.[21] Unlike Julia, or Viola in *Twelfth Night*, who do new things in their disguises, Kent becomes Caius in order to go

---

[18] See, for example, Russell A. Peck, "Edgar's Pilgrimage: High Comedy in *King Lear*," *Studies in English Literature*, 7 (1967), 224; Willard Farnham, *The Shakespearean Grotesque: Its Genesis and Transformations* (Oxford, 1971), p. 119; R. B. Heilman, *This Great Stage: Image and Structure in "King Lear"* (Baton Rouge, La., 1948), p. 186.

[19] In the old *King Leir*, the Gallian King woos Cordella disguised as a palmer, and later he and Cordella are disguised as country folk when they seek Leir; but Perillus, the Kent figure, has no disguise.

[20] See Victor O. Freeburg, *Disguise Plots in Elizabethan Drama* (New York, 1915), p. 159; Freeburg's other examples are all from comedies.

[21] As Leo Kirschbaum has observed in "Banquo and Edgar: Character or Function?" *Essays in Criticism*, 7 (1957), 10.

150   DIVINE AND ABSURD

on doing what he has been doing before. His servant role represents no radical change of outlook, and its freeing powers are
correspondingly limited. As he watches and weeps for Lear, we
easily forget the fact of his disguise. Certainly it permits no sus-
tained escape or detached overview.

Toward the end of the play Cordelia brings Kent's disguise
back to our attention when she asks (IV.vii.6-8) that he cast it off.
He does not do so at this point, and I suspect that the reminder is
there to intensify our sense of things gone wrong when we get
to the final scene. For Kent later confesses who he is to Gloucester and Edgar, and finally, as the convention dictated, reveals
himself to his master in that last scene: "I am the very man." But
here the convention breaks down entirely, as everything else is
breaking down in the shock of Cordelia's death. The bewildered, grief-racked king hardly notices him, never acknowledges his loyal service. As for Kent himself, his loyalty and
sympathy have brought him to the point of death. We are hor-
rifyingly far from the joyous revelation-and-reward scenes of
comedy, and I believe Shakespeare consciously used the convention to measure that distance.

Edgar, more complex, provides another example of the double impact of comic conventions in the play. His disguise as
Poor Tom (also invented by Shakespeare) is more in the comic
tradition than Kent's, a role assumed for self-protection but
functioning as a positive source of new insight. The Bedlam disguise does more than cover Edgar: it *possesses* him in some way.
He elaborates his *persona* far beyond what is required for con-
cealment. Imaginative sympathy creates for Tom a whole mi-
nutely observed milieu of bogs and bridges, newts and rats,
Flibbertigibbet, Smulkin, and Frateretto, of shivering in the cold
wind and being whipped from tithing to tithing. Tom not only
has a present, detailed in his lists of activities and foods and his
whole train of fiends named and differentiated ("of lust, as
Obidicut; Hobbididence, prince of dumbness; Mahu, of stealing; Modo, of murder": IV.i.60-62), but he has a past—wine and
women, gloves in his cap, three suits and six shirts. Poor Tom is
a full character in his own right as well as an image of the poor,
bare, forked animal man, passionate, vain, lustful, fearful, pursued by his demons, cold in an indifferent world. The picture is

KING LEAR   151

bleak enough. But there is nevertheless a certain wild exuber-
ance in Edgar's bizarre world-making. It releases something in
him even while it expands Lear's vision and that of the audience.
The effect is of possibilities opening, rather than the usual tragic
one of possibilities closing. The same inventiveness gives an odd
exhilaration to the scene at Dover, where Edgar as beggar
creates the whole dizzy prospect that is not there from the cliff
where they are not standing, and then Edgar as peasant changes
the beggar into a comic fiend:

                                                his eyes
       Were two full moons; he had a thousand noses,
       Horns whelk'd and waved like the enridged sea.
                                        (IV.vi.69-71)

When we consider that Edgar has already assumed the peasant
role *before* casting off the beggar role (thus puzzling Gloucester at
the beginning of the scene by his improved speech), and that the
exaggerated fiend is yet another disguise imposed retroactively
on the beggar-peasant for Gloucester's benefit, Edgar's pyro-
technics in this scene must seem no less dizzying than the view
from Dover cliff. Later in the same scene, he uses Southern
dialect when talking to Oswald. Looking back afterward one
can see a point to this, some contrast between honest nature and
corrupt civilization.[22] At the time, though, it seems like versatil-
ity for its own sake. Edgar gives the impression of reveling in his
talents for adaptation and in his growing ability to control situations. Quick changes are an important feature of the manipulator's stock-in-trade, and this last switch into dialect feels like a
direct importation from comedy. Other playwrights tended to
use dialect for comic purposes.[23] Shakespeare himself had fun in
Henry V and *The Merry Wives of Windsor* with Welsh, Scottish,
and Irish accents and the broken English of foreigners.

   It is easy to recognize in Edgar the virtuosity of the accomplished disguiser and the unrestrained word-spinning of the
clown, aspects of his role that probably account for the special

[22] Cf. Mack, *"King Lear" in Our Time*, pp. 53-54.
[23] For example *The London Prodigal* (1604), performed by Shakespeare's company and printed in 1605, in which Oliver's Devonshire speech resembles Edgar's dialect in *Lear* (Muir, New Arden ed., p. 185n).

152   DIVINE AND ABSURD

attention he gets on the title page of the 1608 quarto of *King Lear*.[24] It seems to me wrong, however, to set Edgar up as the principal figure in the subplot whose growth in self-knowledge parallels Lear's.[25] Edgar's disguises up until Act v function not primarily for himself but for Lear and Gloucester, as new mirrors to make them see more. In him Lear finds unaccommodated man; through him Gloucester apprehends why "distribution should undo excess" (IV.i.71). When, in his peasant phase, Edgar characterizes himself as

> A most poor man, made tame to fortune's blows,
> Who, by the art of known and feeling sorrows,
> Am pregnant to good pity
>
>   (IV.vi.223-225)

the words interest us as reflecting more on Lear's experience and Gloucester's than on Edgar's. He has certainly suffered fortune's blows and felt deep pity for the two old men; but the play gives no hint that he was lacking in patience or compassion to begin with. Leo Kirschbaum is closer to the mark with his notion of Edgar as a "function" rather than a psychologically consistent character: "His various roles do not tell us more about Edgar. They tell us more about the play in which he is a character."[26]

Yet, agreeing to take this external view of Edgar's diverse parts in a dramatic pattern, one may still find in the shape of his career a significant relation to the world of comedy. It is not just that he survives to rule. More important, he changes from gullible *alazon* to powerful *eiron*, and this transformation helps to raise comic expectations about the whole course of the action as Edgar becomes increasingly effective in it. In notable contrast to the foiled manipulations of Friar Laurence, Edgar's schemes *work*. Every one of them is successful. His way with the despairing Gloucester is reminiscent of the dark comedies, in which destructive impulses like Angelo's lust and Bertram's cruelty could

---

[24] "M. William Shak-speare: His True Chronicle Historie of the life and death of King Lear and his three Daughters. With the unfortunate life of Edgar, sonne and heire to the Earle of Gloster, and his sullen and assumed humor of Tom of Bedlam."

[25] Peck, "Edgar's Pilgrimage," pp. 219-237.

[26] Kirschbaum, "Banquo and Edgar," p. 9.

KING LEAR 153

be acted out within a frame of safety, for the education of the destructive one: "Why I do trifle thus with his despair / Is done to cure it" (IV.vi.33-34). On Edgar's side are not only skill and insight but fortune, which delivers Goneril's incriminating letter into his hands just when he needs it. His Act v entrance in knightly armor, the last of his disguises, comes pat at the final trumpet call—exactly the "castastrophe of the old comedy" that Edmund had joked about at his brother's first entrance (I.ii.128). All the portents for Edgar's comic success are there.[27] Having brought about Gloucester's regeneration, Oswald's downfall, Goneril's exposure, and Edmund's defeat, can he not save Lear and Cordelia? Some apprehension may shadow anticipations of a happy resolution when we learn that Edgar's shedding of his disguise resulted not only in joyful reconciliation of father and son but in the father's death. Still, Gloucester's heart "burst smilingly," and Edmund's reaction to the news promises well: "This speech of yours hath mov'd me, / And shall perchance do good" (v.iii.199-200). What good is within his power except to countermand his order and save Cordelia and Lear?

It is a striking fact that, although Shakespeare's main source for *Lear* was a tragicomedy, he himself added or expanded most of the comic elements I have been discussing: double plot, green world, upended hierarchies, commentary by the Fool, disguise. All together they carry strong suggestions of a final comic ordering—or they would if the outcome of Shakespeare's play were not so well known. As familiarity with *Hamlet* diminishes the uncertainty we ought to be sharing with the hero in the early acts of the play, so familiarity with *Lear* mutes the full effect of these implications of comic pattern. If we did not know what was coming, we would surely recognize and respond to the play's evident thrust beyond madness and misery to growth,

[27] Edgar seems destined to act as an agent of the Providence that typically brings off the comic resolution in what Leo Salingar calls the "exemplary romance" pattern of Shakespeare's early comedies and late tragicomedies: "A family is divided; one of its members, cut off from civilised security and exposed to hazard, suffers with constancy and devotion; at last he or she is redeemed by an unexpected turn of Fortune, and the life of the family begins afresh. In this way Fortune, seemingly hostile and capricious, acts at the end in concert with the latent powers of Nature and obeys a hidden Providence." *Shakespeare and the Traditions of Comedy*, p. 30.

154   DIVINE AND ABSURD

reintegration, and new harmony.[28] We might recognize too that this comic movement, carried on as it is in terms of serious moral issues instead of the more purely social concerns of romantic comedy, points to an analogue with the Christian divine comedy of redemption. It is analogue only, because for reasons that I shall explore later Shakespeare placed the action of *Lear* in an emphatically non-Christian milieu. But in the sequence of pride, fall, recognition of guilt, forgiveness, and reconciliation, Christian audiences might well see something akin to their faith's basic pattern of evitability: sin and its consequences dissolving in new opportunity, the birth of the new man.

Sure enough, the last scene of Act IV brings a moving reconciliation between Lear and Cordelia. The Prodigal Son undercurrent joins with more overt allusions to Cordelia as savior—holy water, going about her father's business, redeeming nature from the general curse.[29] Lear's perception moves from death and hell to new life. And mercy supersedes justice:

> *Lear.* If you have poison for me I will drink it.
> I know you do not love me; for your sisters
> Have, as I do remember, done me wrong:
> You have some cause, they have not.
> *Cor.*   No cause, no cause.
>   (IV.vii.72-75)

The scene is so charged and so satisfying that the unknowing audience could easily forget that Edmund, Goneril, and Regan are still at large, and feel that here was the end of the story. It is only after Lear and Cordelia exit that Shakespeare looks beyond the reunion to remind us of the coming battle.

---

[28] Marvin Rosenberg reports that spectators at a Berkeley production of *Lear* who were unfamiliar with the play found a happy ending "continually possible—even promised." *The Masks of King Lear* (Berkeley and Los Angeles, 1972), p. 10.

[29] IV.iii.30; IV.iv.23-24; IV.vi.208; cf. Bethell, *Shakespeare and the Popular Dramatic Tradition*, pp. 59-61. Nicholas Brooke finds in Cordelia's mixture of "sunshine and rain at once" (IV.iii.18) an anticipation of a redemptive conclusion—"the aftermath of storm . . . watery but astonishingly hopeful." *Shakespeare: "King Lear"* (London, 1963), p. 36.

KING LEAR   155

Kent. 'Tis time to look about; the powers of the kingdom approach apace.

Gent. The arbitrement is like to be bloody.

(93-95)

With this swing from security to fear begins the peculiar
rhythm that dominates the last act of *Lear* and makes it different
from the final acts of all Shakespeare's other tragedies. It is a
very crowded act. As one event or announcement succeeds
another, we are cast up and down by turns, hope alternating
with fear. The battle is done almost before we know it has
started; Edgar lets us down suddenly with the news that Lear
and Cordelia have been defeated and taken prisoner. But hopes
rise again immediately afterwards when Lear appears, not in
despair but serenely happy. His lyrical "let's away to prison"
speech reduces to insignificance the battle and its outcome
("who's in, who's out") and thus *refines* our expectations, redi-
rects them toward a more appropriate resolution. Surely it is
right for the painfully educated new Lear to turn his back on the
vanities of power, rather than to regain his throne by martial victory. Lear imagines his earthly paradise so beautifully that we
forget it will be inside a prison.

For the moment, that is. Then comes another sharp deflection,
from hope back to fear, as Edmund orders Lear and Cordelia
killed. The affairs of Goneril's party hold attention for a while
after that, but soon we have Edgar's fairy-tale entrance as the
Unknown Knight. The duel ends with the satisfactory spectacle
of Edmund fallen. The good ones embrace, the wicked one re-
pents, and Edmund's "the wheel is come full circle" implies a
pattern not only for his own life but for Goneril's and Regan's.
Their deaths come next.

But we do not learn at once who it is that has died. A gentleman rushes in with a bloody knife and the horrified announcement, "She's dead!" Once again the plunge into fear, for surely
we would expect that "she" is Cordelia, whose death we now
remember has been ordered some time back. (I suspect that in
the rush of events we have not thought much of Cordelia and
Lear in the last few minutes; Albany's later exclamation "Great
thing of us forgot!" is not ridiculous, though it looks so on the

156   DIVINE AND ABSURD

printed page.) For a moment, Cordelia in our minds is dead.
Then comes the reprieve—not Cordelia, but Goneril and Regan.

Next, Kent arrives to complete the scene-setting for denoue-
ment. Except for Lear and Cordelia (and the long-missing Fool),
all the major characters not otherwise disposed of are present
now. Hopes rise to a new height as Edmund confesses his order
of execution and urges the others to forestall it.

> *Edm.* Nay, send in time.
> *Alb.*   Run, run, O, run!
>
> .   .   .   .
>
>   Haste thee, for thy life.
>   (*Exit Edgar*)
>
> .   .   .   .   .   .
>
> The gods defend her!
>   (v.iii.247-256)

It is time at last for Lear and Cordelia to enter, and they do. But
Cordelia is dead.

It is shocking, incongruous, an affront to all our preconcep-
tions about fiction. The author has broken the rules. It will not
do to put the blame on Shakespeare's sources,[30] or to search
back over Cordelia's brief stage life for some fault that justifies
her death,[31] or even to assert that the forces unleashed by Lear's
errors must work themselves out regardless of his personal regeneration. They *do* work themselves out, but this rhythm of
hopes which are dashed only to be revived implies the very opposite of *must.* Nor does Cordelia's death in any sense come out

[30] R. W. Chambers argues in *King Lear* (Glasgow, 1940) that the legend included Cordelia's eventual death and that Shakespeare could not change the end
of the well-known story (pp. 10-25). But Cordelia's suicide is not part of Lear's
story. It takes place several years after Lear's own death, when rebel nephews
imprison her. Shakespeare did in fact change the suicide to murder, and the
source play is proof that playwrights did not feel constrained to include in treat-
ments of Lear the final chapter of Cordelia's story.

[31] Explanations like that of Gervinus, that Cordelia erred in using a foreign
invasionary force to rescue her father, convert tragedy into what Frye has called
"a kind of insane cautionary tale" (*Anatomy*, p. 211). The touch of pride and will-
fulness that Coleridge and others have found in Cordelia's initial refusal to cater
to Lear, even if we agree that it is there, does not really dismiss the sense of out-
rage at her death: see New Variorum ed., ed. H. H. Furness (Philadelphia, 1880),
pp. 459-460 and p. 16n.

KING LEAR

of the logic of events. The execution order may be presumed to do so, although Edmund says nothing at the time about his motives. But now he has repented, and the sole artistic rationale for his repentance would seem to be the rescue of Lear and Cordelia. What finally prevents that rescue? Not a deep-seated human motive or a tightly forged chain of necessity, but simple bad timing.

Even now, Shakespeare has not finished playing on our hopes. Lear's agonizing lament over his daughter's body ends in an unexpected way:

> Do you see this? Look on her. Look, her lips.
> Look there, look there!

(310-311)

Is she alive after all? Once more, no. By the time that hope is gone, Lear is dead too. The numb survivors speak their final lines, and the play concludes with a dead march. We might well ask with Kent, "Is this the promis'd end?"[32]

The most celebrated defender of the ending of *King Lear* was Charles Lamb, who proclaimed that Lear's long agony had made "a fair dismissal from the stage of life the only decorous thing for him."[33] In human terms, he is perhaps right about Lear (he does not say why Cordelia had to die too). But the dramatic shaping of the act produces only a dismissal, not a fair one. Had Shakespeare intended to make Lear's death feel "right" in the way Lamb indicates, he would have constructed the latter part of the play very differently. As things stand, it seems monstrously *un*fair that Lear should be cheated out of a serene death in Cordelia's arms because some nameless captain was a little too prompt in carrying out orders.

If we assume that Shakespeare knew what he was doing, he must have been seeking an effect quite unlike that of the usual final movement of a tragedy. One thinks of Hamlet's premonition of death, of Macbeth backed into a corner by Malcolm and

[32] The primary reference of Kent's question is to the end of the world, but Shakespeare may also be calling attention to the happy ending he has promised and then denied. I am indebted to Professor Jon Quitslund of George Washington University for this suggestion. See also Young, *The Heart's Forest*, p. 92; and Goldman, *Shakespeare and the Energies of Drama*, p. 102.

[33] "On the Tragedies of Shakespeare etc.," *Charles Lamb: Prose and Poetry*, ed. George Gordon (Oxford, 1921), p. 89.

158   DIVINE AND ABSURD

Macduff, or Antony and Cleopatra by Octavius. *Othello* is closer
to *Lear* in that so long as Desdemona is alive there is still a chance
to avert disaster. But in *Othello* it is a hypothetical chance, not
one rooted in the play's psychological realities. These dictate
that when Desdemona does in fact wake up in time to protest
her innocence, Othello will be too deep in his obsession to heed
her. Even in *Romeo and Juliet*, where accidental bad timing also
generates the final catastrophe, there is no strong attempt in the
latter part of the play to arouse expectations of a nontragic end.

Comparison with *Romeo* brings out another element in this
uniqueness of *Lear*. Both plays end unhappily because a good
message lags behind the bad message it should annul. In *Romeo*
both messages are well-intended. Balthazar carries the bad one,
but he is not prompted by malice. Pure misfortune hurries him
to Mantua while detaining Friar John with his good message.
In *Lear*, however, Edmund's original order certainly had an evil
intention, and his remand came from a conscious desire to do
good. The operations of chance raise no necessary moral questions, then, in *Romeo*. In *Lear* they cannot be avoided. Is the
force that guides events inimical to good? If so, logic would re-
quire that Edgar and Albany go down too. Does the force, then,
pay no attention to logic or morality, or to any of our modes for
ordering life into significance? Is Cordelia's death not the result
of anything, but merely a grotesque joke?

To have its full effect, the punch line of a joke must be both
unexpected and prepared for. Shakespeare has in fact prepared
for this one, in some peculiar ways. First, he has more than once
called our attention to comic convention and cast doubt on its
"promis'd end." When Edmund greets Edgar's first entrance
with "Pat! He comes like the catastrophe of the old comedy"
(I.ii.128), the main point is to mock good, gullible Edgar. Yet
the sneer also reflects on the artificiality of comic conventions as
such. Later in the play, after a terrible night on the heath, Edgar
himself invokes comic convention, more fully if less directly:

> Yet better thus and known to be contemn'd,
> Than still contemn'd and flatter'd. To be worst,
> The lowest and most dejected thing of fortune,
> Stands still in esperance, lives not in fear.

KING LEAR   159

The lamentable change is from the best;
The worst returns to laughter.

(IV.i.1-6)

This is the traditional premise of all comedy, that the way down
is also the way up. But the next thing Edgar sees is his horribly
mutilated father. "I am worse than e'er I was," he says. So much
for the consolations of comic pattern. Shakespeare planted the
idea only to destroy it. Edgar's image of fortune's wheel has
been anticipated by Kent while he is in the stocks, with the same
supposition, that as night gives way to day, so good will follow,
and even grow from, evil: "Nothing almost sees miracles / But
misery. . . . / Fortune, good night; smile once more; turn thy
wheel" (II.ii.160-161, 168). Events contradict this comic supposition too. Kent goes from the stocks to a deeper kind of suffering and sees his king join him in humiliation. Where in *Othello*
and *Hamlet* Shakespeare made us experience the dark side of
comic *values*, in *Lear* he undermines the basic comic *structure*. Intimations that this structure can fail indirectly jeopardize the
whole redemptive thrust of the play and question the most pro-
found comic assumption of all, the Fortunate Fall.

Still, intimations so momentary and widely dispersed cannot
by themselves prepare the audience for the final blow to conventional expectation. They support a more powerful and insistent
presence in the play, the other kind of comedy which Knight
called grotesque. Cordelia's death is the last and greatest example of pelican displaced to pillicock, moral significance dissolving in absurdity.[34]

The grotesque is easier to recognize than to define. As against
the divine comedy I have been examining, it depends not on the
predictable but on the startling, not on opposite states in sequence but on opposite states perceived all at once. In Philip
Thomson's formula, it is not just that life is "now a vale of tears,
now a circus"; rather, the grotesque implies that "the vale of
tears and the circus are one."[35] It places tragic stature and suffering in uneasy proximity with the laughable, the irrelevant, the

---

[34] Empson compared it to "a last trip-up as the clown leaves the stage." *The
Structure of Complex Words* (Ann Arbor, Mich., 1967), p. 150.

[35] *The Grotesque*, Critical Idiom Series (London, 1972), p. 63.

160   DIVINE AND ABSURD

reductive. In a play this proximity may be spatial and visual—
the king's gestures and accoutrements parodied by those of the
fool, for example—but, as plays are made of words and words
function in sequence, the juxtaposition is likely to be temporal,
one tone jarringly offsetting another.

> *Lear.* O me, my heart, my rising heart! But, down.
> *Fool.* Cry to it, nuncle, as the cockney did to the eels
> when she put 'em i' th' paste alive; she knapp'd
> 'em o' th' coxcombs with a stick, and cried
> 'Down, wantons, down.'
>
> (II.iv.119-123)

The figure before our eyes is an old man on the verge of a heart
attack. On this the Fool superimposes a ludicrous kitchen scene
with a foolish woman struggling to slap down wriggling eels in
a pastry. The degrading image, slipped in all at once between us
and Lear's royal pathos, creates a distance in which there is room
for perspectives other than sympathetic identification. The king
is as stupid as that cockney. His suffering is no more consequential than a spoilt pie. He may give orders all he wants, but he is as
little in control as an inept kitchen wench with a bunch of live
eels. When some or all of this comes through, we feel strain and
disequilibrium. If we laugh, it is uneasily, without release.

In the ambiance of comedy the conjunction of king and kitch-
enmaid would delight and liberate. Even in *Lear* itself, a few
minutes before this interchange, the counterpoint of Kent's
earthy insults with Oswald's civilized self-importance has pro-
duced pleasure without tension. The difference is that we have
no stake in Oswald's self-importance, or in the dignity of Regan
and Cornwall, who later come in for some of Kent's comic
bluntness. We do have a stake in Lear's importance. His hurt and
large spirit have been made real for us. Incongruity becomes
grotesquerie when the emotional commitment we have made to
one element is threatened by admixture with another, disjunct
element.

Conceptions of the grotesque usually include some notion of a
striking departure from the expected order or norm. Individual
importance and uniqueness are the norm for a tragic hero. By
diverging from these, contradicting them, the grotesque endan-

KING LEAR

gers the tragic sense; it hints subversively that the hero is not so different from everyone else, or that his suffering does not really matter much. The Fool gets across both ideas with his cockneys and eels, but his favored line with Lear is the first of the two. His talk reconstructs the exalted in terms of homely images (eels and eggs), homely situations ("thou mad'st thy daughters thy mothers . . . thou gav'st them the rod, and put'st down thine own breeches"), and the commonplace wisdom of proverbs ("Fathers that wear rags / Do make their children blind; / But fathers that bear bags / Shall see their children kind").[36] As mirrored in this reductive foolery, Lear is not primarily a king but any father without "bags," any old man who was fool enough to give away his land. His experience is not peculiar to royalty or uniquely his, but is common to other men and even to snails and hedge-sparrows. Like the clowns of comedy, the Fool is close to nature—a common-sense, pragmatic nature that has comically little to do with that deity from whom Lear solemnly calls down curses on Goneril. As the Fool's talk of crabs and snails in I.iv makes a reductive coda to Lear's grandiose "Hear, Nature, hear" declamation, so later on, in the storm, his small boundaries and his practicality contract drastically the huge visions of universal chaos invoked by Lear:

> Lear. Blow, winds, and crack your cheeks; rage, blow.
> You cataracts and hurricanoes, spout
> Till you have drench'd our steeples, drown'd the cocks.
> You sulph'rous and thought-executing fires,
> Vaunt-couriers of oak-cleaving thunderbolts,
> Singe my white head. And thou, all-shaking thunder,
> Strike flat the thick rotundity o' th' world;
> Crack nature's moulds, all germens spill at once,
> That makes ingrateful man.
> Fool. O nuncle, court holy-water in a dry house is better than this rain-water out o' door.
>
> (III.ii.1-11)

---

[36] I.iv.157-158; 171-173; II.iv.47-50.

DIVINE AND ABSURD

Cataracts and hurricanoes unexpectedly shrink into the prosaic "rain-water out o' door." What is needed is a dry house, not an apocalypse. However magnificent Lear's words and actions here, we cannot shut out another sense of him as an impotent old man comically at odds with reality, giving orders to the universe.

The Fool has the clown-habit of pulling the grandly remote down to the physical and near. In the next juxtaposition, Lear reasons largely with the elements about kingdoms and moral obligations while the Fool reflects on codpieces, lice, and corns. He contracts the universe to four walls—the dry house he wants so much—as his doggerel contracts the roll of Lear's blank verse. Later still, Lear reads in the destitute Tom of Bedlam his own condition of loss and betrayal, and assumes that Tom too has suffered from grasping daughters: "Could'st thou save nothing? Would'st thou give 'em all?" And again the Fool jolts us without warning into the smaller dimension, the immediate physical fact: "Nay, he reserv'd a blanket, else we had been all sham'd" (III.iv.64–65). That first sweeping "all" collapses to something countable, a stock of clothes and household goods with one blanket subtracted. By the Fool's giggling irrelevance, the moving representative of unaccommodated man is made also a potential social embarrassment. The line may be directly addressed to the audience, in which case the perspective shifts still another way. If the Fool's "we" is felt to include themselves, the spectators are pushed back from their preoccupation with Lear's ordeal, made aware of themselves as observers of an act of make-believe—which is also a social occasion bound by social rules.

The text does not make it clear whether the Fool is here taking advantage of the custom that allowed clowns a special relationship with the audience. He is certainly doing so at two other points, the end of I.v and the end of III.ii. In the first instance he stays behind Lear a moment to threaten girls in the audience who laugh at him with loss of their virginity. In the second, he indulges in a comic prophecy which breaks the dramatic illusion even more decisively. Not only does the Fool speak to the audience in terms of its own time (brewers, priests, heretics, cutpurses, bawds), but he calls attention to the artificiality of his

KING LEAR   163

stage self. The prophetic speech plays on verses which exist in
the audience's present, outside the play world.[37] The Fool
"foresees" this audience present as well as the Arthurian age,
which is far future for the play world but long past for the audience: "This prophecy Merlin shall make, for I live before his
time." Both scene endings open up a gap between the spectators, momentarily aware of themselves as spectators, and the
action onstage, and to that extent diminish by distance the impact of Lear's experience. The second gives a special dimension
to the distance, a dimension of time. S. L. Bethell thought that
Shakespeare by the Fool's Merlin-prophecy brought play world
and real world together.[38] But if we have been directly experi-
encing the play world, does it not have just the opposite effect,
to displace the events of *Lear* from their present immediacy into
long-ago remoteness? In such a broad sweep of time, one man's
perplexity and pain do not count for much. For a moment, like
the gravedigger in *Hamlet*, we see that one as simply part of the
many.

These flashes of grotesquerie last long enough to make us feel
the vulnerability of Lear's tragic stature, but not so long as to
destroy it. Not that the Fool has a monopoly on the grotesque,
by any means. It is built into the very nature of events and especially into the characterization of Lear himself. The early acts
show us an incongruity verging on the comic between the king's
towering emotions and the petty incidents that cause them:
slights from a servant, some knights subtracted from his retinue,
his own servant put in the stocks. While Goneril and Regan will
eventually try to have Lear destroyed, the initial confrontations
of father and daughters are really little more than domestic
squabbles. The stocks are humiliating for Kent but hardly in-
struments of torture, and the Fool invites a comic response to
Kent's discomfiture: "Ha, ha! he wears cruel garters" (II.iv.7).
Recognizing that rudeness to Lear or to his representative is an
attack on his personal worth, one sees simultaneously that these

[37] Steevens observed that the verses are a parody of the pseudo-Chaucerian
"Merlin's Prophecy," which Shakespeare probably found in Thynne's edition of
Chaucer; see Dover Wilson's note to this passage in *King Lear*, New Cambridge
ed. (Cambridge, 1960).

[38] *Shakespeare and the Popular Dramatic Tradition*, pp. 85-86.

164   DIVINE AND ABSURD

slights are far from the titantic cruelties that might fittingly pro-
voke curses and bring on madness. The disproportion of cause
to effect comes out clearly when Lear complains of Goneril,

> She hath abated me of half my train;
> Look'd black upon me; struck me with her tongue,
> Most serpent-like, upon the very heart

and then curses her:

> All the stor'd vengeances of heaven fall
> On her ingrateful top! Strike her young bones,
> You taking airs, with lameness
>
> .   .   .   .
>
> You nimble lightnings, dart your blinding flames
> Into her scornful eyes. Infect her beauty,
> You fen-suck'd fogs, drawn by the pow'rful sun
> To fall and blast her pride.

                                        (II.iv.157–166)

Similarly, Lear's dramatic outburst " 'Tis worse than murder" must seem a ludicrous overreaction to the stocking of his
servant, especially when Shakespeare has built up to it by a kind
of Jones-and-Bones routine between the king and Kent.

> *Lear.* No.
> *Kent.* Yes.
> *Lear.* No, I say.
> *Kent.* I say, yea.
> *Lear.* No, no; they would not.
> *Kent.* Yes, they have.
> *Lear.* By Jupiter, I swear, no.
> *Kent.* By Juno, I swear, ay.

                                        (II.iv.14–21)

Sir John Gielgud told Marvin Rosenberg that audiences at his
1940 production of *Lear* laughed at these exchanges whether
they were "played for comedy" or not.[39]

In some of this, *King Lear* anticipates *Antony and Cleopatra*,
where the protagonists are often comically undercut by com-

___
[39] *The Masks of King Lear*, p. 155.

KING LEAR

ments from their subordinates as well as by their own petty behavior. What differentiates *Lear* and makes the term *grotesque* applicable to it but not to *Antony*? For one thing, multiple perspective seems built into the conceptions of Antony and Cleopatra, especially Cleopatra with her "infinite variety." Because we are invited constantly to detachment, the comic commentary does not jar in the startling way of *Lear*.[40] Moreover *Lear* is special in the pervasive nonsense quality of its incidental comedy. Although it is possible on close analysis to find wayward meanings in the Fool's snatches of rhyme and his tales of cockneys and eels, our first impression each time, I suspect, is one of derailment—not just from gravity of tone but from the very logic of discourse. Songs and jokes do not answer protests and curses; they simply exist beside them unreconciled. At its most extreme, the grotesque comedy in *Lear* questions not only the protagonists' stature but the order and purpose of all human existence. Beginning with brief effects in the early acts, this questioning becomes more insistent in the trial of Goneril and Regan and the Dover cliff scene, and it finally breaks out full force when the divine comedy pattern shatters on the senseless death of Cordelia.

The trial of Goneril and Regan is introduced casually. Nevertheless, when Lear announces, "I will arraign them straight," and summons his justicers (III.vi.20-22, 36-38), his words call to mind the most orderly of processes, and the most teleological. Each step in a trial is logical; each moves events further toward the judgment which is the point of the whole thing. But Lear's process begins to break down almost as soon as it starts. When he formally presents his first charge against Goneril, it comes out in a farcical image: "I here take my oath before this honourable assembly she kick'd the poor King her father" (46-48). We are back in the world of domestic bickering, with a shrewish

---

[40] In *The Common Liar*, Janet Adelman proposes that the comic perspectives in *Antony* act with other distancing devices to prevent full audience engagement with the lovers through most of the play (chap. 1), but disappear, along with other means of undercutting, towards the end of the play, so that in their last moments we are allowed to take Antony and Cleopatra at their own grand valuation (pp. 158-159). Absurd and heroic are sequential in *Antony*, simultaneous in *Lear*.

166 DIVINE AND ABSURD

housewife Goneril taking out some bad temper on her useless old father. It is rather like the Fool's sudden contractions of scope, and all the more absurd here because we have recently learned from Gloucester that Goneril and Regan have in fact gone far beyond small domestic cruelties and are actively seeking their father's death. Then the defendant escapes, dogs bark, and the muddled Lear abruptly abandons law for medicine: "Then let them anatomize Regan; see what breeds about her heart. Is there any cause in nature that make these hard hearts?" (74-76). The doctors cannot answer any more than the judges could, and Lear drifts off into nonsense: "We'll go to supper i' th' morning." Indeed, the nonsense element has been there all along. Lear and his fellow judges are mad. They must act out the trial in the absence of the defendants, using stools as substitutes, as Launce in *Two Gentlemen of Verona* acted out his family farewells with shoes, hat, and staff for *dramatis personae*.[41] Nahum Tate dropped the trial scene when he rewrote *Lear*. In fact, this scene may have given trouble even in Jacobean productions. Its omission from the Folio text suggests that it was not always acted,[42] and indeed, both actors and audiences may have difficulty coping with pathos that trembles constantly on the edge of farce.

Absurdity again jostles deeply felt emotion in IV.vi, especially when the elaborate buildup to Gloucester's suicide ends in a pratfall. Tate retained this scene, but he presumably allowed "Gloster" more dignity in his fall. There is no stage direction to suggest how; perhaps he swooned. At any rate, the Tate who found the Fool too gross a violation of decorum was not likely to invite laughter at this point. Nineteenth-century productions regularly omitted Gloucester's ineffectual leap, bringing Lear on early to forestall it.[43] Even in our own century many productions blunt the effect somewhat because their realistic sets make the audience aware from the start that the climb to the top of the cliff is pretend, like the trial of Goneril and Regan. Harry Levin has pointed out that Shakespeare's bare stage would have given no

[41] Hallett Smith points out the parallel in *Shakespeare's Romances* (San Marino, Calif., 1972), p. 125.
[42] Muir, New Arden ed., p. xlviii.
[43] Odell, *Shakespeare from Betterton to Irving*, II, 196-197, 295.

KING LEAR   167

clue that Edgar was practicing a deception, and that an audience
used to accepting verbal scene-painting as the true setting would
not be sure until the fall itself that Gloucester was not in fact
going over a cliff. Gloucester's puzzlement about the ease of the
climb might raise suspicions, and Edgar's aside "Why I do trifle
thus with his despair . . ." certainly gives assurance that he has
some plan in mind for preventing his father's death; but the audience could not know what it was.[44] In the stage conditions for
which it was written, this scene gives not just a spectacle of absurdity but an experience of it. Ideally we should be "with"
Gloucester as he prepares solemnly for his end, right up to the
moment when the abortive leap violently separates our perspective from his.

It is an extremely odd theatrical effect, a comic parenthesis in
what is recognizably the serious moral climax of the Gloucester
plot. Odder still, it is in no sense detachable from the whole.
"Parenthesis" is really inexact, for Edgar's whole scenario requires that Gloucester go through with his purpose seriously and
be foiled nevertheless. Only after he has acted out his death wish
will he be open to the judgment "Thy life's a miracle," and its
corollary lesson of patient acceptance. Only then can the
"fiend," thousand noses and all, be exorcised. In Gloucester's
suicide attempt the grotesque confronts the comedy of redemption head-on.

The scene which follows between Gloucester and Lear offers
grotesquerie in varying intensities. Some effects will depend on
the actor's interpretation. "Every inch a king" and "kill, kill
kill" can be absurd in the mouth of a shaky, feeble Lear, as can
the "sa, sa" exit line if delivered playfully. Less equivocal are
Lear's jesting images for the mutilated Gloucester—Goneril with
a white beard, blind Cupid. This last must clash violently with
the visual pathos of Gloucester's savaged face. From the alien
world of "sugared sonnets" it calls up the convention of the love
god taking aim at the gallant who has scorned love's power.
"No, do thy worst, blind Cupid; I'll not love" (137). To *hear* this
while *seeing* two human ruins is to be stretched taut between
laughter and pain.

[44] Levin, "The Heights and the Depths: A Scene from *King Lear*," in *More
Talking of Shakespeare*, ed. John Garrett (London, 1959), pp. 97-99.

DIVINE AND ABSURD

Lear is, of course, mad at this time. Madness was probably the most acceptable objective correlative Shakespeare could have chosen for a sense of cosmic absurdity. In any case, there is no precedent for the king's mental breakdown in the many previous versions of the Lear story.[45] As far as we know, the mad Lear— like the Fool and the pseudo-madman Tom—was Shakespeare's invention. In the context of certified insanity, his audience presumably could tolerate a good deal of unorthodox questioning and illogic that they might otherwise find too disturbing.

Does this strain of grotesquerie prepare us for the final absurdity of Cordelia's death? Not directly, certainly. The essence of grotesque, after all, is that it intrudes unexpectedly. And, as we have seen, the rhythm of Act v keeps renewing hope until Lear enters carrying the dead Cordelia. On the other hand, the earlier shocks and dislocations have a similar spirit. They will probably connect with each other somehow, so that later ones reverberate beyond their particular moments. Subjective responses must vary from one spectator to the next (or, in the same spectator, from one occasion to the next), yet surely there is a common element of unease, unease not at the center of consciousness but around the edges, waiting to close in at the shattering nonsequitur of Cordelia's death.

If I am right, then Shakespeare has, in a way, prepared us for the end even while necessarily leaving us unprepared and open to shock. The question remains, to what purpose? Are we supposed to feel that the last shocking joke is the point, that the intimations of positive moral evolution in the divine comedy pattern were there only to show up the folly of perceiving order in an orderless universe? Or should we see Cordelia's death and Lear's last agony as underlining the pain of the human condition but leaving the redemptive pattern more or less intact? Probably critical opinion still leans more toward the second alternative, al-

---

[45] New Arden ed., p. xliii n. Shakespeare may conceivably have got the idea from the analogous Robert of Sicily stories, in which it is part of Robert's humiliation to be scorned as a fool or a madman, or from the real case of Sir Brian Annesley and his three daughters: see Lillian H. Hornstein, "*King Robert of Sicily:* Analogues and Origins," *PMLA*, 79 (1964), 13-21; Mack, "*King Lear*" *in Our Time*, pp. 49-51; and, on the Annesley parallel, Muir, New Arden ed., p. xliii n., citing G. M. Young.

KING LEAR

though Barbara Everett, Nicholas Brooke, William Elton, and John D. Rosenberg, among others, have argued for more pessimistic readings.[46] At one extreme, R. W. Chambers celebrates *Lear* as Shakespeare's *Purgatorio*; at the other, Jan Kott proclaims it Shakespeare's *Endgame*.[47] The play's stage history shows something of the same split. While eighteenth- and nineteenth-century productions generally cut or prettified the grotesque elements, some twentieth-century ones have opted emphatically for absurdity—notably that of Peter Brook in 1962.

The pessimists have sequence on their side, certainly. In terms of events, blind chance, or malevolent fate, has pretty much the last word. After the play action has come to its grim close, one can look back over the whole to see what happens to purpose and plan on several levels. On the surface, several characters initiate plots of some sort, to get power or love, to save or destroy. None of them, good or bad, ultimately succeeds. On a deeper level are the obscurely motivated wanderings of Lear and Gloucester. These *acquire* a purpose not intended by the wanderers and only partly engineered by Edgar, a positive pattern seemingly ascribable to an orderly, though awesome, providence that guides faulty men through suffering to wisdom. Taken together, these levels suggest a universe like that of *Hamlet*, in which human schemes go awry while some power beyond the human directs events toward a larger order. In *Lear*, however, there is still another level, one only suggested in *Hamlet*, to which belong those grotesque incongruities that mock all human dignity and meaning. The grotesquerie might have been contained, if not resolved, in a framing order, as the graveyard scene is in *Hamlet*. But Act IV, with Lear and Gloucester secure in their re-

[46] Everett, "The New *King Lear*," *Critical Quarterly*, 2 (1960), 325-339; Brooke, "The Ending of *King Lear*," in *Shakespeare 1564-1964*, ed. Edward A. Bloom (Providence, R.I., 1964), pp. 71-87; Elton, *"King Lear" and the Gods*, passim; Rosenberg, "King Lear and His Comforters," *Essays in Criticism*, 16 (1966), 135-146. Everett, Elton, and Rosenberg all canvass the optimistic criticism before arguing against it.

[47] Chambers, *King Lear*, pp. 47-52; Kott, *Shakespeare Our Contemporary*, 2nd ed. (London, 1967), pp. 100-133. Wilson Knight has it both ways, in separate essays in *The Wheel of Fire*, presenting an optimistic purgatorial interpretation in "The *Lear* Universe" and exploring the implications of absurdity in "*King Lear* and the Comedy of the Grotesque." Knight does not integrate the two views.

170   DIVINE AND ABSURD

demption, is not the end of the story. When Cordelia and Lear
die as they do, the play seems finally to say, "This universe, after
all, has no concern for men's moral growth, in fact has no mind;
those momentary janglings that you shuddered at before shrug-
ging them off as peripheral—they are the point." Pelican yields
to pillicock.

The play does say this, but it says more. Even Brook, who
more or less realized the *Endgame-Lear* on stage, found he had to
cut or undermine certain parts of the text that worked against
the Beckettian bleakness. The practical compassion shown by
Cornwall's servants to the blinded Gloucester was omitted, as
was Edmund's repentant "some good I mean to do, / Despite of
mine own nature" (v.iii.243-244); and Edgar's (or Albany's)
couplets that conclude the play were spoken against a rumble of
thunder presaging another storm.[48] Brook's decisions help to
define the affirmative element in *Lear*. The servants can do little
enough for Gloucester, yet their disinterested impulse to help offers more hope for the human spirit than Brook's vision would
allow. Since we know nothing beforehand of these nameless
men and see nothing of them afterward, their act may perhaps
imply something about humanity in general. In any case, its significance is in its quality rather than its efficacy. Those who find
values affirmed amid the despair of *Lear* tend to locate them in
the characters as opposed to the course of events, in the constant
loyal goodness of some and the spiritual growth of others.
Without ignoring the Gonerils and Oswalds who exist alongside
the Cordelias and Kents, without denying that the good go
down as well as the corrupt, this view finds meaning "not in
what becomes of us, but in what we become."[49]

Brook's impulse to sabotage the final speech points us to
another aspect of affirmation in *Lear*:

> The weight of this sad time we must obey;
> Speak what we feel, not what we ought to say.

[48] See Robert Speaight, "Shakespeare in Britain," *Shakespeare Quarterly*, 14
(1963), 419; and Charles Marowitz, "*Lear* Log," *Encore*, 10 (January-February
1963), 28-29. The quarto gives the last lines to Albany, the folio to Edgar. Most
modern editors assign them to Edgar.
[49] Mack, "*King Lear*" *in Our Time*, p. 117. Heilman's equivalent value is "the
quality of [the good characters'] living." *This Great Stage*, p. 289.

KING LEAR   171

The oldest hath borne most; we that are young
Shall never see so much nor live so long.

(v.iii.323-326)

While the words are muted and sad enough, their message is not
despair. If the first line is meant as a response to Kent's speech
just before, in which he rejects a share in rule and in life itself,
then "we must obey" counters "my master calls me; I must not
say no." That is, we must accede to life, not death. At any rate,
the word *obey* suggests order, as does the balanced form of the
last three lines. And the order sought is significantly different
from the hypocritical forms with which the evil began in Act I.
"What we ought to say," with its reminder of the love test,
yields to "what we *feel*."[50] This speech is probably Edgar's; Albany has already showed the same spirit in his attempts to provide for the future of the state. First he aspires to a moral settling
of accounts: the king will be restored, friends will be rewarded,
enemies will be punished (298-304). He breaks off to witness yet
another horror, Lear's last agony. Although events once again
have mocked human orderings, Albany, instead of subsiding
into despair, tries again to pick up the pieces: "Friends of my
soul, you twain / Rule in this realm and the gor'd state sustain"
(319-320). Starting as a passive neutral, Albany has, during the
course of the action, defined himself by choosing human fellowship as the only alternative to men's preying upon one another
like monsters of the deep. Now left, by Lear's defeat and
Cornwall's death, sole ruler of Britain, he gives up the
throne—first to the rightful king, and then after Lear has died to
Kent and Edgar, presumably out of a sense of his own unworth-
iness. Again this last scene recalls the first, again with a significant difference: Albany's unselfish offer of power is the opposite
of Lear's self-serving abdication.[51] Although in order that this
structural point be made Albany must decline active participation in rule, his words here—"friends of my soul . . . the gor'd
state sustain"—express continued concern for the private and

[50] My italics. For a different reading of this line see Brooke, "The Ending of
King Lear," p. 85.

[51] As Dover Wilson points out in the notes to the New Cambridge edition,
"The play ends as it began, with resignation of the throne—but of a very different sort."

172   DIVINE AND ABSURD

public bonds that tie men together. Enid Welsford has observed that in the early part of *Lear* the bad characters are firmly allied while the good are divided among themselves; toward the end the reverse is true.[52] Albany's words to Edgar and Kent throughout the scene have underlined that community of the good, even surrounded by terrifying disorder. As for the bad characters, Goneril has preyed on Regan and on herself, and Edmund has departed further from the solidarity of evil at the last, to make common cause with the good. Edmund's impulse to save Cordelia and Lear is ineffective, as future events may frustrate Albany's hopes for the gored state, but the impulse itself marks Edmund's reentry (or entry) into the human community.

The final movement of *Lear*, then, is not all pillicock. Some elements counter the pervasive absurdity. Yet this negative, rather grudging formulation will not do for the many readers and spectators who find the play exalting. Are Bradley and all the others who see transcendent victory at the end simply refusing to face the bleak facts? Certainly the facile optimism of some finds sweetness in the uses of adversity with too little attention to the actual experience of the two old men—grinding agony, exhaustion, death. Others import back into the story the Christian otherworldly comfort that Shakespeare so rigorously excluded from it, so that they can imagine Lear and Cordelia united again beyond the grave. There is exaltation in *Lear*, I believe, but it is *tragic* exaltation. Far from depending on the next world, its premise is that this world—imperfect, limiting, indifferently cruel, perhaps senseless—is all there is. Lear's universe is preeminently the scene of tragic heroism as I described it in the Introduction,[53] and Lear himself is the unaccommodated but also unaccommodating hero. "Pour on; I will endure" (III.iv.18). He does more than that. Mocked and trivialized by his Fool and by his own silliness, battered by storms within and without, Lear keeps on asking. His pursuit of justice does not stop with the half-truth that he is more sinned against than sinning, or with the abortive trial of Goneril and Regan, or even

[52] Cited by Irving Ribner, *Patterns in Shakespearian Tragedy* (New York, 1960), p. 135n.
[53] See above, pp. 12-14.

KING LEAR 173

with his anarchic intuition that all are guilty and hence none can justly punish: "Handy-dandy,which is the justice, which is the thief?" This question, with all the reservations it implies about human justice, is allowed to stand; and no divine justice comes to answer the later, more terrible question, "Why should a dog, a horse, a rat have life, / And thou no breath at all?"[54] Yet in a world where "none does offend," Lear has nevertheless insisted on his moral responsibility, offering himself to Cordelia for punishment because he has wronged her: "You have some cause." Not finding morality outside, he has created it inside. Like other tragic heroes, Lear in adversity realizes more and more of his self. The final words of the play pay tribute to that fullness of enduring and learning: "the oldest," Lear, has suffered and lived more fully than any who come after him will. Like Hamlet in particular—not the Hamlet who saw heaven ordinant and divinity shaping our ends but the Hamlet of the graveyard scene—Lear seems in his energetic, questing response to absurdity to be *creating* a self, defining it against nothingness.

Creation is a divine act. It may perhaps seem strange to talk of human beings performing divine acts in a play whose characters appeal so often to the gods. Religion is omnipresent in *Lear*.[55] Its content, however, is problematic. Scholars have tried to piece together a consistent theology from the many religious invocations and explanations, but with little success. The comments contradict each other; and the action confirms Gloucester's "as flies to wanton boys are we to th' gods" at least as much as it confirms Edgar's "the gods are just." In fact, if we mean by "gods" anything more than "the way things turn out," they do not seem to exist in the play at all. Omnipresent yet nonexistent, the gods invoked in *Lear* carry a dual meaning, indicating simultaneously that men need a divinity greater than their own selves and that those selves are after all the only source of that divinity. Any divine comedy they achieve is self-generated, without support from a larger order.

Notice, for example, that prayers to these gods are almost

---

[54] III.ii.59–60; III.vi; IV.vi.154–155; V.iii.306–307.

[55] Other pagan plays—*Timon, Antony, Coriolanus*—invoke the gods more frequently than *Lear* but mainly in an exclamatory way; none seeks so relentlessly to *explain* them.

174   DIVINE AND ABSURD

never answered. Lear exhibits from time to time the patience he
has prayed for, Cordelia's appeal that her father be restored to
his senses meets with some short-range success, and Edgar does
eventually prosper as the remorseful Gloucester twice prays he
will.[56] One could say, more doubtfully, that Edmund's goddess
Nature stands up for bastards, at least for a while. In general,
though, prayers go unanswered so regularly that asking for a di-
vinely initiated action just about guarantees it will not happen.
The gods do not strike Goneril blind and lame, do not keep Lear
from madness or even from humiliating tears, do not find out
and punish their enemies in the storm, do not crack Nature's
molds and destroy the world, do not reward Gloucester's kindness to Lear or keep him from further despair after his attempted
suicide, do not cause the right side to win the battle, and most of
all do not save Cordelia from death.[57] Either the heavens are
empty or their divinities are perverse, alien to any moral system
we can understand. At times the result is so ironically at odds
with the prayer that one suspects a malicious intelligence behind
it. The reward for Gloucester's kindness is his savage blinding
by Cornwall; the stormy blasts and eye-piercing flames that Lear
calls down on Goneril fall in fact on himself and Gloucester.

On the other hand, it gradually becomes apparent that images
of the gods in *Lear* have a close subjective relation to the characters who offer them. Kind and protective themselves, Kent and
Cordelia see the gods as kind and protective. Edgar and Albany,
who value justice, see them as just. For Lear in his anger at his
elder daughters, they are wrathful and punishing, but after he is
reborn into humility, they smile on self-sacrifice. For Gloucester after he has sheltered Lear from the storm, the gods are kind;
when he despairs they are wantonly cruel; after he is brought
from despair to acceptance they are "ever-gentle."[58]

Edmund's goddess Nature is clearly a projection of his own

[56] II.iv.270; IV.vii.14-17; III.vii.91; IV.vi.40.

[57] II.iv.161-164; I.v.43-44; II.iv.276-277; III.ii.49-51; III.ii.6-8; III.vi.5;
IV.vi.220-221 (cf. v.ii.8-10); v.ii.2; v.iii.256.

[58] I.i.182; IV.vii.14; v.iii.170; IV.ii.78-80; I.iv.275-289; II.iv.160-166; v.iii.20-
21; III.vii.34; IV.i.37-38; IV.vi.219. I share the premise that the characters' religious conceptions reflect their own natures with various critics, e.g. J. C. Max-
well, "The Technique of Invocation in *King Lear*," *Modern Language Review*, 45
(1950), 142-147; Knights, *Some Shakespearean Themes*, pp. 132-133; Elton, "*King
Lear*" *and the Gods*, passim. My conclusions differ from theirs, however.

KING LEAR   175

lawless, amoral energy. His address to her in the second scene of
Act I serves dramatically to introduce him to the audience, but
after this speech, which in any case is more self-definition than
plea, Edmund forgets he has a tutelary deity. He refers to things
divine only twice, to bolster his pose of righteousness when he is
doing down first his brother and then his father:

> . . . I told him [Edgar] the revenging gods
> 'Gainst parricides did all their thunders bend.
>
> (II.i.45–46)

> O heavens! that this treason were not, or not I the
> detector!
>
> (III.v.11–12)

Aside from these pious frauds practiced on Gloucester and
(rather unnecessarily, one would think) on Cornwall, Edmund
is as silent on religious matters as the other bad characters are.
Regan has one conventional exclamation (II.iv.166), while
Goneril and Oswald say nothing of the gods. It would appear
that besides differentiating images of the divine according to
temperament and moral condition of the imager, the play distinguishes more generally between the good characters who invoke their gods in earnest and the bad ones who call on them
hypocritically or not at all. This might indicate that the gods are
real after all, but I think there is a better explanation.

The strongest evidence that men make divinities rather than
the other way round is that again and again conclusions about
what the gods are like and what they should do follow and grow
out of *human* initiatives. A good example is Lear's meditation
on poverty during the storm. He says, "I'll pray," but then he
talks not to gods but to men, the poor naked wretches and those
in power who should be taking thought for them.

> Poor naked wretches, wheresoe'er you are,
> That bide the pelting of this pitiless storm,
> How shall your houseless heads and unfed sides,
> Your loop'd and window'd raggedness, defend you
> From seasons such as these? O, I have ta'en
> Too little care of this! Take physic, pomp;
> Expose thyself to feel what wretches feel,

176   DIVINE AND ABSURD

> That thou mayst shake the superflux to them,
> And show the heavens more just.
>
> > (III.iv.28-36)

The gods come in only at the end, and they come as result rather than cause. When human rulers like Lear learn to distribute wealth justly, then the heavens will be revealed as just.

Words and action follow this pattern at several significant points. When Albany hears that Cornwall has been killed for blinding Gloucester, he says,

> > This shows you are above,
> > You justicers, that these our nether crimes
> > So speedily can venge!
> >
> > > (IV.ii.78-80)

Does it show any such thing? A *man* has punished Cornwall, not the "visible spirits" sent down from heaven that Albany conceives as the proper agents of retribution (IV.ii.46-47). What "proves" the existence of heaven is a purely human action. The scene of Cornwall's punishment itself ends in a similar way:

> *2 Serv.* Let's follow the old Earl and get the Bedlam
> To lead him where he would . . .
>
> .   .   .   .
>
> *3 Serv.* Go thou. I'll fetch some flax and whites of eggs
> To apply to his bleeding face. Now heaven help
> him!
>
> > (III.vii.102-106)

First comes the desire to help; then it is projected onto the gods.

In the Dover cliff scene, we actually watch Edgar invent new gods for his father. Picking him up after his "leap," Edgar proclaims Gloucester's life a miracle and instructs him about the makers of that miracle: "Think that the clearest gods, who make them honours / Of men's impossibilities, have preserved thee" (IV.vi.73-74). Both the impossibility and the miraculous preservation, of course, are Edgar's own work. He is converting his father away from the casual murderer-gods Gloucester has earlier called up from his despair.[59] Interestingly, Gloucester him-

---

[59] Edgar is also prolific in inventing fiends who objectify Poor Tom's condition.

KING LEAR   177

self has shown an impulse toward a more positive belief soon
after the "flies to wanton boys" pronouncement, in a speech that
more or less parallels Lear's meditation on social justice. Like
Lear, he is stirred by his own misery to feel for others:

> Here, take this purse, thou whom the heavens' plagues
> Have humbled to all strokes. That I am wretched
> Makes thee the happier. Heavens, deal so still!
> Let the superfluous and lust-dieted man
> That slaves your ordinance, that will not see
> Because he does not feel, feel your power quickly;
> So distribution should undo excess,
> And each man have enough.
>
> (IV.i.65–72)

What has happened to him seemed senseless only a moment ago,
yet now he perceives a purpose in it: heaven strikes at the com-
fortably hard-hearted ones to make them, in Edgar's later
phrase, "pregnant to good pity." Why does Gloucester see this
just now and not before? Because he has felt the good pity and
initiated, by himself, the distribution that undoes excess—"take
this purse." He finds meaning in heaven's act only through his
own act.

Religion in *King Lear*, then, does not contradict heroic self-
creation but reinforces it. Men make gods in their own images.
Shakespeare is not Marlowe, however, and the play does not
celebrate the all-sufficient ego. Edgar's insistence that his father
attribute his rescue from death to the "clearest gods" reminds us
that, even though the gods have no objective reality, it is a sign
of moral health to invoke them. The implication is that men
must create gods out of themselves but not make self their god.
They need to refer their lives to larger ideals of order and community, even if the order receives no support from an indifferent
universe, and community cannot save them from undeserved
suffering.[60]

[60] Wilson Knight, who sees a progress in *Lear* from a groping sort of natural
religion to the revelation of supreme love, recognizes man's creation of gods as,
at most, an "insistent need in humanity to cry for justification to something beyond its horizon." *Wheel of Fire*, p. 188. But it is hard to see god-making as an
early, inadequate stage of religious evolution when Lear is still doing it in the
play's last scene.

178   DIVINE AND ABSURD

In a sense, *King Lear* is a play about religion in the making. Shakespeare created for it a thoroughly pagan milieu quite unlike that of his source play, which is steeped in Christian allusion and assumption. The play world of *Lear* is emphatically, if not totally, primitive[61] Elton thinks that Shakespeare de-Christianized the story in order to make his own play demonstrate the breakdown of belief in Providence. He sees the "poor naked wretches" speech as an indictment of cosmic injustice, with Lear's recognition of his own injustice as an incidental irony.[62] I would argue rather that this recognition is central: it is Lear's acknowledgment that if justice is to exist, he as man and ruler must make it happen. Cosmic injustice is still there, but all is not therefore cheerless, dark, and deadly. Shakespeare's decision to examine man's ethical and metaphysical position in the universe without the *donnés* of Christian revelation is in line with the general tendency of his maturing art. Charlton points out, for example, that in *Richard III* it is assumed that the wages of sin is death, while *Macbeth*, in the next decade, reveals the internal necessity of that principle, by demonstrating its roots in "the bare rudiments of human nature."[63] One sees the same impulse to discard orthodox frameworks and start with human beings alone in the development of Shakespeare's political drama. The divine scheme of sin and retribution that is prominent in the *Henry VI-Richard III* tetralogy is much less noticeable in the *Richard II-Henry V* group, where problems of government are explored mainly in human terms. Shakespeare went farther in the same direction when he abandoned English history, with its patriotic imperatives, for the emotional neutrality of Rome. In *Julius Caesar*, *Antony and Cleopatra*, and especially *Coriolanus*, he used that freedom to address fundamental questions about the individual's relation to the state without any prior assumption in favor of the state. He could hardly ask whether English prosper-

---

[61] There are occasional anomalies—Edgar is Lear's godson; Lear sees Cordelia as a soul in bliss—and the speeches of Poor Tom and the Fool, as well as some of Lear's in IV.vi, allude to conditions of contemporary life. Overall, however, the impression is of a primitive, non-Christian society in which social structures and institutions are few, towns do not exist, and physical nature is very immediate and fearsome. See Charlton, *Shakespearian Tragedy*, pp. 218-224.

[62] *"King Lear" and the Gods*, pp. 225-226.

[63] *Shakespearian Tragedy*, p. 141.

ity and continuity were worth all they demanded (though perhaps he comes close to asking it through Hal's rejection of Falstaff). He could and did question the value of Rome. *Hamlet*, after some flirtation with absurdity, finally asserts an external guiding providence; five years later, in *Lear*, Shakespeare removes providential sureties and leaves his characters alone to destroy themselves or to create a positive ethic out of their own need. The play's values of love, forgiveness, and fellow-feeling gained through suffering are indeed those preached by Christianity. The point is that, rather than being handed down from on high, they take root in and grow up from the ground of human desperation. Furthermore, in an apparently random universe with no afterlife in which ultimate justice is meted out, following that ethic must be its own reward. Victories won through it are personal, limited, and nonenduring.

In the Introduction I suggested as the shaping emotion of tragedy a tension between recognition of death's rightness and protest against its wrongness. This is to say that tragedy's ground is the disputed border—or no-man's-land—between a just and orderly pattern for life on the one hand and an amoral patternlessness on the other. Shakespeare in *King Lear* is not rewriting the *Purgatorio* or anticipating *Endgame*; he is setting one vision against the other, and in their uneasy coexistence lies the play's peculiar tragic force. Dante and Beckett at their respective poles offer not tragedy but two kinds of comedy. What is important to realize here is that each kind in its way diminishes man somewhat. He is either a figure in a preestablished scheme, following the way laid out for him by a higher intelligence, or he is an aimless atom in a universe of aimless atoms. Where the two comic visions are held in balance, with neither dominating, individual choice and perseverance have special significance. The universe of tragedy, and preeminently of *Lear*, intimates pattern but fails to complete it; some pieces of the jigsaw are forever missing, and some of those on hand will never fit. Man is heroic in these circumstances when, like Lear, he has the capacity to create a larger self even out of the destructive element—to make his own meaning.

Index

Absurdity, *see* Shakespeare: *Hamlet*, fusion of comic and tragic in graveyard scene; and *King Lear*, grotesque comedy
Adam and Eve, fall of, 9, 13-14
Adelman, Janet, 132n, 165n
Amadís de Gaul, 37-38
Ariosto, Ludovico, 72
Aristotle, 8, 10, 41, 44n
Arthurian romance, 37-38
Auden, W. H., 50, 138

Bacon, Sir Francis, 19
Bandello, Matteo, 57n
Barber, C. L., 27n, 71
Battenhouse, Roy W., 147n
Beaumont, Francis, *The Knight of the Burning Pestle*, 38
Beckett, Samuel, *Endgame*, 169, 170, 179
Bergson, Henri, 113
Bethell, S. L., 68-69, 163
Blake, William, 11
Booth, Stephen, 105, 122
Bradley, A. C., 75, 92, 94, 130-131, 139, 172
Brook, Peter, 25, 169, 170
Brooke, Arthur, 57n
Brooke, Nicholas, 154n, 169
Burke, Kenneth, 84n

Cervantes, *Don Quixote*, 38
Chambers, E. K., 121n
Chambers, R. W., 156n, 169
Chapman, George, 7; *Bussy D'Ambois*, 23; *Eastward Ho*, 38
Charlton, H. B., 58, 59, 178
Charney, Maurice, 105

Cinthio, Giraldi, 57n, 58, 83
Clemen, Wolfgang, 105
Coleridge, Samuel Taylor, 106
Colie, Rosalie, 95
Comedy:
—conventions, 7, 18-40; (summarized, 36-37); chaotic middle, 25, 48; character types, 42-45, 61-62, 64-65, 107-115; character types as clowns, 30-33, 39-40, 42-46, 79-80, 127-128, 148-149, 162; character types as manipulators, 21-24, 39, 42, 45-47, 64, 66-67, 75-76, 84, 122-124, 129, 133-134, 152-153; consciousness of play-artifice, 35-36, 52; courtship plot, 19, 36, 37, 39, 71, 73; disguise, 21-24, 36, 38, 39, 45, 47, 116-117, 149-153; elastic time, 28-29, 36, 38-39, 52, 64-67; evasion of death, 19-20, 36; evasion of law, 25-26, 48, 50-51; fictive plot, 41; fortune, 19, 36, 37-38, 39; magic, 21-23, 36, 38, 45, 51, 75-76, 84, 122; multiple perspectives, 30, 31-32, 34-36, 39-40 (*see also* principles and assumptions underlying: alternative realities and perspectives; eiron over alazon); multiple plots, 29-30, 40, 140-142; in prose romance, 37-38; reversing of social hierarchies, 26-28, 36-37, 39, 146-147; in Roman comedy, 39-40; verbal play, 32-34, 37, 40, 46, 48-51, 52
—principles and assumptions underlying, 41-54; age yielding to youth, 43-44, 46, 143-146; alternative realities and perspectives, 42-43, 51-54, 91-105, 114-117, 122, 134-136; continuity of life, 41-42, 44, 46, 47,

182 INDEX

—principles and assumptions (*cont.*)
50-51, 64, 65, 128-129, 143-144;
drive toward mating, 43-44, 46, 51,
73-89; eiron over alazon, 44-48, 51,
91, 94, 105, 114-117, 121, 134,
152-153; "evitability," 41, 52, 58,
121-122, 154; flexibility and accommodation, 24-25, 45-48 (*see also*
eiron over alazon); "natural law,"
21, 23, 25, 42, 48; rejection of singleness as common premise, 51-53,
82-83, 116
—relation to moral instruction, 42, 44
—romantic *vs.* satiric, 18, 40, 54n
—roots in fertility rites, 27, 44, 45-46
—Shakespeare's early mastery of, 3-4
Comic relief, 4-5
Conventions, 15-16; *see also* Comedy:
conventions
Cornford, F. M., 44

Dante, 138, 169, 179
The Dead Man's Fortune, 20n
De Quincey, Thomas, 68
Dickey, Franklin, 19n, 57n
Diomedes, 40
Donatus, 11, 40
Donne, John, 15-16
Doran, Madeleine, 7n, 39, 56

Eliot, T. S.: "The Hollow Men," 121;
"The Love Song of J. Alfred Pruf-
rock," 106
Elton, William, 169, 178
Empson, William, 53, 97n, 159n
Enright, D. J., 148
Erasmus, 134
Evanthius, 40, 41
Everett, Barbara, 169

Fair Em, 17, 18, 21, 24, 25, 27, 32, 44
Fergusson, Francis, 110
Fiedler, Leslie, 89n
Freud, Sigmund, 48-49, 50, 52, 106
Friar Bacon and Friar Bungay, see
Greene, Robert
Frye, Northrop, 9, 44-45, 59, 71, 108n

Geoffrey of Monmouth, 145
George a Green, *see The Pinner of
Wakefield*
Gervinus, G. G., 156n
Gielgud, Sir John, 164
Giraldi Cinthio, *see* Cinthio, Giraldi
Giraudoux, Jean, *La folle de Chaillot*,
112
Goethe, *Wilhelm Meisters Lehrjahre*,
115
Goldman, Michael, 121n, 122
Gorboduc, *see* Norton and Sackville
Gosson, Stephen, 19, 37
Granville-Barker, Harley, 68, 69n
Greene, Robert: *Friar Bacon and Friar
Bungay*, 17, 18, 19-22, 24, 28, 31,
51; *James the Fourth*, 18, 20, 22-23,
24, 27, 28, 29, 30, 31, 33, 34, 35, 37,
42; *Menaphon*, 38; *Orlando Furioso*,
18, 19-20, 25, 28, 29, 42, 48
Greg, W. W., 97n, 121n

Hadas, Moses, 37n
Harbage, Alfred, and S. Schoenbaum,
18, 139
Hawkes, Terence, 77n
Hazlitt, William, 75
Heilman, Robert B., 77n
Heliodorus, *Aethiopian History*, 37
Heroic, *see* Tragedy, the heroic in
Higgins, John, 145
Honigmann, E.A.J., 79n, 103n
Hubler, Edward, 87
Huizinga, Johan, 34

James, D. G., 94
James the Fourth, *see* Greene, Robert
Jaspers, Karl, 97n, 116, 134
John a Kent and John a Cumber, *see*
Munday, Anthony
John of Bordeaux, 18, 21, 31, 43n
Johnson, Samuel, 3, 4, 116, 134, 140
Jonson, Ben, 7; *The Case is Altered*,
50n; *Eastward Ho*, 38; *The Staple of
News*, 37
Joyce, *Ulysses*, 106

INDEX

183

King Leir, 139, 144-145, 149n
Kirschbaum, Leo, 152
Kitto, H.D.F., 131n
Kittredge, G. L., 114n
A Knack to Know a Knave, 18, 19, 30, 31
A Knack to Know an Honest Man, 18, 20, 24, 26, 29, 31, 35, 43n
Knight, G. Wilson, 138, 159, 169n, 177n
Knights, L. C., 106n
Kott, Jan, 169
Kozintsev, Grigori, 145
Kyd, Thomas: *The Spanish Tragedy*, 29, 35-36

Lamb, Charles, 157
Langer, Susanne K., 10, 13, 46-47, 51
Levin, Harry, 57n, 112, 166-167
Lewis, C. S., 102n
Locrine, 29
The London Prodigal, 151n
Long, Michael, 140n
Lower, Charles B., 69n
Lyly, John: *Gallathea*, 47n; *Midas* (prologue), 19; *Mother Bombie*, 17

Mack, Maynard, 13, 94n, 127, 140n, 143n
Mack Jr., Maynard, 131n
Marlowe, Christopher, 177; *Doctor Faustus*, 23
Marston, John, *Eastward Ho*, 38
Mason, H. A., 57n
McElroy, Bernard, 96n, 119n, 144n
McFarland, Thomas, 113n
Mehl, Dieter, 29n
Montaigne, Michel de, 95
Mucedorus, 17, 18, 21-22, 29, 30, 31
Munday, Anthony, *John a Kent and John a Cumber*, 18, 21, 22, 29
Murry, John Middleton, 89n

Norton and Sackville, *Gorboduc*, 29
Nosworthy, J. M., 57n
Nowottny, Winifred, 77n

The Old Wives' Tale, *see* Peele, George
Orlando Furioso, *see* Greene, Robert

Painter, William, 57n
Palmerin romances, 37-38
Peele, George, *The Old Wives' Tale*, 18-20, 22, 25, 28-29, 30-32, 43, 107
The Pinner of Wakefield, 18, 22, 30, 31, 32
Plato: *Republic*, 8, 14; *Symposium*, 51
Plautus, 39-40
Porter, Henry, *The Two Angry Women of Abington*, 18, 19, 25, 27, 29, 31, 33, 43-45
Prince, F. T., 4
Prodigal Son, 147-148, 154
Prosser, Eleanor, 97n, 135n

Rabkin, Norman, 122n
Raphael, D. D., 8
Richards, I. A., 8
Romances, comic conventions in, 37-38
Rosenberg, John D., 169
Rosenberg, Marvin, 154n, 164
Rossiter, A. P., 5, 11n
Rymer, Thomas, 3

Salingar, Leo, 56n, 153n
Schlegel, A. W., 141n
Schücking, Levin L., 92n
Servius, 41
Shakespeare:
—*All's Well that Ends Well*, 67, 72n, 73, 133, 152-153
—*Antony and Cleopatra*, 6-7, 41-42, 89, 109n, 114, 158, 164-165, 173n, 178
—*As You Like It*, 47, 49, 51, 53, 71-73, 93, 117, 142-143
—*The Comedy of Errors*, 18, 19, 24n, 25-28, 30, 35, 73n
—*Coriolanus*, 12, 15, 24n, 113, 173n, 178
—*Cymbeline*, 67n
—*Hamlet*, 4, 5, 6, 7, 8, 10, 12, 13, 24, 35-36, 41-42, 69, 89-90, *91-136*, 138, 143, 144, 157, 159, 169, 173,

184 INDEX

—*Hamlet* (*cont.*)
179; antic disposition as disguise, 24, 116-117; clowns, 127-129; conflict between eiron's multiple awareness and alazon's certainty, 91-98, 115, 116, 118-119, 134-136; "evitability," 121-122; failure of manipulator, 122-124, 129, 133-134; fusion of comic and tragic in graveyard scene, 117, 125-129; open questions, 101-105; Osric as comic character, 110-112, 114, 132-133; Polonius as comic character, 107-112, 114-115, 132-133; reflector-characters for objective-subjective dilemma, 98-101; rejection of singleness, 116; revenge, 135n; Rosencrantz and Guildenstern as comic characters, 112-115, 132-133; structure, 117-125; subjective interpretations, 106-107, 113-115; summary of operations of comedy, 132-136

—*Henry IV*, parts 1 and 2, 67n, 178, 179

—*Henry V*, 151, 178

—*Henry VI*, parts 1, 2, and 3, 128n, 178

—*Julius Caesar*, 3, 12, 33, 178

—*King Lear*, 4, 5, 6, 7, 10, 12, 14, 24, 69, 78, 90, 136, *137-179*; age yielding to youth, 143-146; Christian overtones, 154; disguise, 24, 148, 149-153; double plot, 141-142; Edgar as eiron and manipulator, 152-153; ending, 155-158, 168-172; Fool, 148-149, 160-163; green-world structure, 142-143; grotesque comedy, 138, 159-168; inversion of hierarchies, 146-147; Lear as *senex*, 144; preceded and followed by comedies, 139-140; redemptive comedy, 138-157; religion and the heroic, 173-179; tragedy derived from two kinds of comedy, 137-139, 179

—*Love's Labour's Lost*, 3-4, 18, 20-22, 26-27, 30-33, 35-36, 43, 71, 72, 107

—*Macbeth*, 12, 13, 68, 110, 114, 157-158, 178

—*Measure for Measure*, 67, 133, 152-153

—*The Merchant of Venice*, 47, 51, 61, 73

—*The Merry Wives of Windsor*, 73n, 151

—*A Midsummer Night's Dream*, 18, 19, 21, 22, 24n, 25-27, 30, 31, 35-36, 43, 45, 46, 48, 51, 53, 59-60, 71-73, 142

—*Much Ado about Nothing*, 24n, 67, 75

—*Othello*, 3, 4, 6, 7, 12, 56-57, *70-90*, 93-94, 107, 132-134, 143-144, 158-159; Iago as clown, 79-80; Iago as manipulator, 75-76, 84-85; Iago as enemy of love, 80, 84-85; illumination of by Shakespeare's poems, 85-88; initial comic structure, 73-75; novella source, 56-57; questioning of comic assumptions, 73-88; universal dimension, 88-89

—"The Phoenix and Turtle," 87-88

—*The Rape of Lucrece*, 4

—*Richard II*, 58, 128, 178

—*Richard III*, 58, 178

—*Romeo and Juliet*, 4-8, 12, 33, 56-57, *57-70*, 88, 89, 107, 109, 132, 133, 140n, 152, 158; comic and tragic time, 64-67; comic world shifting to tragic world, 59-64, 70; Friar Laurence and Nurse as comic characters irrelevant to tragic world, 64-68; fusion of comic and tragic, 68-69; Mercutio as comic character, 61-62; novella source, 56-57; tragedy of fate, 69-70; Tybalt as alazon, 60-61

—Sonnet 35, 85-86

—Sonnet 36, 88

—Sonnet 57, 85

—Sonnet 116, 87

—Sonnet 130, 16

—Sonnet 138, 86-87

—*The Taming of the Shrew*, 18, 21, 25, 27, 29-30, 31, 33, 34-35, 43, 45-47, 51, 73, 75

INDEX

—*Timon of Athens*, 173n
—*Titus Andronicus*, 3-4, 24n, 58
—*Troilus and Cressida*, 89, 133
—*Twelfth Night*, 49-50, 51, 72, 149
—*The Two Gentlemen of Verona*, 18, 22, 24-27, 29, 31, 32, 34, 43-45, 47, 61, 71-72, 149, 166
—*Venus and Adonis*, 4
—*The Winter's Tale*, 67
Sidney, Sir Philip, *Arcadia*, 19, 37-38
Skulsky, Harold, 100n
Soliman and Perseda, 19, 35-36
Spencer, Theodore, 82n
Stauffer, Donald, 124
Steevens, George, 163n
Swinburne, Algernon Charles, 75

The Taming of a Shrew, 17, 18, 21, 25, 29, 31, 35
Tate, Nahum, 139-140, 166
Terence, 39-40
Thomas, Henry, 39n
Thomson, Philip, 159
Tillyard, E.M.W., 122n
Tractatus Coisilianus, 44n
Tragedy: as address to death, 9-10, 41;

as generator of opposed emotions, 8-11, 13-14; the heroic in, 11-14, 129-130, 135-136, 172-179; law in, 58
The Two Angry Women of Abington, *see* Porter, Henry

Ur-*Hamlet*, 104n

Waldock, A.J.A., 123n
Webster, John, *The Duchess of Malfi*, 48
Welsford, Enid, 172
Wilson, John Dover, 92n, 97n, 101, 102, 103, 114n
Women in comedy, *see* Comedy, conventions, reversing of social hierarchies
Woodes, Nathaniel, *The Conflict of Conscience*, 17
Wright, Louis B., 39n

Young, David, 140n, 142

Zeffirelli, Franco, 69n

Library of Congress Cataloging in Publication Data

Snyder, Susan.
  The comic matrix of Shakespeare's tragedies.

  Includes index.
  1. Shakespeare, William, 1564-1616—Tragedies.
2. Comic, The.   I. Title.
PR2983.S58   822.3′3   79-84018
ISBN 0-691-06404-0